Leaving Richard's Valley

Michael DeForge

Drawn & Quarterly

 drawnandquarterly.com. 9781770463431. First edition: March 2019. Printed in China. 10 9 8 7 6 5 4 3 2 1. Cataloguing data available from Library and Archives Canada. Published in the USA by Drawn & Quarterly, a client publisher of Farrar, Straus and Giroux. Orders: 888.330.8477. Published in Canada by Drawn & Quarterly, a client publisher of Raincoast Books. Orders: 800.663.5714. Published in the United Kingdom by Drawn & Quarterly, a client publisher of Publishers Group UK. Orders: info@pguk.co.uk. Produced with the support of the City of Toronto through the Toronto Arts Council. Drawn & Quarterly acknowledges the support of the Government of Canada and the Canada Council for the Arts for our publishing program.

TORONTO ARTS COUNCIL | FUNDED BY THE CITY OF TORONTO

Canada

Leaving Richard's Valley

EVERYONE WHO LIVES HERE LOVES RICHARD
I LOVE RICHARD BECAUSE HE WAS IN A MOVIE
I LOVE RICHARD BECAUSE HE PAYS FOR MY PIANO CLASS!
I LOVE RICHARD BECAUSE HE LOVES ME

Leaving Richard's Valley

R
RICHARD TAKES CARE OF US
IF YOU DON'T LOVE RICHARD, YOU'RE PROBABLY REALLY MESSED UP
R
R
BUT LOVING RICHARD MAKES MESSED UP PEOPLE BETTER
R
I REALLY LIKE WATCHING RICHARD KISS MY MOM
I USED TO HATE WATCHING MY DAD KISS MY MOM. IT WOULD MAKE ME FEEL GROSS. WHEN I WATCH RICHARD KISS MY MOM, I FEEL SO HAPPY
R
R

Leaving Richard's Valley

EVERYONE WHO LIVES HERE LOVES RICHARD AND IF YOU DON'T LOVE RICHARD THEY DON'T LET YOU IN
ONCE YOU'RE LET IN, YOU HAVE TO RUB THESE STONES ON YOU. THEY RID YOU OF ALL YOUR TOXINS
WE DON'T WANT TO POISON RICHARD
ALL OUR DRINKING WATER RUNS THROUGH THESE STONES
RICHARD MAKES MEDICINE FOR US
R

Leaving Richard's Valley

EVEN BABIES BORN IN THE VALLEY NEED TO BE RUBBED WITH STONES
I WAS RECENTLY A BABY
TOXINS ARE EVERYWHERE
TOXINS MAKE IT HARD FOR RICHARD TO BREATHE. THAT'S WHY THE VALLEY IS THE SAFEST PLACE FOR US
STILL, SOME TOXINS STILL SLIP THROUGH. I FEEL SICK TO MY STOMACH IMAGINING ALL THE POISON WHIPPING AROUND THE AIR!
WHIPPING AROUND AS WE SPEAK!

Leaving Richard's Valley

WHAT'S WRONG?
I DRANK TOO MUCH WATER!

Leaving Richard's Valley

RICHARD HAS JOBS FOR ALL OF US
R
I COULDN'T ASK FOR A BETTER BOSS!
R
IF YOU'RE LAZY, YOU CAN'T LIVE IN THE VALLEY
R
MY DAD WAS LAZY AND NOW HE LIVES IN A DIFFERENT STATE
R

Leaving Richard's Valley

FOLKS WHO LIVE IN THE VALLEY: RACCOONS, TODDLERS
BEARS, ADULTS
SPIDERS, ANTS
SNAKES, DOGS

Leaving Richard's Valley

WHERE YOU MIGHT FIND TOXINS: CREEKS AND STREAMS
THE AIR
CONVERSATIONS AND GATHERINGS BETWEEN FEWER THAN THREE PEOPLE
OUR THOUGHTS

Leaving Richard's Valley

RICHARD HAS MANY HUSBANDS AND WIVES. THEY ENFORCE ALL THE RULES AROUND HERE
THIS IS CYNTHIA
REBECCA AND NATHANIEL. I HATE NATHANIEL
MICHELLE, ELENA, AND RAOUL
THIS IS SERENA. SHE IS VERY UNFAIR. SHE ONCE MADE ME DRINK A LOT OF WATER AND GO PEE IN FRONT OF ALL MY FRIENDS
FOR PRACTICALLY NOTHING! IT WAS PUNISHMENT FOR GIVING BREAD TO MY SISTER
(GRAINS ARE FORBIDDEN IN RICHARD'S VALLEY)

Leaving Richard's Valley

RICHARD IS SO HOT
AND SO SMART
I CAN'T BELIEVE THERE WAS A TIME IN MY LIFE WHEN I DIDN'T LOVE RICHARD
HE'S THE MOST THOUGHTFUL MAN I'VE EVER KNOWN
IF ANYTHING WERE TO HAPPEN TO RICHARD, I'D THROW MYSELF INTO THE RIVER
WE'LL NEVER LET ANYTHING HAPPEN TO RICHARD

Leaving Richard's Valley

OHHHHHHHHHH
DO YOU HAVE A STOMACHE ACHE AGAIN?
I THINK IT'S THE WATER. THE WATER IS MAKING ME FEEL SO BAD
DID IT RUN THROUGH THE STONES?
A BUNCH OF TIMES. I THOUGHT MAYBE IT HADN'T BEEN PURIFIED **ENOUGH**, SO I RAN IT THROUGH EVEN MORE STONES
BUT IT MADE ME EVEN WORSE!

Leaving Richard's Valley

I THOUGHT IF THE WATER WAS MAKING ME SICK, I SHOULD STOP DRINKING IT ALTOGETHER
I HAVEN'T DRANK ANYTHING FOR THREE DAYS
YOU'RE SCARING ME!
YOU SHOULD GO. WE CAN'T BE CAUGHT TALKING IN A GROUP OF TWO
RICHARD WOULD BE MAD

Leaving Richard's Valley

I LOVE HER... CYNTHIA... ONE OF RICHARD'S WIVES
A FORBIDDEN LOVE. A LOVE THAT BETRAYS MY LOVE FOR RICHARD
THAT BETRAYS MYSELF
I CAN'T TAKE THIS AGONY!
ROOT ME OUT, RICHARD! BANISH ME FROM YOUR WOODED PARADISE!

Leaving Richard's Valley

WE'RE GATHERING MEDICINE FOR LYLE THE RACCOON!
HE STILL HAS A STOMACH ACHE
RICHARD ONLY LETS US USE SPECIAL MEDICINE HERE IN THE VALLEY
OUTSIDE, PEOPLE TRY TO TRICK YOU WITH BAD MEDICINE
RICHARD HAS WRITTEN A LOT OF BOOKS EXPLAINING THE DIFFERENCE BETWEEN GOOD AND BAD MEDICINE!

Leaving Richard's Valley

ALL OUR MEDICINE IS MADE FROM PLANTS AND ROOTS FOUND IN THE VALLEY
INGREDIENTS ARE PURIFIED WITH THE SPECIAL STONES, OF COURSE
ALL ACCORDING TO RICHARD'S INSTRUCTIONS
RICHARD ALSO FEEDS US LONGEVITY PILLS!

Leaving Richard's Valley

MANY OUTSIDERS WOULDN'T BELIEVE IT, BUT THERE ARE A TON OF WAYS TO HAVE FUN AND PASS TIME IN THE VALLEY!
DRAWING PICTURES OF RICHARD!
ORGANIZING LEAVES!
PUTTING ON SKITS AND PLAYS!
MAKING LISTS OF ALL THE BAD THINGS I'VE DONE!
IMAGINING ME AND RICHARD AS THE ONLY TWO SURVIVORS AFTER THE APOCALYPSE!

Leaving Richard's Valley

WHY WON'T YOU ANSWER ME? IT'S BEEN MONTHS SINCE I CONFESSED MY LOVE FOR YOU
SAY SOMETHING! ANYTHING! MOCK ME! KISS ME! SHUN ME! SLAP MY FACE!
YOU HAVEN'T TOLD RICHARD YET, OR I'D BE BANISHED ALREADY
WHY? DO YOU HAVE FEELINGS FOR ME AFTER ALL?
OR DO YOU JUST LIKE WATCHING ME TWIST IN THE WIND?
I'M FINE WITH IT... ALL I'VE EVER WANTED IS TO HOLD YOUR ATTENTION

Leaving Richard's Valley

* SOB *

Leaving Richard's Valley

ME AND MY PARENTS AND MY BROTHER AND SISTER USED TO LIVE ON BLOOR STREET
A BIKE COURIER RAN OVER MY SISTER. IT MADE MY PARENTS FIGHT ALL THE TIME
IT GOT BETTER WHEN THEY TOOK US TO THE VALLEY AND EVEN BETTER WHEN MY DAD LEFT THE VALLEY
I DON'T REMEMBER MUCH ABOUT BLOOR STREET

Leaving Richard's Valley

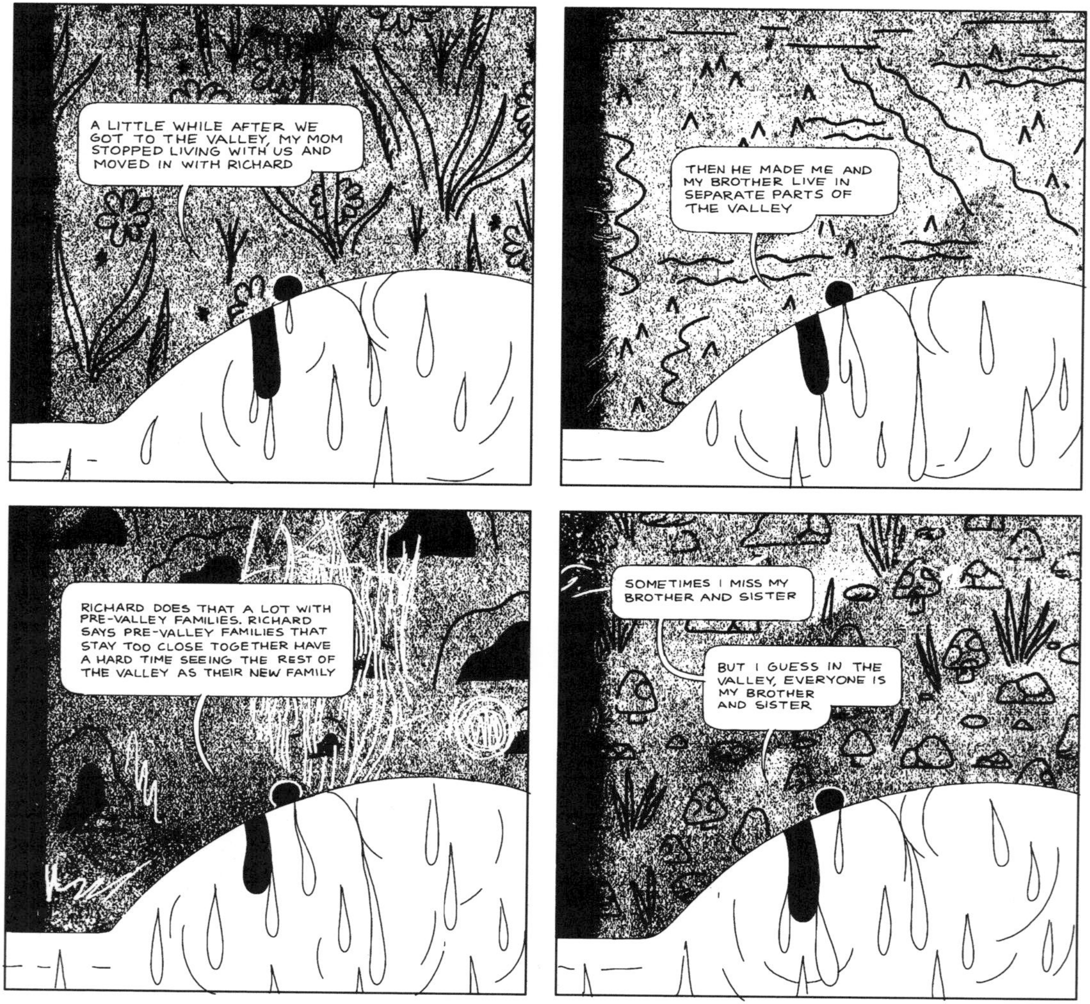
A LITTLE WHILE AFTER WE GOT TO THE VALLEY, MY MOM STOPPED LIVING WITH US AND MOVED IN WITH RICHARD
THEN HE MADE ME AND MY BROTHER LIVE IN SEPARATE PARTS OF THE VALLEY
RICHARD DOES THAT A LOT WITH PRE-VALLEY FAMILIES. RICHARD SAYS PRE-VALLEY FAMILIES THAT STAY TOO CLOSE TOGETHER HAVE A HARD TIME SEEING THE REST OF THE VALLEY AS THEIR NEW FAMILY
SOMETIMES I MISS MY BROTHER AND SISTER
BUT I GUESS IN THE VALLEY, EVERYONE IS MY BROTHER AND SISTER

Leaving Richard's Valley

HELLO, MY LOVE! ARE YOU--

Leaving Richard's Valley

WHEN SOMEONE DIES IN THE VALLEY, WE RUB PURITY STONES ON THEIR BODY
THEN COVER THEM IN THOSE STONES TO KEEP OUT IMPURE FORCES FROM BOTH THE NATURAL AND MATERIAL WORLD
RICHARD BELIEVES A TOXIN-FREE MIND CAN STAY ACTIVE FOR DECADES AFTER ITS BODY DIES
HE BRAGS ABOUT ALL THE WONDERFUL INSIGHTS AND INVENTIONS HE'LL COME UP WITH LONG AFTER WE PUT HIM TO THE GRAVE

Leaving Richard's Valley

SNAKE MARK DIDN'T SHOW UP TO THE FUNERAL. I CAN'T BELIEVE IT
I WISH I COULD HAVE ATTENDED
THAT'S HORRIBLE. I HEARD MARK HAD A BIT OF A THING FOR CYNTHIA
IT WAS SO OBVIOUS
LORD
CAN YOU IMAGINE BETRAYING RICHARD LIKE THAT? SO AWFUL
HOW CAN HE EVEN SHOW HIS FACE IN THE VALLEY AGAIN?
I GUESS SOME CREATURES FALL BEYOND THE REACH OF RICHARD'S GRACE

Leaving Richard's Valley

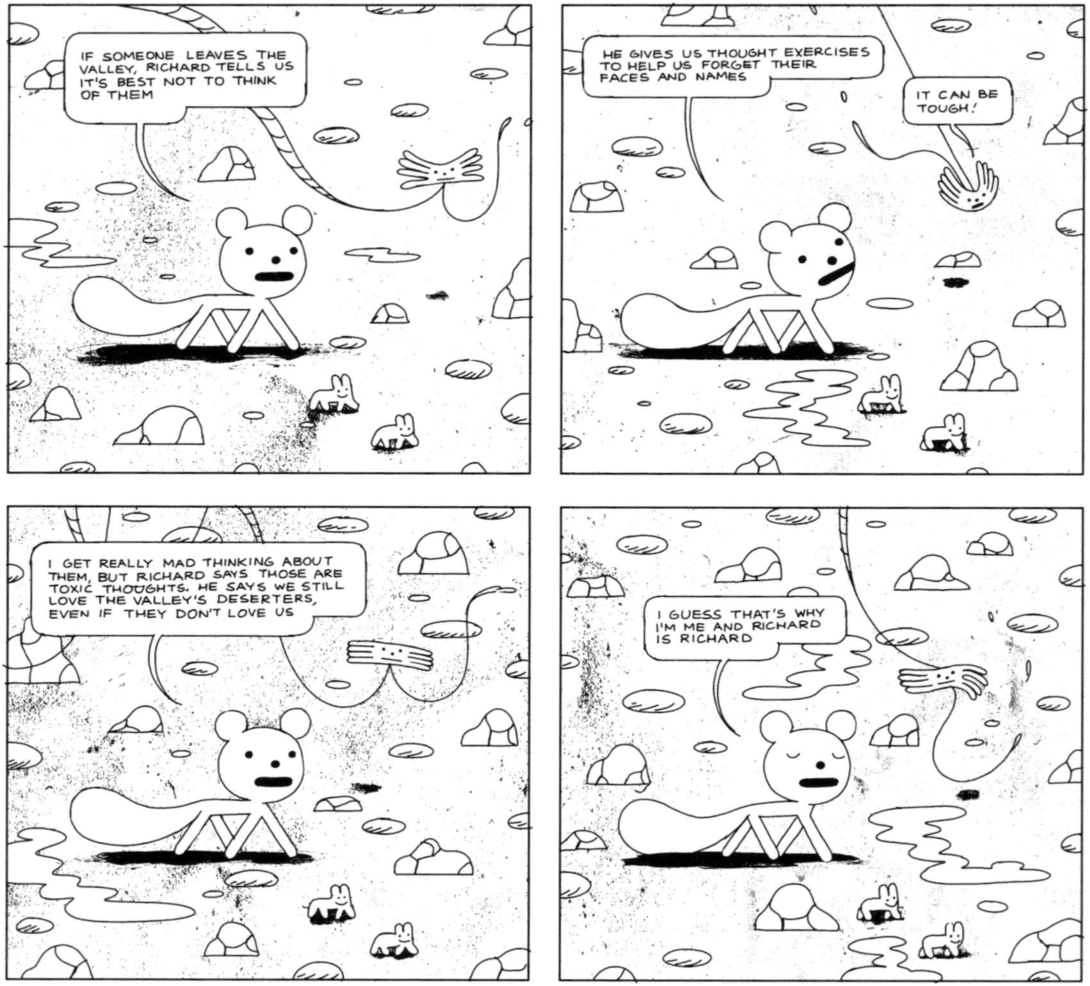
IF SOMEONE LEAVES THE VALLEY, RICHARD TELLS US IT'S BEST NOT TO THINK OF THEM
HE GIVES US THOUGHT EXERCISES TO HELP US FORGET THEIR FACES AND NAMES
IT CAN BE TOUGH!
I GET REALLY MAD THINKING ABOUT THEM, BUT RICHARD SAYS THOSE ARE TOXIC THOUGHTS. HE SAYS WE STILL LOVE THE VALLEY'S DESERTERS, EVEN IF THEY DON'T LOVE US
I GUESS THAT'S WHY I'M ME AND RICHARD IS RICHARD

Leaving Richard's Valley

WHY HELLO
I'M JULIANNE NAPKIN AND I'M AN INTERNATIONAL MODEL
OOOH
WOW
YAY
I TRAVEL FAR AND WIDE TO BE PHOTOGRAPHED! I'M COURTED BY FAMOUS POP STARS! I'M TWENTY TWO YEARS OLD
OHH
WOO!
* SAY THAT OUR BOYFRIEND IS A DJ *
MY BOYFRIEND IS A DJ! HE HAS AN APARTMENT ON QUEEN STREET
YAAA
HURRAH

Leaving Richard's Valley

MS. NAPKIN, IS IT TRUE THAT YOU AND RICHARD ARE DATING?
NO, NO, THE TWO OF US ARE JUST FRIENDS
MS. NAPKIN, WHAT BRINGS YOU TO RICHARD'S VALLEY?
MY GOOD FRIENDS OMAR THE SPIDER AND ELLIE SQUIRREL INVITED ME!
MS. NAPKIN, CAN YOU CONFIRM THE RUMOURS THAT SPIDERS AND SQUIRRELS MAKE THE BEST OF FRIENDS?
NO COMMENT!

Leaving Richard's Valley

IT WAS NICE TALKING WITH ALL OF YOU, BUT IT'S TIME FOR ME TO GO!
GASP
!!
OMAR?! ELLIE SQUIRREL?! WHERE DID YOU COME FROM?
WHERE DID MS. NAPKIN GO?!!
I MISS HER! SO MUCH!
WEHHH

Leaving Richard's Valley

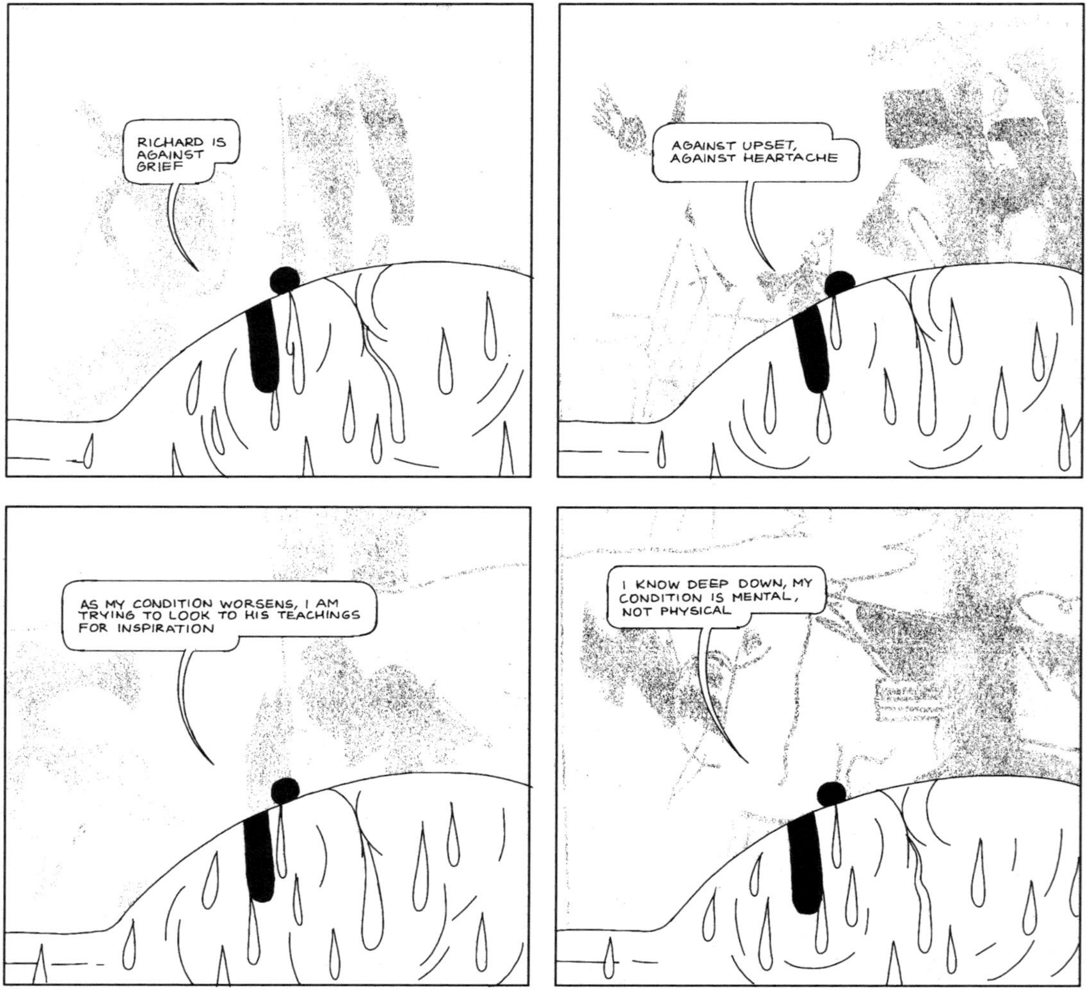
RICHARD IS AGAINST GRIEF
AGAINST UPSET, AGAINST HEARTACHE
AS MY CONDITION WORSENS, I AM TRYING TO LOOK TO HIS TEACHINGS FOR INSPIRATION
I KNOW DEEP DOWN, MY CONDITION IS MENTAL, NOT PHYSICAL

Leaving Richard's Valley

I'M WORRIED ABOUT MY BROTHER LYLE
WHAT IF THE VALLEY IS THE CAUSE OF HIS ILLNESS?
I KNOW RICHARD WILL FIGURE OUT HOW TO FIX IT
BUT WHY DOES LYLE HAVE TO SUFFER SO MUCH IN THE MEANTIME?!

Leaving Richard's Valley

WHAT ARE YOU DOING?
COLLECTING ACORNS FOR RICHARD
THOSE ARE MY ACORNS. I GATHERED THEM
THEY'RE THE VALLEY'S ACORNS, AND WE LIVE IN RICHARD'S VALLEY
BUT I'LL TELL HIM YOU HELPED
OK

Leaving Richard's Valley

I MET RICHARD IN THE 90s. HE WAS ROOMMATES WITH MY COLLEGE BOYFRIEND, WALLACE, WHO WORKED AT SUSPECT VIDEO WITH ME
THEY STARTED HOLDING WEEKLY GATHERINGS AT THEIR APARTMENT. WALLACE WOULD PICK SOME CRAZY MOVIE FROM THE STORE, SCREEN IT, AND THEN HE AND RICHARD WOULD GIVE A LITTLE LECTURE ABOUT WHAT WE SAW
WHENEVER RICHARD SPOKE, SOMETHING WOULD HAPPEN TO THE ROOM. IT WAS LIKE THIS PULSING, ELECTRIC THING
PEOPLE STARTED SHOWING UP JUST TO HEAR RICHARD. THEY STOPPED AIRING MOVIES. I BROKE UP WITH MY BOYFRIEND

Leaving Richard's Valley

Leaving Richard's Valley

RICHARD MAKES US A SPECIAL STEW FOR SPECIAL OCCASIONS
SO GOOD!
IT MAKES YOU REALLY EXCITED FOR A WHILE, THEN YOUR STOMACH HURTS
I LOVE STEW
SOMETIMES I THINK ABOUT LEAVING THE VALLEY, BUT THE IDEA OF LOSING RICHARD'S STEW IS TOO SCARY

Leaving Richard's Valley

Leaving Richard's Valley

RIBBIT
HAHA
WHAT
RIBBIT RIBBIT
HA HA HA
WHAT ARE YOU DOING?!
RIBBIT RIBBIT RIBBIT RIBBIT RIBBIT RIBBIT
AAA
WHY ARE YOU TALKING LIKE THIS?!
RIBBIT RIBBIT
THIS IS REALLY SPOOKY!

Leaving Richard's Valley

...
IT'S WHAT I'VE ALWAYS FEARED
ALL MY FRIENDS ARE HAVING A LOT OF FUN WITHOUT ME
LEAVING ME ALL ALONE! SICK, SAD, AND VERY TEDIOUS

Leaving Richard's Valley

OH BOY
I THINK I HAD TOO MUCH STEW
I FEEL LIKE WE OVERDID IT
ONE OF RICHARD'S VALLEY'S RARE OPPORTUNITIES TO OVERDO IT

Leaving Richard's Valley

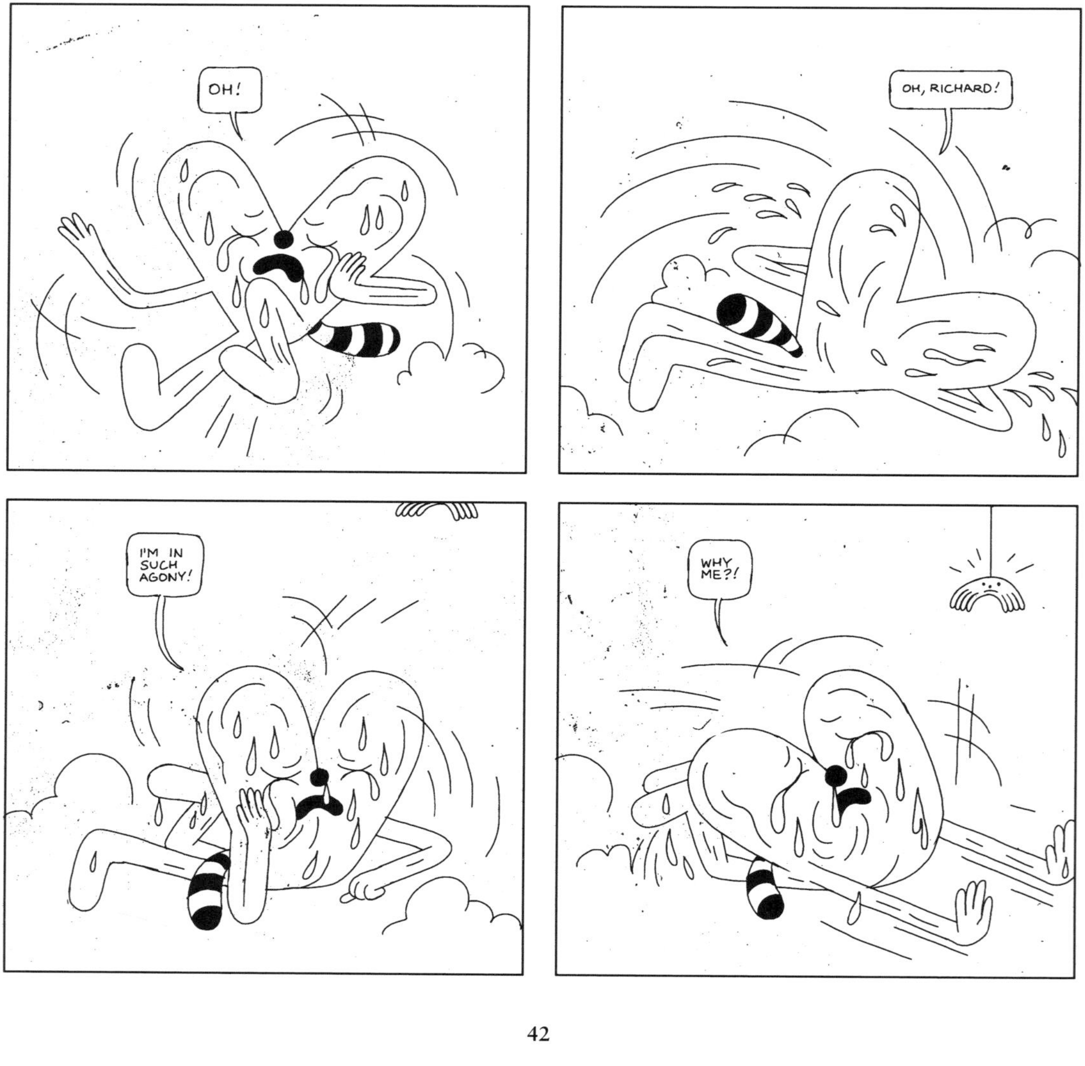
OH!
OH, RICHARD!
I'M IN SUCH AGONY!
WHY ME?!

Leaving Richard's Valley

I'M REALLY SCARED FOR LYLE!
RICHARD WILL FIX HIM...!
HE CAN FIX ANYTHING
...
I DON'T KNOW... RICHARD'S WATER IS MAKING HIM SICKER! RICHARD'S MEDICINE IS MAKING HIM SICKER!
I THINK OMAR IS ONTO SOMETHING
CAN LYLE EVEN UNDERSTAND US RIGHT NOW?
...
IT'S IN RICHARD'S HANDS NOW
IT'S IN **OUR** HANDS! WE CAN BRING LYLE **REAL** WATER- WATER THAT HASN'T BEEN TOUCHED BY PURIFYING STONES!
...
!!!
I THINK... **WE SHOULD DISOBEY RICHARD!**
...

Leaving Richard's Valley

I'M TELLING!
I'M TELLING RICHARD!
I'M TELLING! I'M TELLING!
I'M GONNA TELL ON ALL OF THEM!

Leaving Richard's Valley

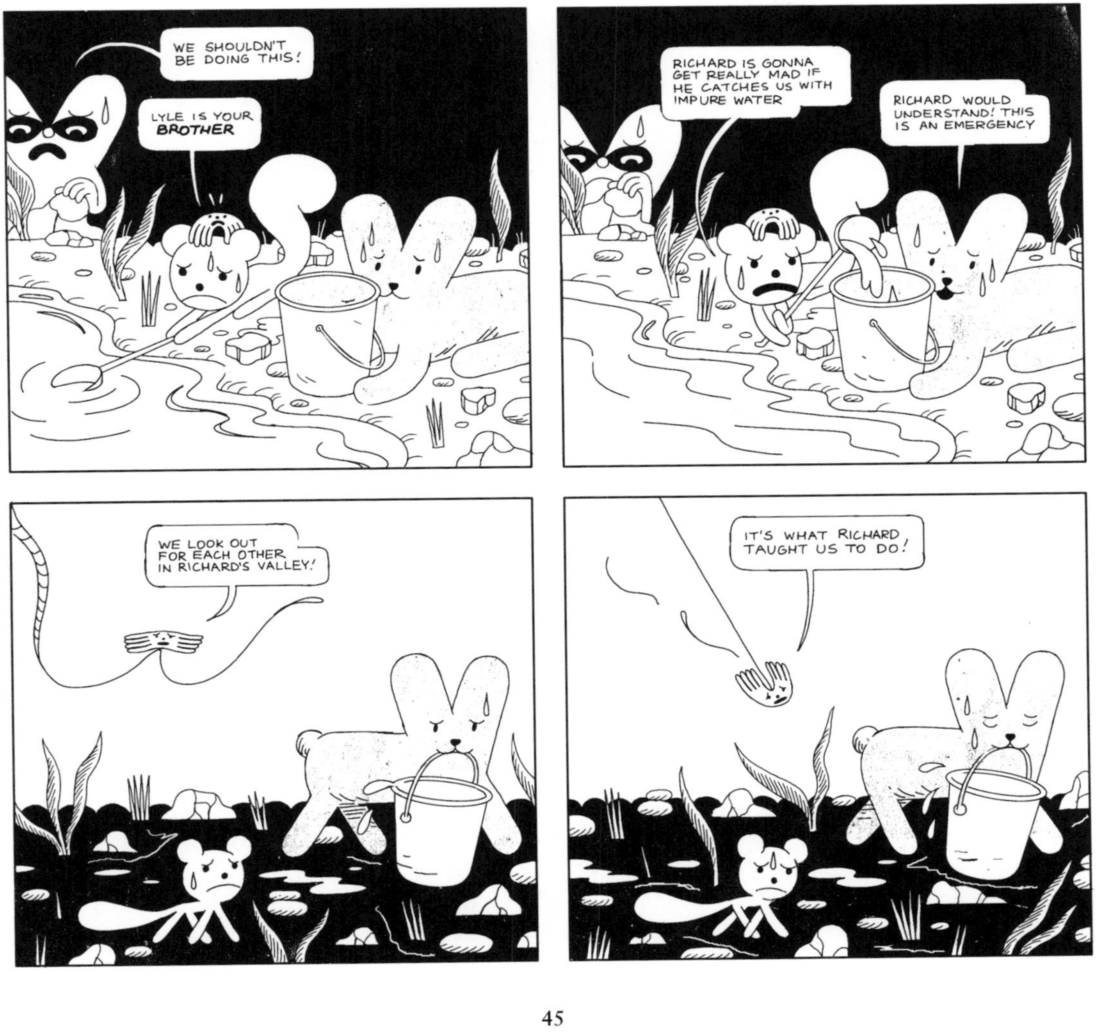
WE SHOULDN'T BE DOING THIS!
LYLE IS YOUR BROTHER
RICHARD IS GONNA GET REALLY MAD IF HE CATCHES US WITH IMPURE WATER
RICHARD WOULD UNDERSTAND! THIS IS AN EMERGENCY
WE LOOK OUT FOR EACH OTHER IN RICHARD'S VALLEY!
IT'S WHAT RICHARD TAUGHT US TO DO!

Leaving Richard's Valley

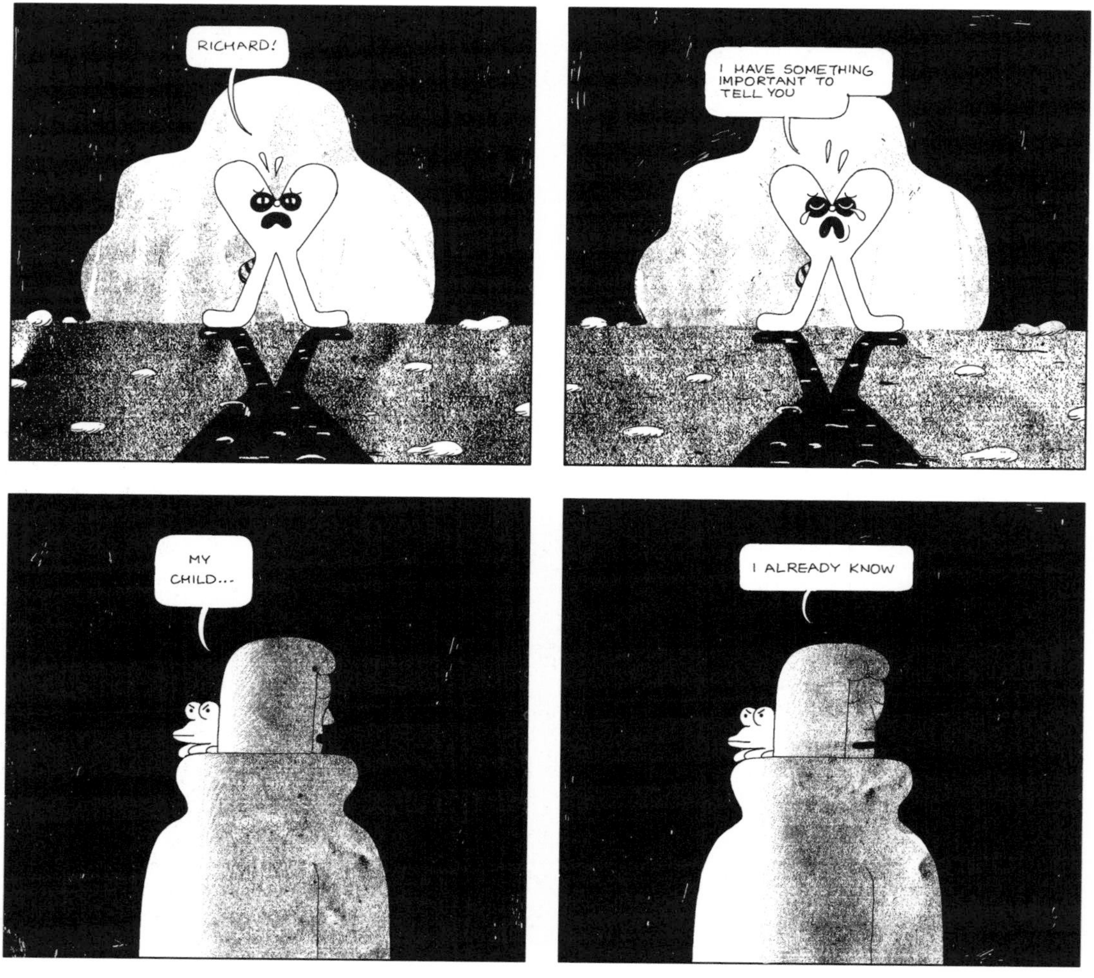
RICHARD!
I HAVE SOMETHING IMPORTANT TO TELL YOU
MY CHILD...
I ALREADY KNOW

Leaving Richard's Valley

Leaving Richard's Valley

THIS IS IT! I'M ABOUT TO DIE. HERE I COME, DEATH!
GLUG GLUG!

Leaving Richard's Valley

LYLE!
IT WORKED!
AHH!
WHAT-- WHAT HAPPENED?
WE WERE SO SCARED FOR YOU
DID RICHARD SAVE ME...?

Leaving Richard's Valley

SOMETIMES I LOOK UP AT THE STARS AND IMAGINE A GIANT TELESCOPE STARING BACK AT ME
STUDYING MY EVERY MOVE
WATCHING ME MAKE THE WORST CHOICES OF MY LIFE
LEARN FROM MY MISTAKES, SPACE FOLK! LET ME BE A TEACHABLE MOMENT IN YOUR SPACE ACADEMIES!
MOMMY! EWW! A SNAKE!

Leaving Richard's Valley

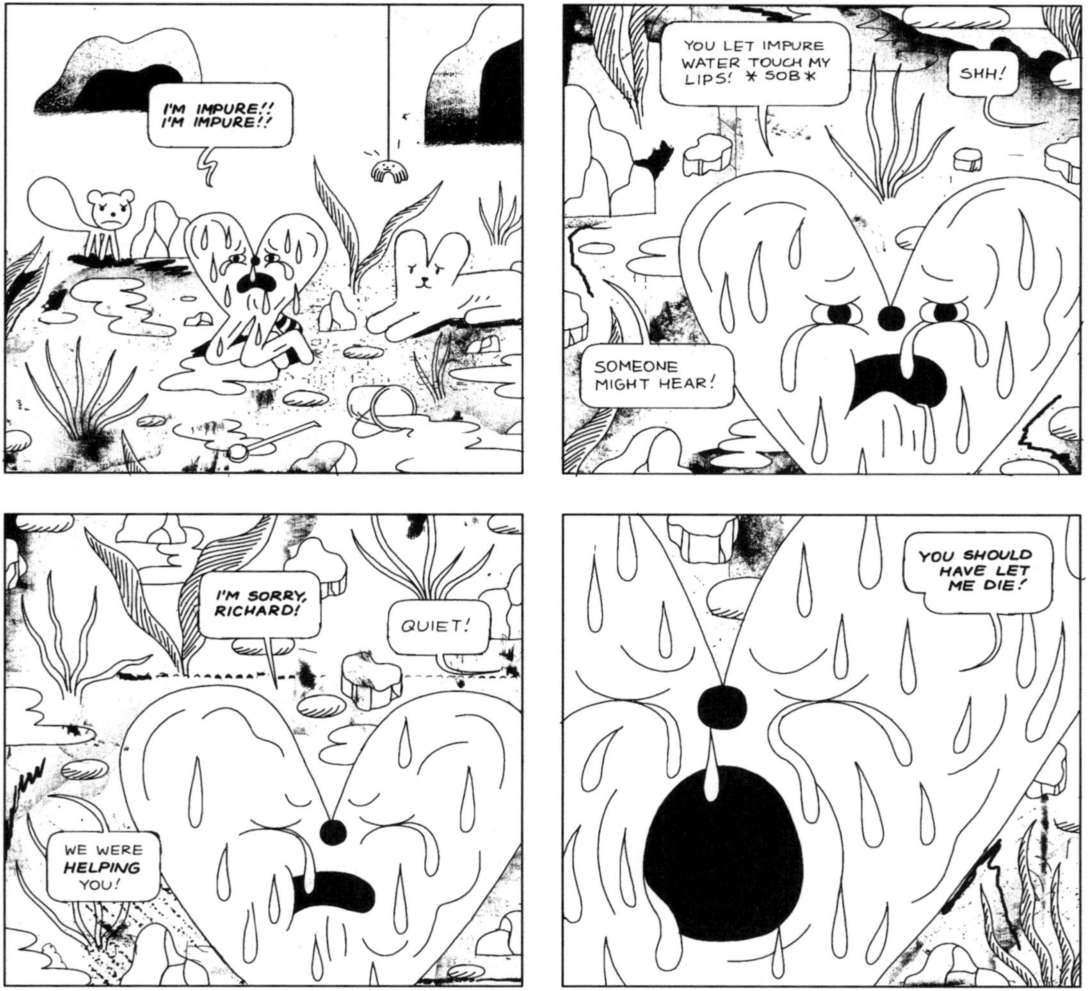
I'M IMPURE!!
I'M IMPURE!!
YOU LET IMPURE WATER TOUCH MY LIPS! *SOB*
SHH!
SOMEONE MIGHT HEAR!
I'M SORRY, RICHARD!
QUIET!
WE WERE HELPING YOU!
YOU SHOULD HAVE LET ME DIE!

Leaving Richard's Valley

DON'T TALK LIKE THIS, LYLE!
I KNEW WE SCREWED UP! I KNEW IT!
YOU'RE OUR FRIEND!
I NEVER WANTED THIS. HOW COULD YOU
I'D RATHER BE DEAD THAN HAVE TO SPEND ANOTHER MOMENT LIVING AWAY FROM RICHARD'S LIGHT
WE MESSED UP! WE'RE SCREWED!
ARE WE BEING OVERLY DRAMATIC

Leaving Richard's Valley

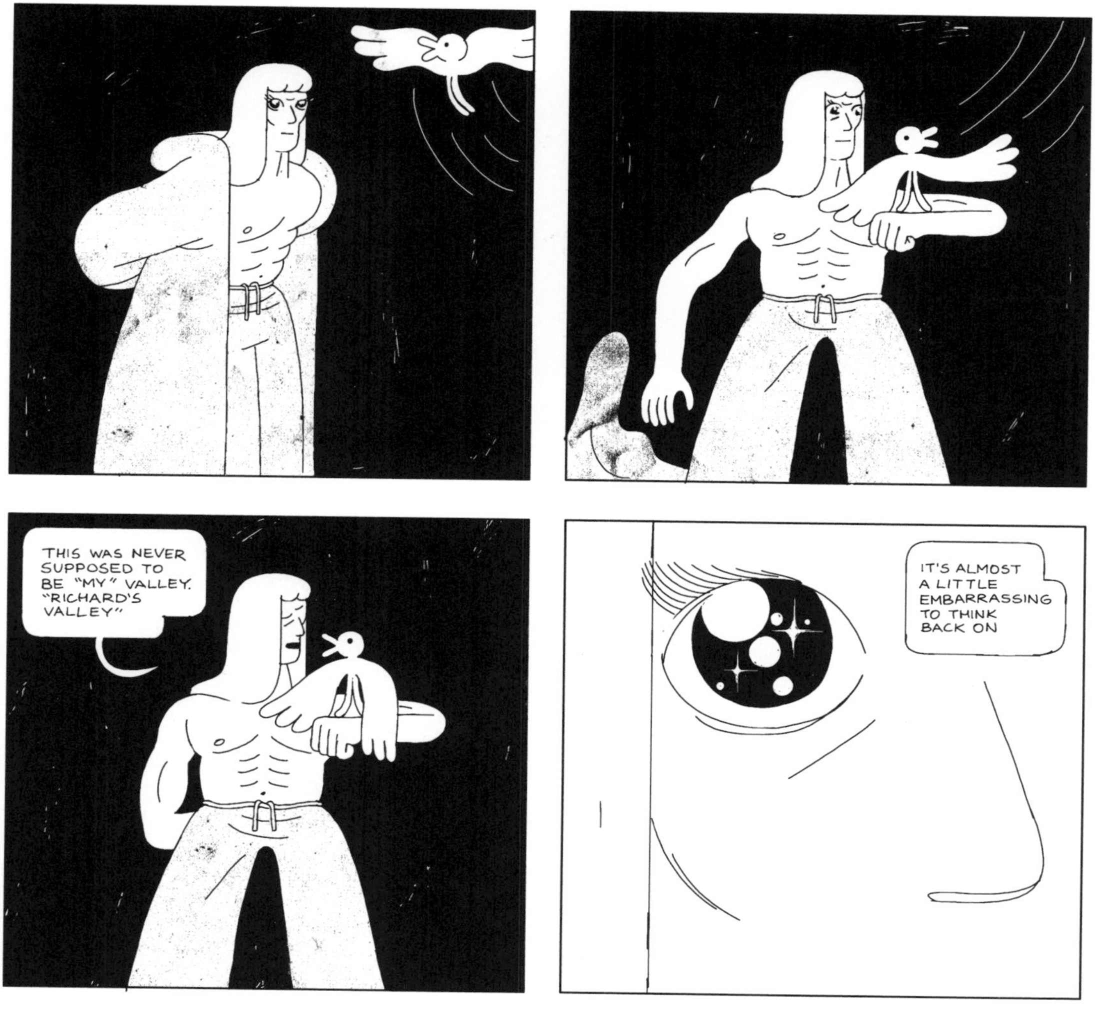
THIS WAS NEVER SUPPOSED TO BE "MY" VALLEY. "RICHARD'S VALLEY"
IT'S ALMOST A LITTLE EMBARRASSING TO THINK BACK ON

Leaving Richard's Valley

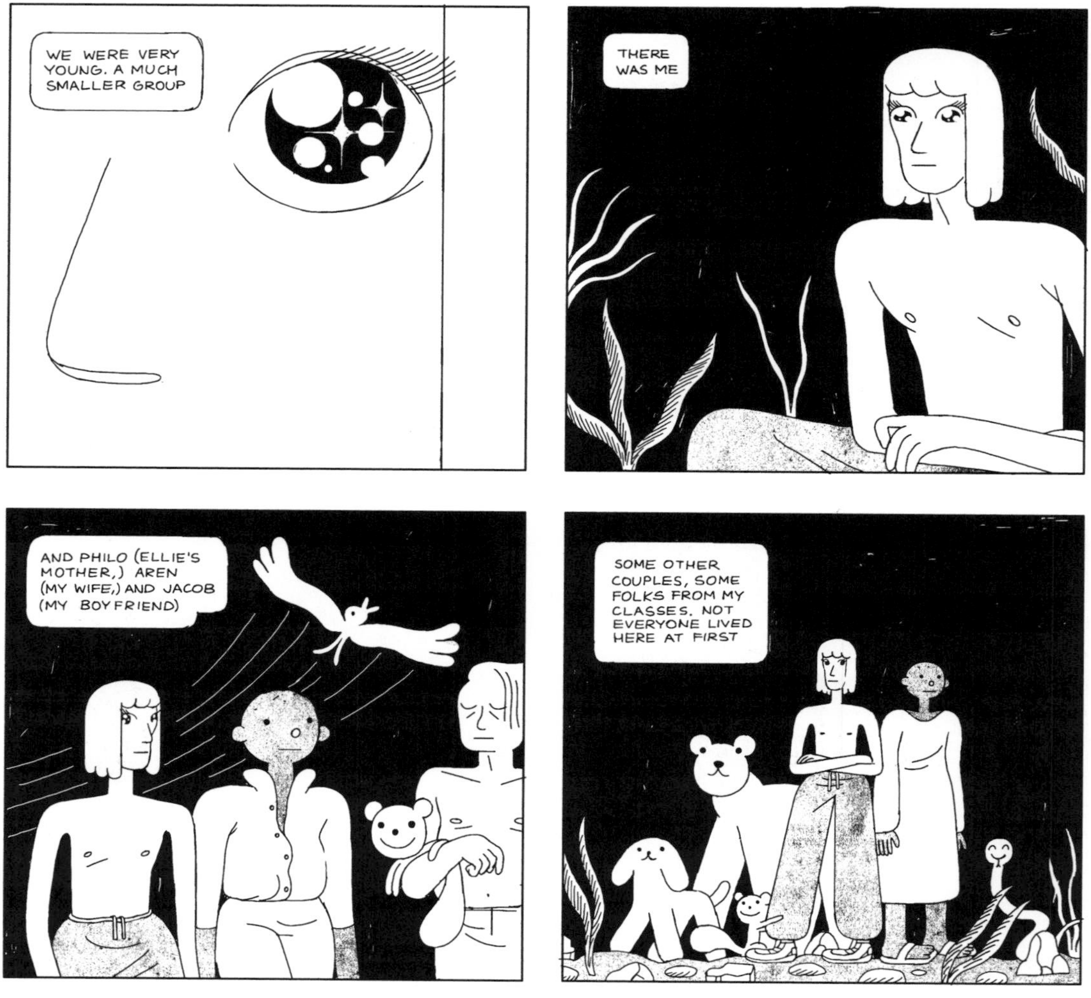
WE WERE VERY YOUNG. A MUCH SMALLER GROUP
THERE WAS ME
AND PHILO (ELLIE'S MOTHER,) AREN (MY WIFE,) AND JACOB (MY BOYFRIEND)
SOME OTHER COUPLES, SOME FOLKS FROM MY CLASSES. NOT EVERYONE LIVED HERE AT FIRST

Leaving Richard's Valley

SOME WOULD STILL LIVE IN THE CITY, AND JUST COME TO THE VALLEY TO SIT IN ON DISCUSSIONS

I WOULDN'T LEAD EVERY DISCUSSION. WE WERE JUST TRYING TO LEARN ABOUT THE VALLEY. EACH PERSON OR ANIMAL COULD HOLD THE FLOOR AND SPEAK TO THEIR OWN EXPERIENCES

WE DIDN'T HAVE RULES YET

WE JUST WANTED TO SEE IF IT WAS POSSIBLE - A TOXIN-FREE HABITAT WITHIN THE CITY

Leaving Richard's Valley

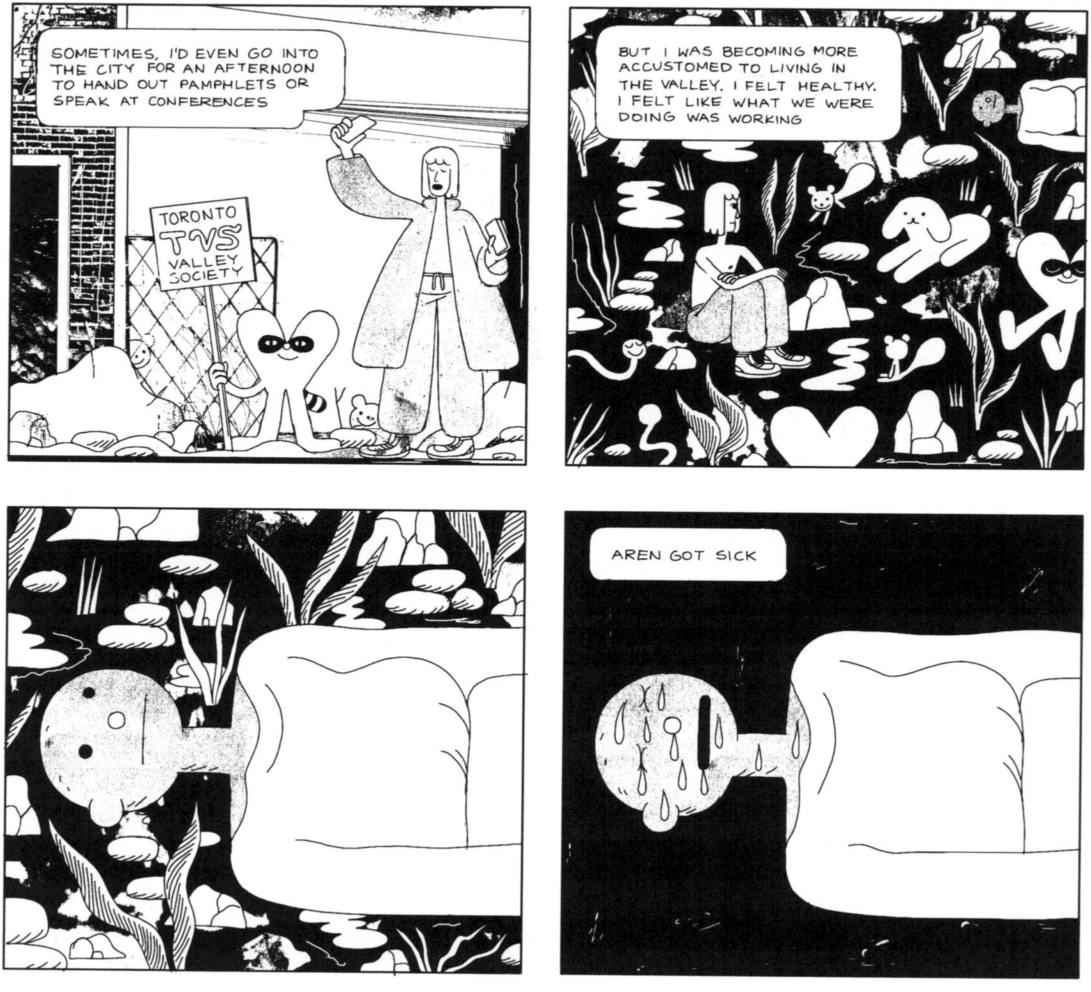
SOMETIMES, I'D EVEN GO INTO THE CITY FOR AN AFTERNOON TO HAND OUT PAMPHLETS OR SPEAK AT CONFERENCES
TORONTO
TVS
VALLEY SOCIETY
BUT I WAS BECOMING MORE ACCUSTOMED TO LIVING IN THE VALLEY. I FELT HEALTHY. I FELT LIKE WHAT WE WERE DOING WAS WORKING
AREN GOT SICK

Leaving Richard's Valley

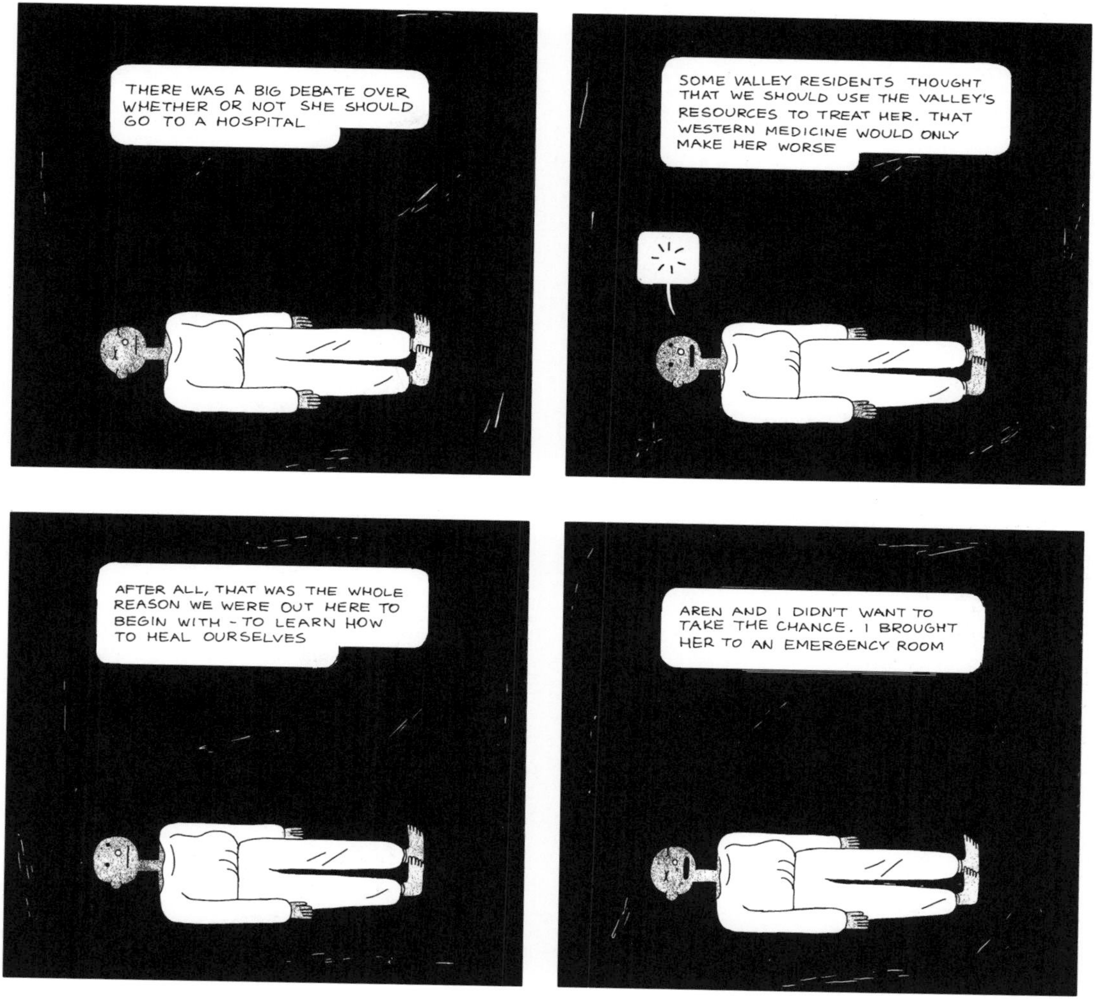

THERE WAS A BIG DEBATE OVER WHETHER OR NOT SHE SHOULD GO TO A HOSPITAL
SOME VALLEY RESIDENTS THOUGHT THAT WE SHOULD USE THE VALLEY'S RESOURCES TO TREAT HER. THAT WESTERN MEDICINE WOULD ONLY MAKE HER WORSE
AFTER ALL, THAT WAS THE WHOLE REASON WE WERE OUT HERE TO BEGIN WITH - TO LEARN HOW TO HEAL OURSELVES
AREN AND I DIDN'T WANT TO TAKE THE CHANCE. I BROUGHT HER TO AN EMERGENCY ROOM

Leaving Richard's Valley

THERE WERE COMPLICATIONS AT THE HOSPITAL
THEY MISDIAGNOSED HER WITH A RESPIRATORY INFECTION
SHE DIED WHILE STILL UNDER THEIR CARE. SHE ACTUALLY HAD PNEUMONIA
THE VALLEY GOT A LOT STRICTER AFTER THAT. I HAD TO SET UP SOME BOUNDARIES...

Leaving Richard's Valley

MOMMY! I DIDN'T KNOW THIS PARK HAD SNAKES!
IT'S GROSS!
STAY AWAY FROM IT, DEAR
I THINK THAT SNAKE HAS EMOTIONAL ISSUES
THIS USED TO BE A NICE PARK!

Leaving Richard's Valley

Leaving Richard's Valley

I'M REALLY SCARED
I CAN'T SLEEP
RICHARD'S GONNA SEE THE BAGS AROUND OUR EYES AND THE JIG WILL BE UP!
INNOCENT PEOPLE SLEEP! GUILTY PEOPLE DON'T!
WHAT WOULD JULIANNE NAPKIN DO?!

Leaving Richard's Valley

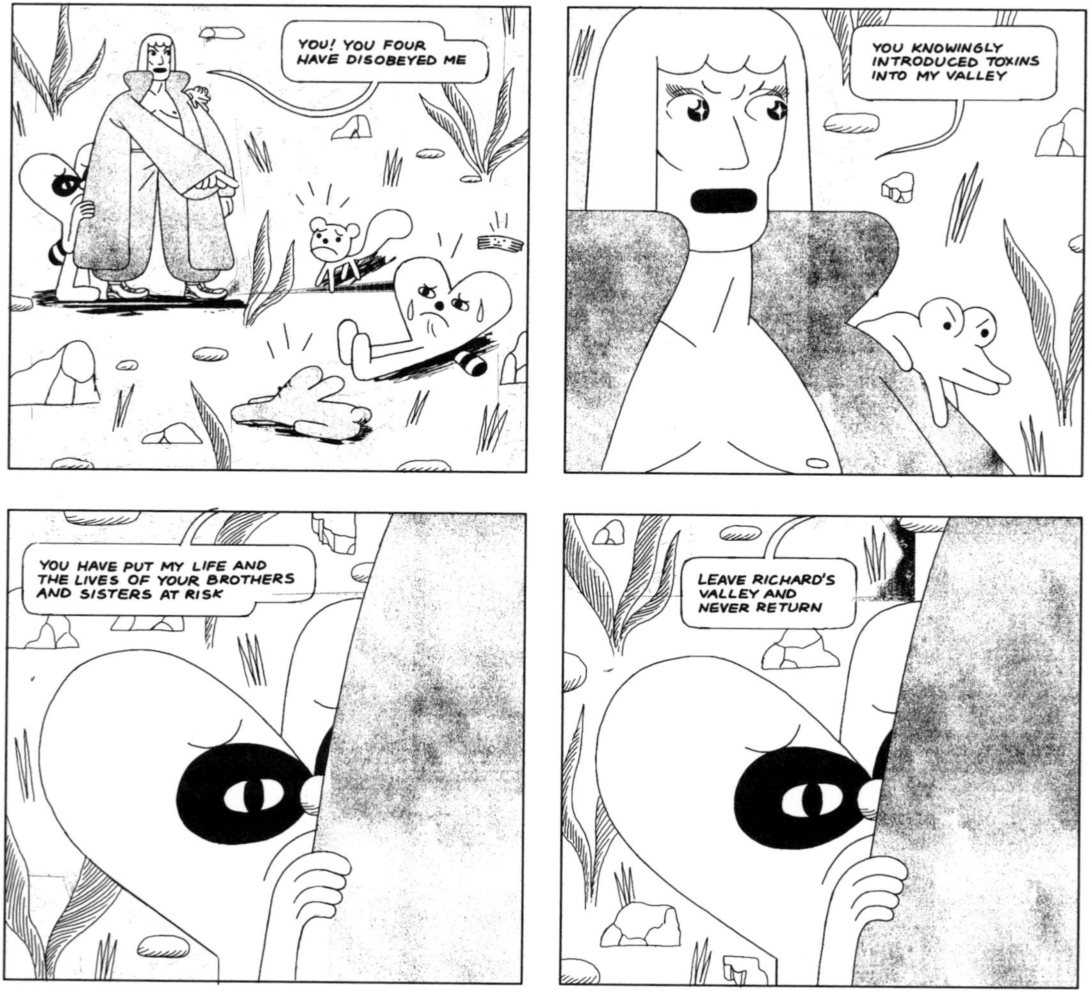
YOU! YOU FOUR HAVE DISOBEYED ME
YOU KNOWINGLY INTRODUCED TOXINS INTO MY VALLEY
YOU HAVE PUT MY LIFE AND THE LIVES OF YOUR BROTHERS AND SISTERS AT RISK
LEAVE RICHARD'S VALLEY AND NEVER RETURN

Leaving Richard's Valley

WE NEEDED TO SAVE LYLE! HE WAS DYING
LYLE WAS NEVER IN TRUE DANGER. THE VALLEY WOULD HAVE HEALED HIM
I WOULD HAVE HEALED HIM. YET YOU DOUBTED ME AND YOU DOUBTED THE VALLEY
LET ME STAY! DRAIN MY BLOOD! LET ME DIE IN THE VALLEY, UNDER YOUR CARE-- WHERE I BELONG!
YOU ARE TOO SHROUDED IN DARKNESS FOR MY LIGHT TO EVER REACH YOU AGAIN. YOU ALL ARE

Leaving Richard's Valley

R

Leaving Richard's Valley

...
...
...
SOMEBODY SAY SOMETHING

Leaving Richard's Valley

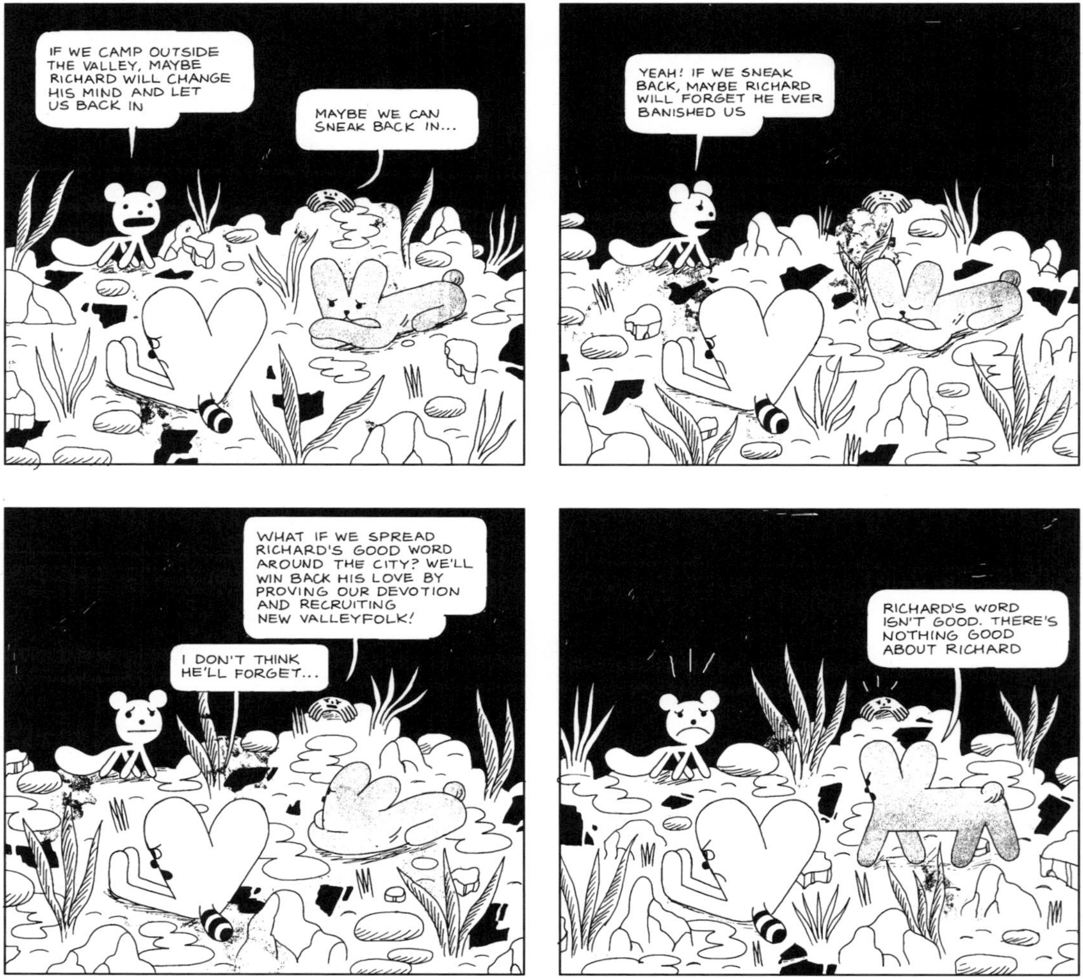

IF WE CAMP OUTSIDE THE VALLEY, MAYBE RICHARD WILL CHANGE HIS MIND AND LET US BACK IN
MAYBE WE CAN SNEAK BACK IN...
YEAH! IF WE SNEAK BACK, MAYBE RICHARD WILL FORGET HE EVER BANISHED US
WHAT IF WE SPREAD RICHARD'S GOOD WORD AROUND THE CITY? WE'LL WIN BACK HIS LOVE BY PROVING OUR DEVOTION AND RECRUITING NEW VALLEYFOLK!
I DON'T THINK HE'LL FORGET...
RICHARD'S WORD ISN'T GOOD. THERE'S NOTHING GOOD ABOUT RICHARD

Leaving Richard's Valley

WE DIDN'T BETRAY RICHARD. RICHARD BETRAYED US
HE LET OUR DEAR FRIEND LYLE SUFFER!
BUT HE WAS TESTING US--
WE GAVE EVERYTHING TO RICHARD! HE WAS THE ONE WHO PUSHED US AWAY. WE HAD NO CHOICE
STOP TALKING LIKE THIS
NO MORE RICHARD. IT'S JUST US FROM NOW ON

Leaving Richard's Valley

I'VE BETRAYED MY BROTHER
YOU PROTECTED YOUR FRIENDS
I'M ALONE IN THIS WORLD
YOU'RE SURROUNDED BY FAMILY
I'M A COWARD
YOU'RE A HERO
LYLE WAS MY BLOOD
BLOOD MEANS CRUD

Leaving Richard's Valley

...
THESE ALL LOOK LIKE RICHARD'S HUSBANDS AND WIVES
WHY ARE THEY SO FAR OUTSIDE THE VALLEY?
I DON'T EVEN RECOGNIZE MOST OF THEM
DID THEY LEAVE TOO? DID RICHARD KICK THEM OUT?

Leaving Richard's Valley

WHY ARE YOU SO SAD?
I LOST THE LOVE OF MY LIFE. I HAD TO FLEE FROM MY HOME
HEY, ARE YOU ONE OF THOSE RICHARD PEOPLE?! THOSE RICHARD'S VALLEY PEOPLE?!
THAT'S SO CRAZY... EVERYONE IN THE PARK IS TOTALLY OBSESSED WITH YOU GUYS

Leaving Richard's Valley

THERE'S SO MUCH LITTER IN THIS PARK
I CAN ALREADY FEEL THE TOXINS CREEPING INSIDE MY BODY!
HOW CAN ANYONE OUTSIDE THE VALLEY STAND TO LIVE LIKE THIS?
HOW DARE YOU JUDGE US?!
YOU RICHARD WEIRDOS THINK YOU'RE ALL SO SPECIAL. WELL, I KNOW THE SECRET TO HOW YOU KEEP THE VALLEY CLEAN
BY SWEEPING YOUR TRASH ONTO THE REST OF THE PARK!
BARK BARK BARK

Leaving Richard's Valley

ARE YOU MAD AT ME, ELLIE?
I KNOW YOU THOUGHT GIVING LYLE THAT WATER WAS A BAD IDEA, BUT I PUSHED FOR IT...
I'M NOT MAD AT YOU, OMAR
I'M MAD AT THE SITUATION
I LOVE RICHARD THE MOST BUT I STILL LOVE YOU THE SECOND-MOST

Leaving Richard's Valley

I HOPE YOU FORGIVE US ONE DAY, LYLE
RICHARD ALWAYS TAUGHT FORGIVENESS
SORT OF
DON'T YOU DARE SPEAK HIS NAME!
THINGS AREN'T SO BAD IN THE REST OF THE PARK
YOU SHOULD BE THANKING YOUR FRIENDS!
SO ARE YOU SUPPOSED TO BE A DOG OR SOMETHING

Leaving Richard's Valley

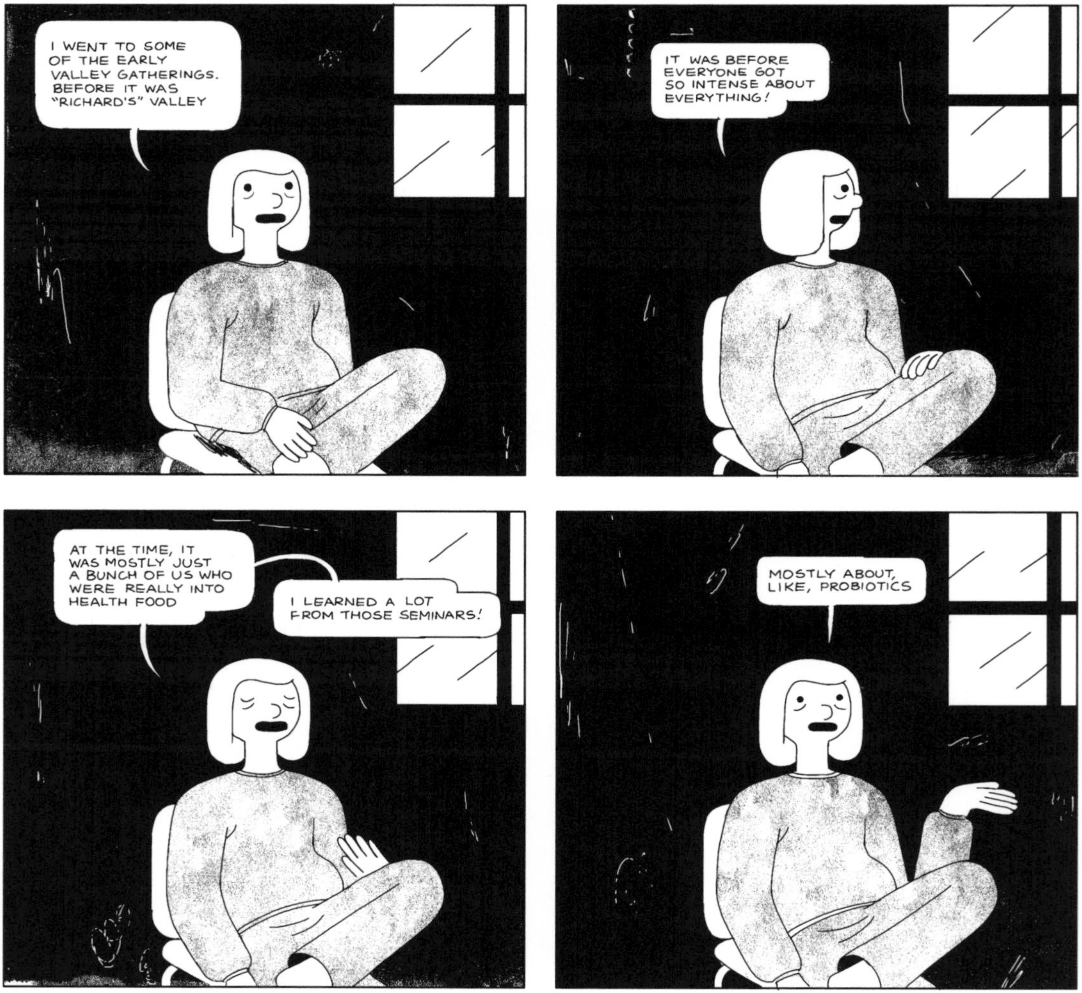
I WENT TO SOME OF THE EARLY VALLEY GATHERINGS. BEFORE IT WAS "RICHARD'S" VALLEY
IT WAS BEFORE EVERYONE GOT SO INTENSE ABOUT EVERYTHING!
AT THE TIME, IT WAS MOSTLY JUST A BUNCH OF US WHO WERE REALLY INTO HEALTH FOOD
I LEARNED A LOT FROM THOSE SEMINARS!
MOSTLY ABOUT, LIKE, PROBIOTICS

Leaving Richard's Valley

I DESERVE THIS. PUNISHMENT FOR LOVING ABOVE MY STATION!
HM. I CAN SEE THE VALLEY FROM UP HERE
THERE'S FOUR MISSING...
ROMANTICS LIKE ME, PERHAPS?

Leaving Richard's Valley

WHAT IS ALL THIS?
IF THIS PARK IS GOING TO BE OUR NEW HOME, I FIGURE WE'LL NEED FURNITURE!
HERE ARE OUR BEDS FROM NOW ON!
CHAIRS AND A SOFA!
DON'T MIND ME, I'M JUST UNWINDING ON THIS SOFA! RELAXING ON MY SOFA AFTER A LONG DAY!

Leaving Richard's Valley

HA HA
TRAITORS. FAKERS. ALL OF THEM!
LET 'EM LEAVE. GOOD RIDDANCE!
ONE DAY, IT WILL BE JUST ME AND RICHARD LEFT! TOGETHER AT LAST! THE WAY IT SHOULD BE!

Leaving Richard's Valley

IS THERE ANYTHING I CAN DO FOR YOU TODAY, RICHARD?
YOU'RE SO WONDERFUL, RICHARD. SUCH A WARM PRESENCE IN ALL OF OUR LIVES
I'M NOT FIT TO SNIFF YOUR PIT!
DON'T BE SILLY, CAROLINE. YOU HAVE A SPECIAL PLACE IN MY HEART
AS DOES EVERYONE IN THE VALLEY

Leaving Richard's Valley

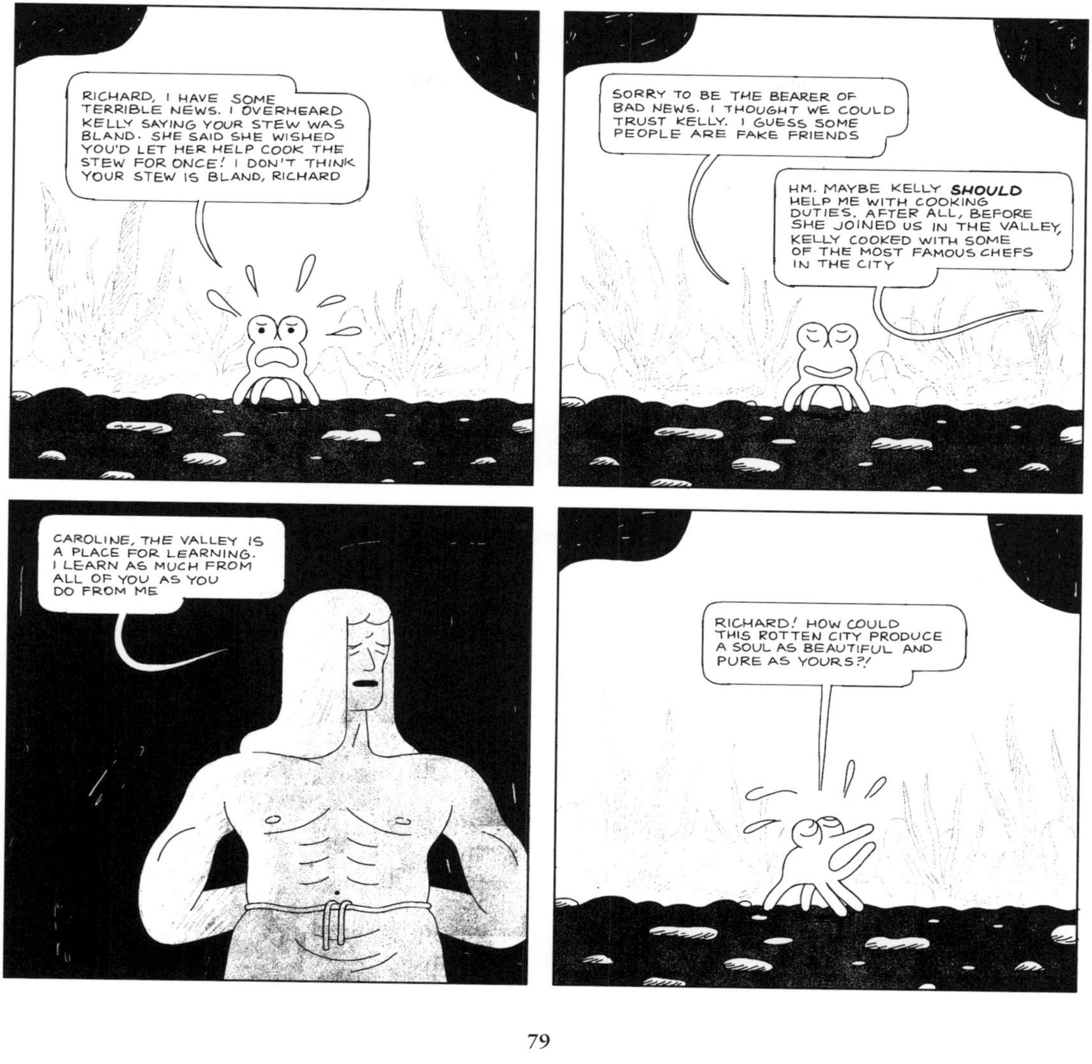
RICHARD, I HAVE SOME TERRIBLE NEWS. I OVERHEARD KELLY SAYING YOUR STEW WAS BLAND. SHE SAID SHE WISHED YOU'D LET HER HELP COOK THE STEW FOR ONCE! I DON'T THINK YOUR STEW IS BLAND, RICHARD
SORRY TO BE THE BEARER OF BAD NEWS. I THOUGHT WE COULD TRUST KELLY. I GUESS SOME PEOPLE ARE FAKE FRIENDS
HM. MAYBE KELLY **SHOULD** HELP ME WITH COOKING DUTIES. AFTER ALL, BEFORE SHE JOINED US IN THE VALLEY, KELLY COOKED WITH SOME OF THE MOST FAMOUS CHEFS IN THE CITY
CAROLINE, THE VALLEY IS A PLACE FOR LEARNING. I LEARN AS MUCH FROM ALL OF YOU AS YOU DO FROM ME
RICHARD! HOW COULD THIS ROTTEN CITY PRODUCE A SOUL AS BEAUTIFUL AND PURE AS YOURS?!

Leaving Richard's Valley

WHAT WAS RICHARD LIKE?
I HEARD HE'S A HUNDRED YEARS OLD
MY MOM HAD SOME OF RICHARD'S OLD CDS. THEY'RE GOOD
I HEARD HE LOCKED YOU ALL UP TO KEEP YOU IN THE VALLEY
ARE YOU, LIKE, ALL MARRIED TO EACH OTHER OR SOMETHING?
IS RICHARD YOUR GOD?
IS IT TRUE YOU'RE ALL RELATED?
I HEARD RICHARD DOESN'T EAT
DOES RICHARD STILL PLAY GUITAR? DID YOU EVER JAM?
I HEARD RICHARD ONLY LIVES OFF SUNSHINE AND WATER
DO YOU MISS THE VALLEY?
DOES RICHARD STILL WRITE NEW SONGS?
ARE YOU ALL MESSED UP IN THE HEAD FROM LIVING THERE?

Leaving Richard's Valley

DO YOU EVER HAVE ONE OF THOSE DAYS
WHERE YOU START THINKING ABOUT HOW WONDERFUL RICHARD IS AND BEGIN TO WEEP UNCONTROLLABLY
I'M GONNA GO SEE WHAT RICHARD IS UP TO

Leaving Richard's Valley

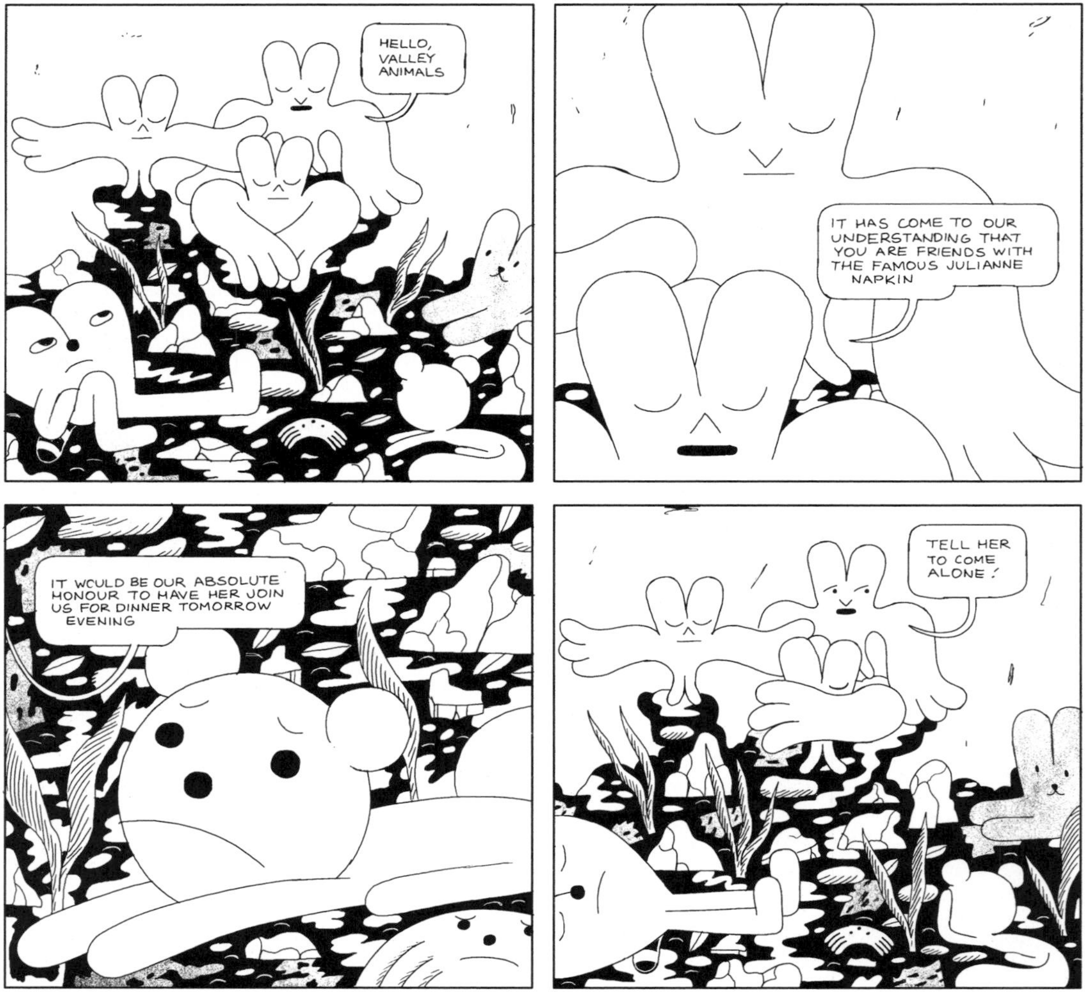

HELLO, VALLEY ANIMALS
IT HAS COME TO OUR UNDERSTANDING THAT YOU ARE FRIENDS WITH THE FAMOUS JULIANNE NAPKIN
IT WOULD BE OUR ABSOLUTE HONOUR TO HAVE HER JOIN US FOR DINNER TOMORROW EVENING
TELL HER TO COME ALONE!

Leaving Richard's Valley

With love,
J.N.

Leaving Richard's Valley

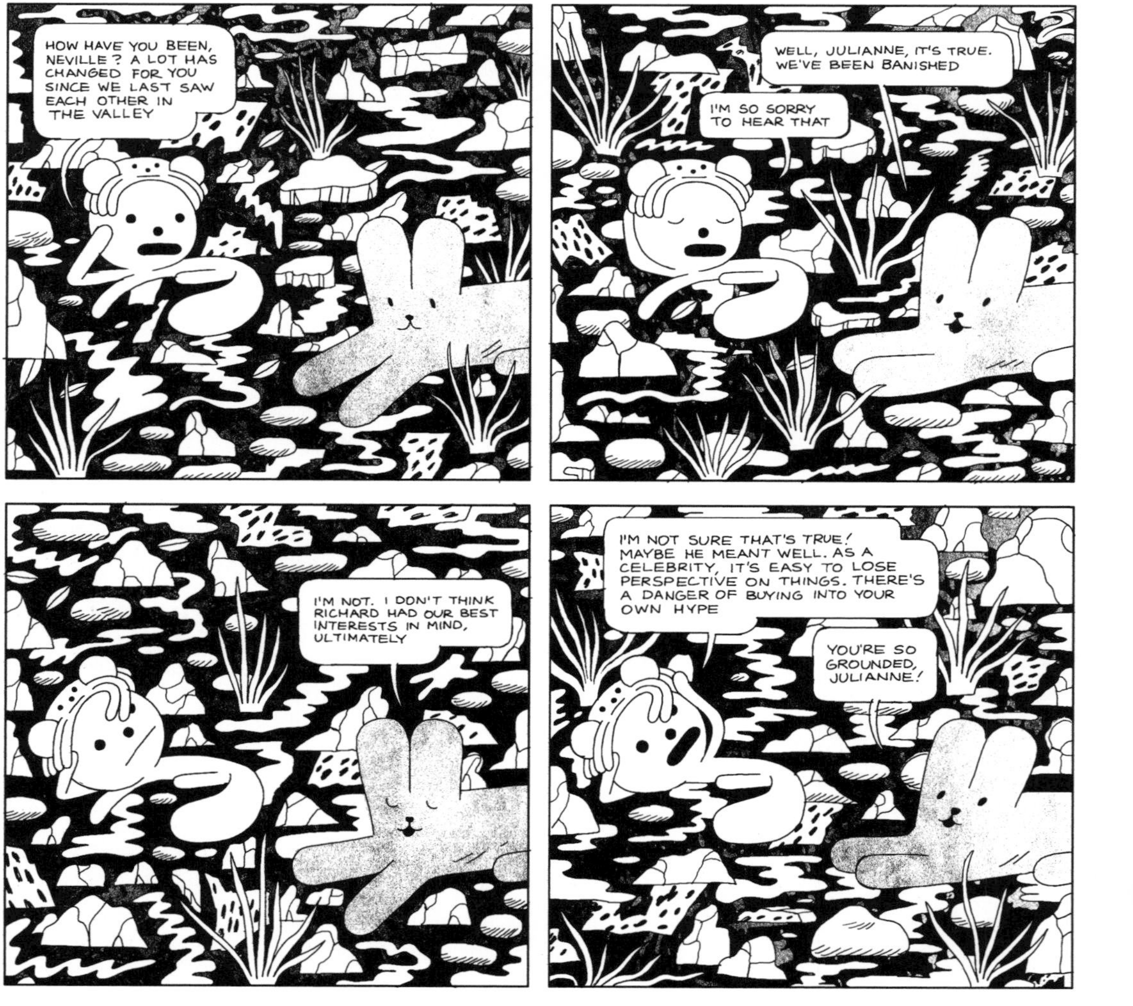
HOW HAVE YOU BEEN, NEVILLE? A LOT HAS CHANGED FOR YOU SINCE WE LAST SAW EACH OTHER IN THE VALLEY
WELL, JULIANNE, IT'S TRUE. WE'VE BEEN BANISHED
I'M SO SORRY TO HEAR THAT
I'M NOT. I DON'T THINK RICHARD HAD OUR BEST INTERESTS IN MIND, ULTIMATELY
I'M NOT SURE THAT'S TRUE! MAYBE HE MEANT WELL. AS A CELEBRITY, IT'S EASY TO LOSE PERSPECTIVE ON THINGS. THERE'S A DANGER OF BUYING INTO YOUR OWN HYPE
YOU'RE SO GROUNDED, JULIANNE!

Leaving Richard's Valley

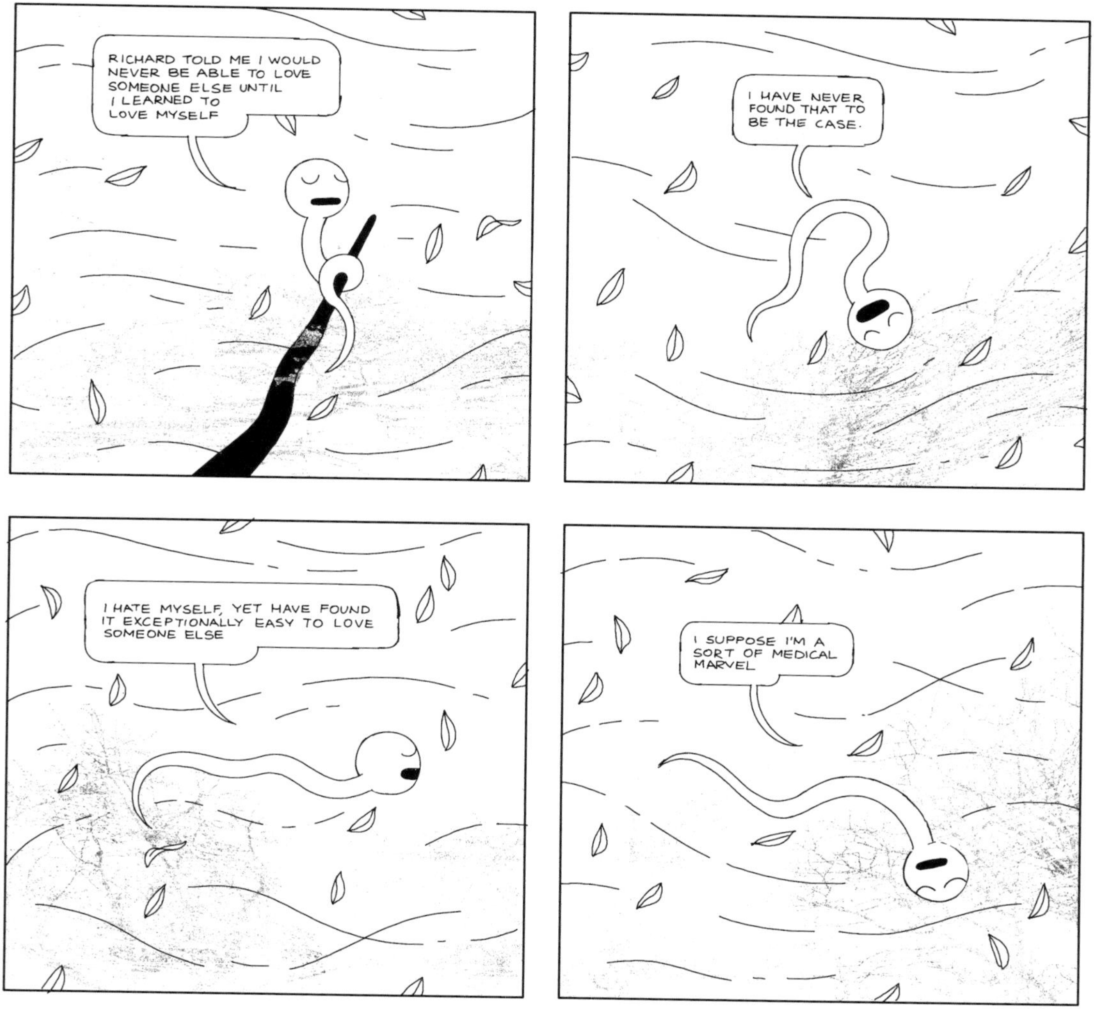
RICHARD TOLD ME I WOULD NEVER BE ABLE TO LOVE SOMEONE ELSE UNTIL I LEARNED TO LOVE MYSELF
I HAVE NEVER FOUND THAT TO BE THE CASE.
I HATE MYSELF, YET HAVE FOUND IT EXCEPTIONALLY EASY TO LOVE SOMEONE ELSE
I SUPPOSE I'M A SORT OF MEDICAL MARVEL

Leaving Richard's Valley

GOSH... IT'S ONLY BEEN A FEW DAYS, BUT I MISS SO MANY OF OUR OLD FRIENDS FROM THE VALLEY
MAYBE YOU SHOULD HAVE THOUGHT ABOUT THAT BEFORE YOU DISOBEYED RICHARD
WELL,
I HOPE WE SEE THEM AGAIN SOMEDAY

Leaving Richard's Valley

LONELINESS
IS A CLOAK YOU WEAR
A DEEP SHADE OF BLUE... IS ALWAYS THERE
THE SUN AIN'T GONNA SHINE ANYMORE

THE MOON AIN'T GONNA RISE IN THE SKY
THE TEARS ARE ALWAYS CLOUDING YOUR EYES
WHEN YOU'RE WITHOOOOUUT LOVE
BAAAABYYY
LONELY
WITHOUT YOU BABY

Leaving Richard's Valley

GIRL, I NEED YOU
I CAN'T GO OOOONNN
THE SUN AIN'T GONNA SHINE ANYMORE
THE SUN AIN'T GONNA SHINE ANYMORE
THE MOON AIN'T GONNA RISE IN THE SKY
THE MOON AIN'T GONNA RISE IN THE SKY
THE TEARS ARE ALWAYS CLOUDING YOUR EYES
THE TEARS ARE ALWAYS CLOUDING YOUR EYES
WHEN
YOU'RE
WITHOUT
LOVE

Leaving Richard's Valley

OMIGOSH! NEVILLE! LYLE! WE'VE BEEN REUNITED!
...
IT'S SO NICE TO SEE FAMILIAR FACES. PEOPLE IN THIS PARK CAN BE SO **MEAN**
OH...
A JOGGER ALMOST STEPPED ON ME!
SO WHAT'S THE PLAN? WHERE ARE WE LIVING THESE DAYS
DON'T TELL HIM

Leaving Richard's Valley

WHAT A BEAUTIFUL PERFORMANCE, JULIANNE!
TRULY STUNNING
MAY WE ASK YOU SOMETHING?
WHY DO YOU ASSOCIATE WITH THOSE RICHARD'S VALLEY PEOPLE?
THEY'RE SO ODD
IS IT RESEARCH? FOR SOME SORT OF FILM ROLE?
ARE YOU BEING BLACKMAILED?

Leaving Richard's Valley

WHAT'S YOUR NAME?
OMAR
OK, I'M PAUL

HOW DID THE TWO OF YOU MEET JULIANNE NAPKIN?
JULIANNE, ELLIE, AND I ARE ALL BEST FRIENDS
WE'VE KNOWN EACH OTHER SINCE WE WERE BABIES
IS IT WEIRD THAT JULIANNE HAS GOTTEN SO FAMOUS?
A LITTLE. SOMETIMES I WORRY SHE'LL OUTGROW US
SHE HAS THIS WHOLE OTHER WORLD WE'LL NEVER BE A PART OF
BUT I COULD NEVER ABANDON MY ROOTS!
JULIANNE!?

Leaving Richard's Valley

Leaving Richard's Valley

IS HE STILL FOLLOWING US?
WHY DON'T YOU WANT HIM AROUND?
HE WAS A VALLEY FRIEND. WE'RE NOT IN THE VALLEY ANYMORE... NO THANKS TO YOU...
I GUESS YOU HAVE A POINT. THE VALLEY APPARENTLY HAS A LOT OF NEGATIVE CONNOTATIONS WITH THE REST OF THE PARK
WE STAND A BETTER CHANCE OF INTEGRATING IF WE DISTANCE--
IS HE GONE YET?

Leaving Richard's Valley

WHAT MAKES ME SO UNIQUELY UNLOVABLE?
MY MONOTONOUS VOICE? MY LACK OF ARMS?
I WISH I COULD PUT A HAND ON THE SHOULDER OF A FRIEND... LEAN IN, AND WITH A WARM, SINGSONG INTONATION
ASK THEM QUESTIONS ABOUT COMPUTERS

Leaving Richard's Valley

ME AND RICHARD? WE DON'T HAVE TIME FOR THE SNAKE MARKS OF THE WORLD
("SNAKES MARK OF THE WORLD?")
I'VE KNOWN MARK SINCE THE POND DAYS. HE'S ALWAYS BEEN A DREAMER
A SITTER. A STEWER. NOT ME, PAL! NOT CAROLINE!

Leaving Richard's Valley

WELCOME TO RICHARD'S VALLEY! WHAT BRINGS YOU HERE, STRANGERS?
HAVE YOU COME TO LEARN ABOUT ALL THE SECRETS OUR VALLEY POSSESSES? TO UNLOCK ITS GENTLE MYSTERIES? OR DID YOU SIMPLY HAPPEN BY OUR HAPPY HOME ON A ROMANTIC STROLL THROUGH THE PARK?
I WILL INTRODUCE YOU TO RICHARD, THE LEADER OF OUR MERRY BAND, WHO WILL THUSLY--
WAIT
WHERE ARE YOU GOING?

DOES THE REST OF THE PARK SEEM JUDGEY TO YOU?
YEAH
NOT PAUL, THOUGH
YEAH, PAUL IS COOL
MAYBE WE'RE NOT READY FOR LIFE OUTSIDE THE VALLEY, OMAR!

Leaving Richard's Valley

ANOTHER PARK?
MAYBE
A SIDEWALK?
GOD FORBID
A DUPLEX? A CONDO?
HMM
THE WATER?
CAN'T SWIM

Leaving Richard's Valley

WHY DON'T YOU WANT TO STAY IN THE PARK, OMAR? DON'T YOU LIKE IT HERE?
I LIKED RICHARD'S VALLEY. THE PARK IS DIFFERENT. ANIMALS AREN'T NICE LIKE THEY ARE IN THE VALLEY
I'M NICE
THAT'S TRUE
WHERE WILL YOU GO?
DUNNO. NEVILLE HAS IDEAS

Leaving Richard's Valley

HAVE YOU EVER THOUGHT THAT MAYBE THE VALLEY ISN'T JUST A **PLACE...**
IT'S MORE LIKE AN **IDEA...**
YES
YES

Leaving Richard's Valley

WHERE DO RACCOONS NORMALLY LIVE, LYLE?
I'VE BEEN IN THE VALLEY SO LONG IT'S HARD TO REMEMBER. TRASH CANS? PILES OF LEAVES?
I DON'T WANNA LIVE IN TRASH
DON'T KNOCK IT 'TIL YOU'VE TRIED IT

Leaving Richard's Valley

Leaving Richard's Valley

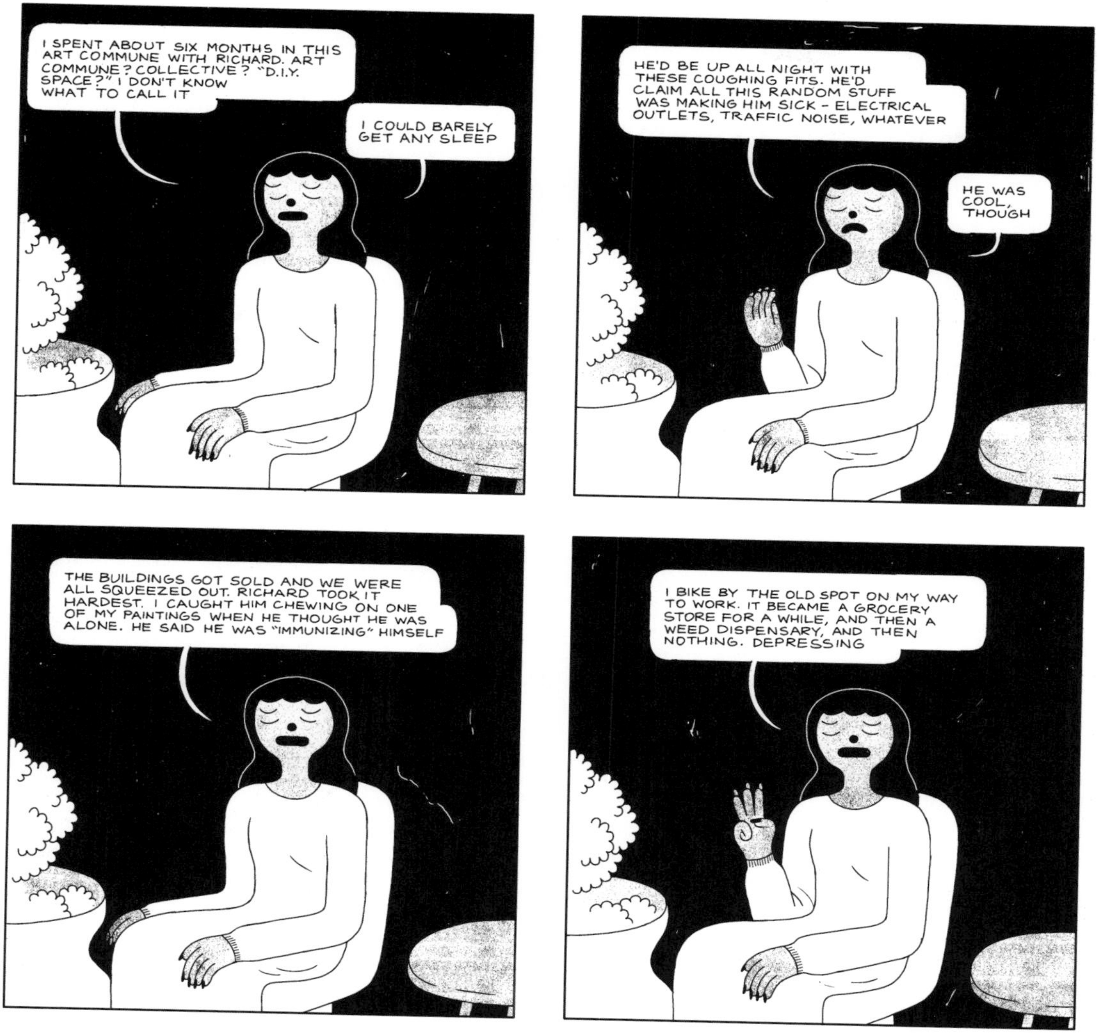
I SPENT ABOUT SIX MONTHS IN THIS ART COMMUNE WITH RICHARD. ART COMMUNE? COLLECTIVE? "D.I.Y. SPACE?" I DON'T KNOW WHAT TO CALL IT
I COULD BARELY GET ANY SLEEP
HE'D BE UP ALL NIGHT WITH THESE COUGHING FITS. HE'D CLAIM ALL THIS RANDOM STUFF WAS MAKING HIM SICK - ELECTRICAL OUTLETS, TRAFFIC NOISE, WHATEVER
HE WAS COOL, THOUGH
THE BUILDINGS GOT SOLD AND WE WERE ALL SQUEEZED OUT. RICHARD TOOK IT HARDEST. I CAUGHT HIM CHEWING ON ONE OF MY PAINTINGS WHEN HE THOUGHT HE WAS ALONE. HE SAID HE WAS "IMMUNIZING" HIMSELF
I BIKE BY THE OLD SPOT ON MY WAY TO WORK. IT BECAME A GROCERY STORE FOR A WHILE, AND THEN A WEED DISPENSARY, AND THEN NOTHING. DEPRESSING

Leaving Richard's Valley

WHY DO I HAVE TO BE LIKE THIS
CAN'T I BE MORE LIKE LYLE?
LYLE IS SO BRAVE. HE'S FACED DOWN ILLNESS... EXILE... HE STAYS STEADFAST AND CALM WHILE THE REST OF HIS GROUP JUST TITTERS ABOUT
LYLE... BRAVE LYLE... BRAVE, BEAUTIFUL LYLE...

Leaving Richard's Valley

RICHARD NEVER LET ME SPIN WEBS THIS BIG
HE DIDN'T LIKE GETTING THEM IN HIS HAIR
THIS IS NICE

Leaving Richard's Valley

WHY DON'T YOU MARRY ME BIII-IIILL
I LOVE YOU SO, I ALWAYS WILL
AND IN YOUR VOICE I HEAR A CHOIR OF CAROUSEEE-ELLS
BUT AM I EVER GONNA HEAR THOSE WEDDING BELLS

Leaving Richard's Valley

Leaving Richard's Valley

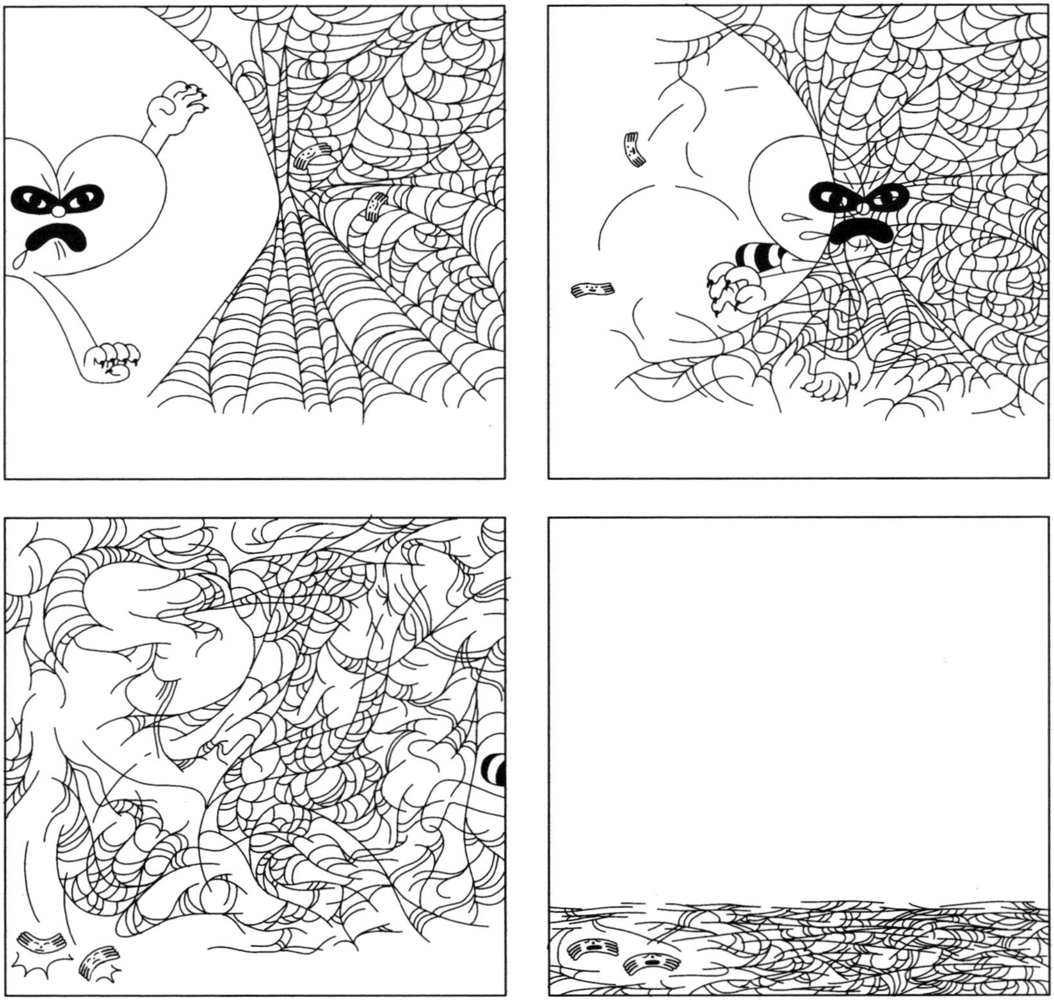

Leaving Richard's Valley

AHH
OH NO! OH GOSH!
...
...
WHAT HAPPENED HERE?!

Leaving Richard's Valley

LYLE! NEVILLE!
A ROTTEN RACCOON KNOCKED OVER OMAR AND OUR FRIEND PAUL!
PAUL'S LEG IS **BROKEN**!!
WE HAVE TO DO SOMETHING!

Leaving Richard's Valley

JULIANNE NAPKIN, WHAT'S WRONG?
OH... YOU BIRDS HAVE TREATED ME SO KINDLY SINCE I ARRIVED HERE
BUT NOT EVERY ANIMAL IN THE PARK HAS GREETED ME AND MY FRIENDS WITH THE SAME GENEROSITY
A CERTAIN RACCOON, FOR INSTANCE...

WHAT HAPPENED TO YOUR TAIL?
BIRDS TOOK IT
I DON'T SEE WHAT THE BIG DEAL WAS... I WAS JUST HORSING AROUND
ROUGHHOUSING! I'M A FERAL RACCOON, WHAT DO THEY EXPECT?!

Leaving Richard's Valley

...HELLO
!
ARE YOU... ONE OF THOSE RICHARD PEOPLE?
YES! YES I AM. YOU LOOK INJURED
MY FRIEND TOLD ME TO COME TO THIS VALLEY
HE TOLD ME THAT RICHARD COULD HEAL MY BROKEN BODY

Leaving Richard's Valley

WELL, WE'RE FINALLY DOING IT. WE'RE FINALLY LEAVING THE PARK
ONCE WE FINISH CROSSING THIS STREET, WE'LL BE OUT OF THE PARK FOR GOOD
WELL, WE'VE DONE IT. WE'VE OFFICIALLY LEFT THE PARK

Leaving Richard's Valley

I THINK THIS WILL BE GOOD FOR US. THAT PARK WAS DANGEROUS
I THINK IT WAS MESSING WITH OUR HEADS
ORDERING THE DE-TAILING OF THAT RACCOON WAS SORT OF STARTLING
I WONDER IF LIVING IN THE VALLEY SO LONG HAS MADE IT IMPOSSIBLE TO LIVE ANYWHERE ELSE
I WONDER IF WE DIED THE SECOND WE LEFT THE VALLEY AND EVER SINCE THEN WE'VE JUST BEEN WANDERING AROUND IN HELL

Leaving Richard's Valley

WHY IS EVERYONE HONKING AT US?
ARE THEY MAD AT US?! WHAT DID WE DO?!
STOP HONKING!
BE NICE TO US, PLEASE!

Leaving Richard's Valley

YOU KNOW
THE MORE YOU HONK, THE SLOWER WE'LL WALK
THE SLOWER YOU WALK, THE MORE WE'LL TOOT
THE MORE YOU TOOT, THE BETTER YOU'LL FEEL
SO EAT BEANS WITH EVERY MEAL

Leaving Richard's Valley

I GUESS I LIKE TRAFFIC JAMS! I GUESS I LOVE THEM!
KEEP HONKING! WON'T HELP!
YOU'RE POISONING THE WORLD WITH THESE GAS GUZZLERS
UGH
SOMEBODY CALL ANIMAL CONTROL
I MOSTLY GUZZLE NUTS AND BERRIES
STOP DANCING!
I WON'T STOP DANCING! MAYBE I'M RABID!

Leaving Richard's Valley

WHAT DO WE WANT
RICHARD
WHEN DO WE WANT IT
I MISS YOU, RICHARD
WHAT DO WE WANT
RICHARD
WHEN DO WE WANT IT
RICHARD, I WANT TO COME BACK

WHY AM I LIKE THIS?
- "I'M SAD, BUT I DON'T KNOW WHY"
- "MY ARMS ARE SORE"
- "I FEEL ITCHY WHENEVER MY PHONE RINGS OR MY STOVE IS TURNED ON"
- "I AM COUGHING"
- "RECEIVING AN E-MAIL GIVES ME A PANIC ATTACK"
Does this describe you? Richard is here to help and here to heal. Come to Richard's Valley for a free learning session. Mixers are held every Tuesday night at 7pm.
NO PHONES

Leaving Richard's Valley

LOVELY LYLE
BOLD AND BRASH
'TIS YOUR LIPS THAT I YEARN TO SMOOCH
AND SHOULD THIS NEVER COME TO PASS
I GUESS I'LL GO JUMP OFF SOME ROOF

Leaving Richard's Valley

RICHARD
LYLE
NEVILLE
ELLIE SQUIRREL
OMAR THE SPIDER
JULIANNE NAPKIN
CAROLINE
SNAKE MARK
PARK BIRDS
PARK SQUIRREL
FERAL RACCOON
LYLE'S BROTHER
AREN (DECEASED)
PAUL
CYNTHIA (DECEASED)
RICHARD'S OTHER SPOUSES

Leaving Richard's Valley

I STARTED WRITING FOR THE VARSITY DURING MY SECOND YEAR OF UNIVERSITY. IF YOU'VE EVER WRITTEN FOR A SCHOOL PAPER IN THE CITY, THERE'S, LIKE, A FIFTY PERCENT CHANCE YOU'VE INTERVIEWED RICHARD OR DONE A STORY ON THE VALLEY AT LEAST ONCE
THEY'RE SUCH AN INSTITUTION HERE THAT IT'S KIND OF LIKE A JOURNALISTIC RITE OF PASSAGE. MOST STUDENTS WILL VISIT AT SOME POINT, EITHER TO GAWK OR GET A FREE MEAL FROM THEIR LEARNING SESSIONS
WHEN I WENT THERE FOR MY INTERVIEW, I TOTALLY SCREWED THE POOCH. I FORGOT ABOUT THE VALLEY'S NO-PHONE POLICY AND BROUGHT MINE AS A RECORDING DEVICE
RICHARD FLIPPED. A BEAR CAME OVER AND ATE MY PHONE. LUCKILY I BROUGHT A NOTEPAD, AND THE REST OF THE INTERVIEW WENT FINE

Leaving Richard's Valley

YOU KNOW, YOU'RE PRETTY LUCKY I WAS THE FIRST ONE YOU MET IN THE VALLEY. DON'T MAKE A BIG DEAL ABOUT THIS, BUT I'M KIND OF THE UNOFFICIAL SECOND IN COMMAND AROUND HERE
OK
I'M A LOT OF THINGS TO RICHARD. HIS ENFORCER, HIS CONFIDANT, ONE OF HIS BEST FRIENDS
OK
I'M SORT OF LIKE RICHARD'S RIGHT HAND
I KNOW YOU'RE SHAPED LIKE A HAND, BUT DON'T GET ANY IDEAS!
HA HA HA
I JUST WANT TO KNOW HOW TO FIX MY ARM

Leaving Richard's Valley

WE'RE CAUSING A RUCKUS! WE'RE CAUSING RUCKUSES NOW!
I THINK IT'S A GOOD DEVELOPMENT
WE SPENT SO LONG UNDER RICHARD'S THUMB
NOW WE HAVE NO LEADER! NO BOSSES! WE CAN FINALLY SELF-ACTUALIZE
I NEVER THOUGHT OF RICHARD AS OUR "BOSS"
TAKE A HIKE, ANIMALS!

Leaving Richard's Valley

WHAT'S THAT NOISE?
?
THE EARTH IS SHAKING!
I'M GETTING SCARED, OMAR!

Leaving Richard's Valley

Leaving Richard's Valley

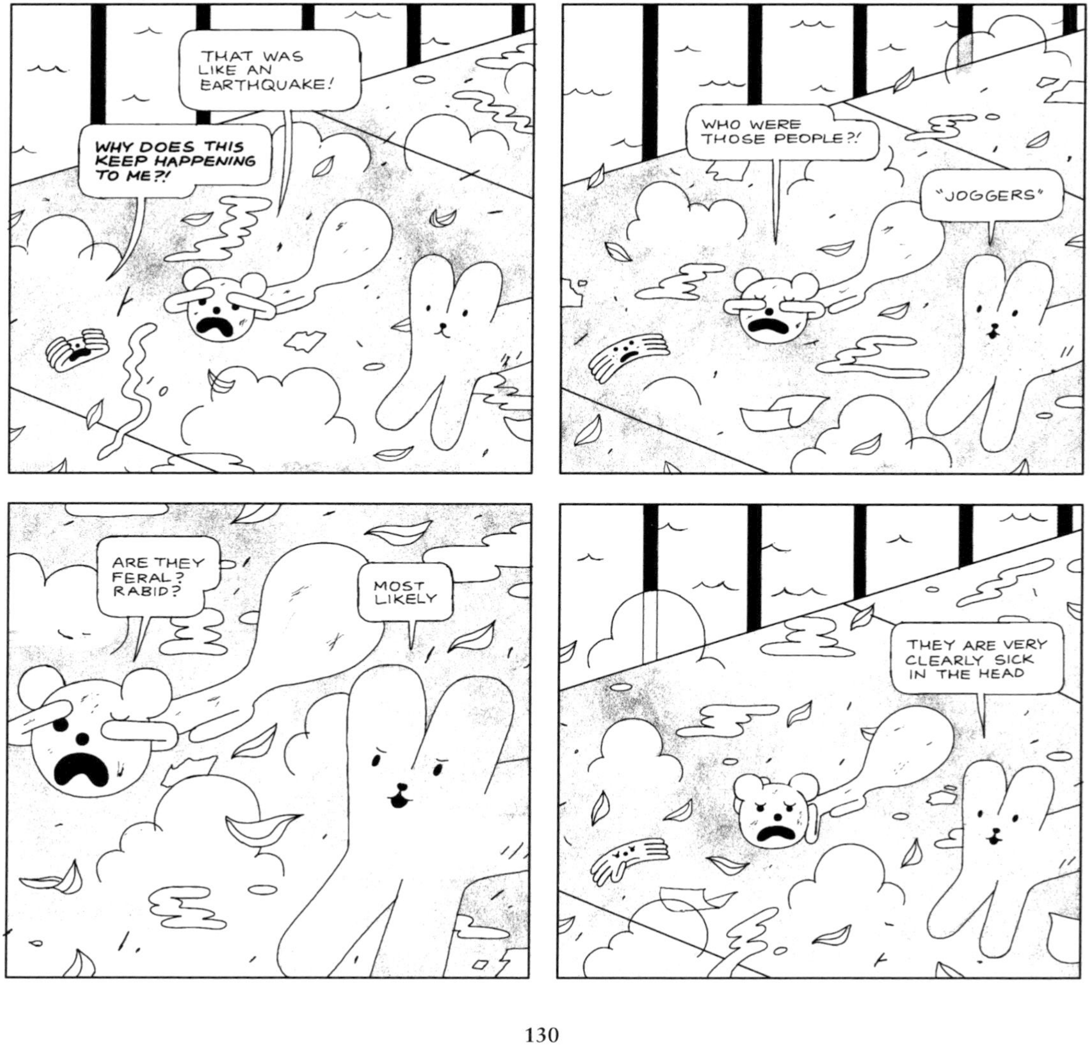
THAT WAS LIKE AN EARTHQUAKE!
WHY DOES THIS KEEP HAPPENING TO ME?!
WHO WERE THOSE PEOPLE?!
"JOGGERS"
ARE THEY FERAL? RABID?
MOST LIKELY
THEY ARE VERY CLEARLY SICK IN THE HEAD

Leaving Richard's Valley

ENERGY SURPLUS
50% OFF SALE
IS THAT A GIANT SQUIRREL?
LOOKS LIKE
I DIDN'T KNOW WE COULD GROW THAT BIG
WELL,
TOXINS AND POISONS FROM THE CITY MUST CAUSE THE ANIMALS HERE TO GROW VERY DEFORMED

Leaving Richard's Valley

EXCUSE ME! MY NAME IS ELLIE. HELLO!
I'M A SQUIRREL LIKE YOURSELF. WE'RE NOT FROM AROUND HERE AND COULD USE SOME HELP!
DO YOU KNOW OF ANY APARTMENTS FOR RENT THAT ARE ANIMAL-FRIENDLY?
OR ANY SORT OF SQUIRREL FRIEND GROUPS OPEN TO NEW MEMBERS?
ENERGY SURPLUS
Everything must go!
Final month!
50% off or best offer!
SALE

Leaving Richard's Valley

"ENERGY SURPLUS: SERVICING YOUR ELECTRONICS NEEDS SINCE 1993."
DON'T TRUST THE GIANT SQUIRREL! HE'S TRYING TO TRICK YOU!
HISSSS
ARE YOU FOLLOWING US?
HISSS
DON'T GO TO THAT ADDRESS! THERE'S NOTHING FOR YOU THERE!

I'M HERE THURSDAYS, FRIDAYS AND SATURDAYS. IT'S JER ON WEDNESDAYS AND SUNDAYS. MY BOSS SAID THERE ISN'T ENOUGH FOOT TRAFFIC TO WARRANT DOING IT OTHER DAYS OF THE WEEK
CLOSING SALE
I'VE HAD WORSE GIGS. I'LL KIND OF MISS BEING "SQUIRREL GUY," THOUGH
"HEY, IT'S SQUIRREL GUY!" "CHECK IT OUT, THAT'S SQUIRREL GUY!"
Your Electronics Needs
MAYBE I'LL JUST KEEP THE DAMN COSTUME

I HAD AN OWNER ONCE. I LOVED HER DEARLY. I GOT SICK AND SHE TOOK ME TO THE VET
I LOVED MY VET. HE COULDN'T CURE ME. HE BROUGHT ME TO RICHARD, HOPING NATURAL MEDICINE WOULD HELP
I LOVED RICHARD, TOO. IT DIDN'T HELP. I'M CLEARLY INCURABLE
WHAT ARE YOU SICK WITH?
IT'S A SORT OF SPIRITUAL ILLNESS, REALLY

Leaving Richard's Valley

I'D LIKE TO BE ANYTHING BUT A SNAKE. A FLEA, PERHAPS! HUGGING YOU TIGHTLY
THE GUM BENEATH YOUR SHOE!
A FLU! A SINUS INFECTION! A RASH!
WHATEVER! I'M NOT PICKY
I THOUGHT YOU WANTED TO INTRODUCE YOURSELF
SOB
I DUNNO. I'M GOOD

Leaving Richard's Valley

LOOK, THEY JUST GIVE ME THE CREEPS. THAT'S ALL
THEY'RE NOT HURTING ANYONE!
THAT WE KNOW OF! THAT WE KNOW OF
LOOK. IF OUR KID DECIDED ONE DAY THAT THEY WANTED TO GO OFF AND JOIN RICHARD'S VALLEY, YOU WOULDN'T BE THE SLIGHTEST BIT CONCERNED?
WAIT, SO NOW YOU WANT TO HAVE KIDS?
PLEASE, I DON'T HAVE THE ENERGY TO RELITIGATE THIS ARGUMENT WHILE I'M MOULTING

Leaving Richard's Valley

Leaving Richard's Valley

WHAT'S YOUR DREAM HOME, OMAR?
A COBWEB STRETCHING FOR MILES AND MILES. WEBS AS FAR AS THE EYE CAN SEE!
THE WEB IS INESCAPABLE
TRY AS THEY MIGHT, NOT A SINGLE FLY WILL EVER DODGE THEIR STICKY INEVITABLE DEMISE
WHAT'S YOURS?
I DUNNO... MAYBE A HOLE IN A TREE
OR A PILE OF CRUMPLED UP NEWSPAPER

Leaving Richard's Valley

MY DREAM HOME? THE PALM OF RICHARDS HAND
A PILE OF DIRT
A COTTAGE
WITH A BIG POOL
AND A GUEST HOUSE FOR ALL MY FRIENDS
AN APPLE'S CORE!

I FEEL AS THOUGH I'VE BECOME THE GROUP'S DE FACTO LEADER
I GUESS IT MAKES SENSE
IN DOG YEARS, I'M THE OLDEST
IT'S A TERRIBLE RESPONSIBILITY. IS THIS HOW RICHARD FELT THIS WHOLE TIME?
HOW DOES HE BEAR IT?
I-- I JUST WANT TO DO A GOOD J-J-JOB--!

I SAY WE HOLD A VOTE TO DECIDE ON WHERE TO GO NEXT
WHY DON'T YOU JUST TELL US, NEVILLE
WE'RE A DEMOCRACY NOW. WE SHOULD ALL HAVE A SAY
JUST DECIDE FOR US. JUST TELL US
I DUNNO
I, FOR ONE, THINK WE SHOULD TRY THIS ENERGY SURPLUS PLACE. THAT LARGE SQUIRREL FRIEND OF ELLIE'S VOUCHED FOR IT, SO IT SEEMS LIKE OUR BEST LEAD
WHATEVER
OK
SURE
LET'S CALL A VOTE!
NEVILLE--

Leaving Richard's Valley

THERE ARE A FEW RULES HERE IN THE VALLEY. NUMBER ONE:
NEVER DO IMPRESSIONS OF OTHER VALLEY FOLK
NUMBER TWO: NEVER MEASURE YOUR HEIGHT
NUMBER THREE: NEVER EXERCISE MORE THAN TWICE A DAY. NUMBER FOUR: NEVER CALL RICHARD "RICK"
NUMBER FIVE: REMEMBER TO HAVE FUN!
NUMBER SIX...

Leaving Richard's Valley

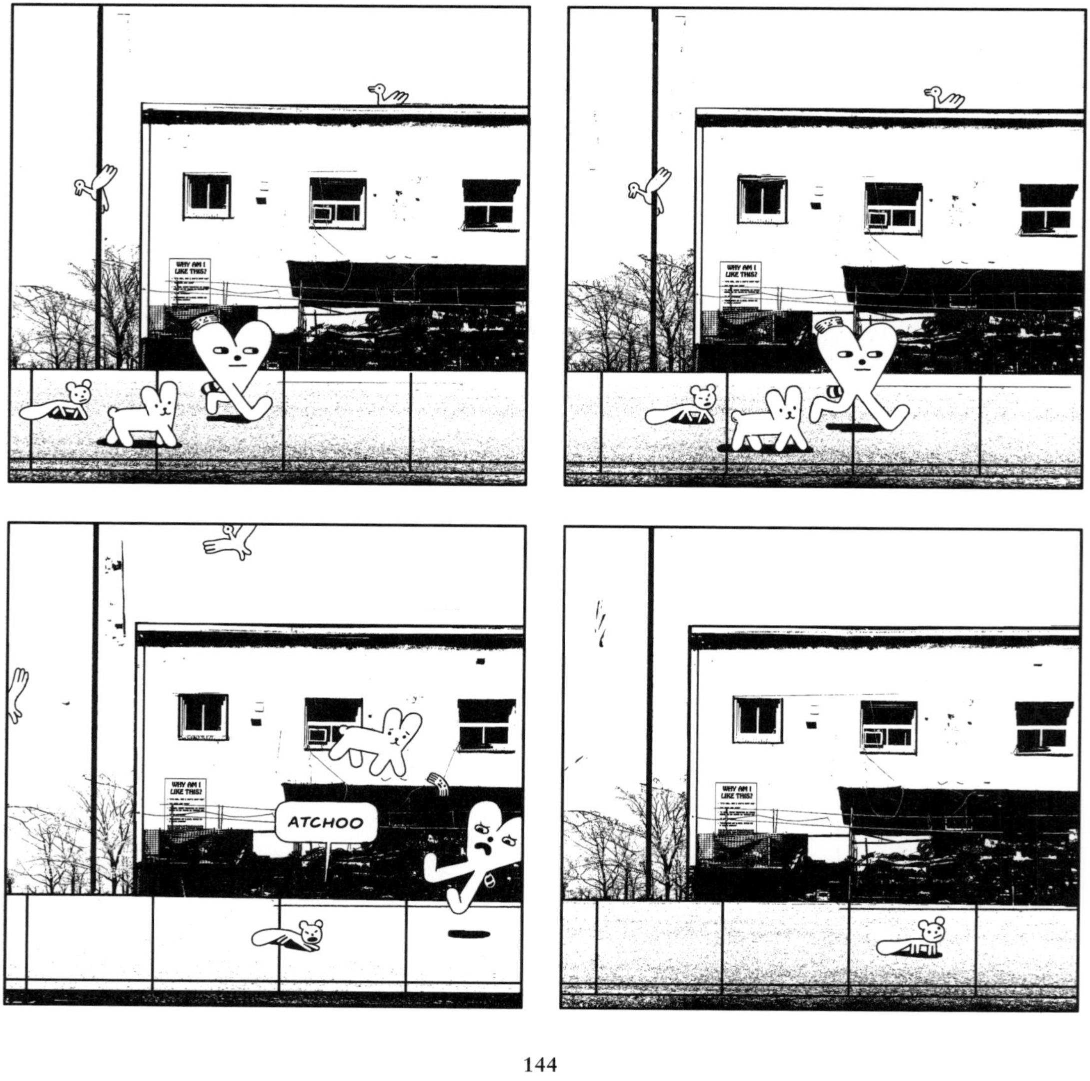
WHY AM I LIKE THIS?
WHY AM I LIKE THIS?
WHY AM I LIKE THIS?
ATCHOO
WHY AM I LIKE THIS?

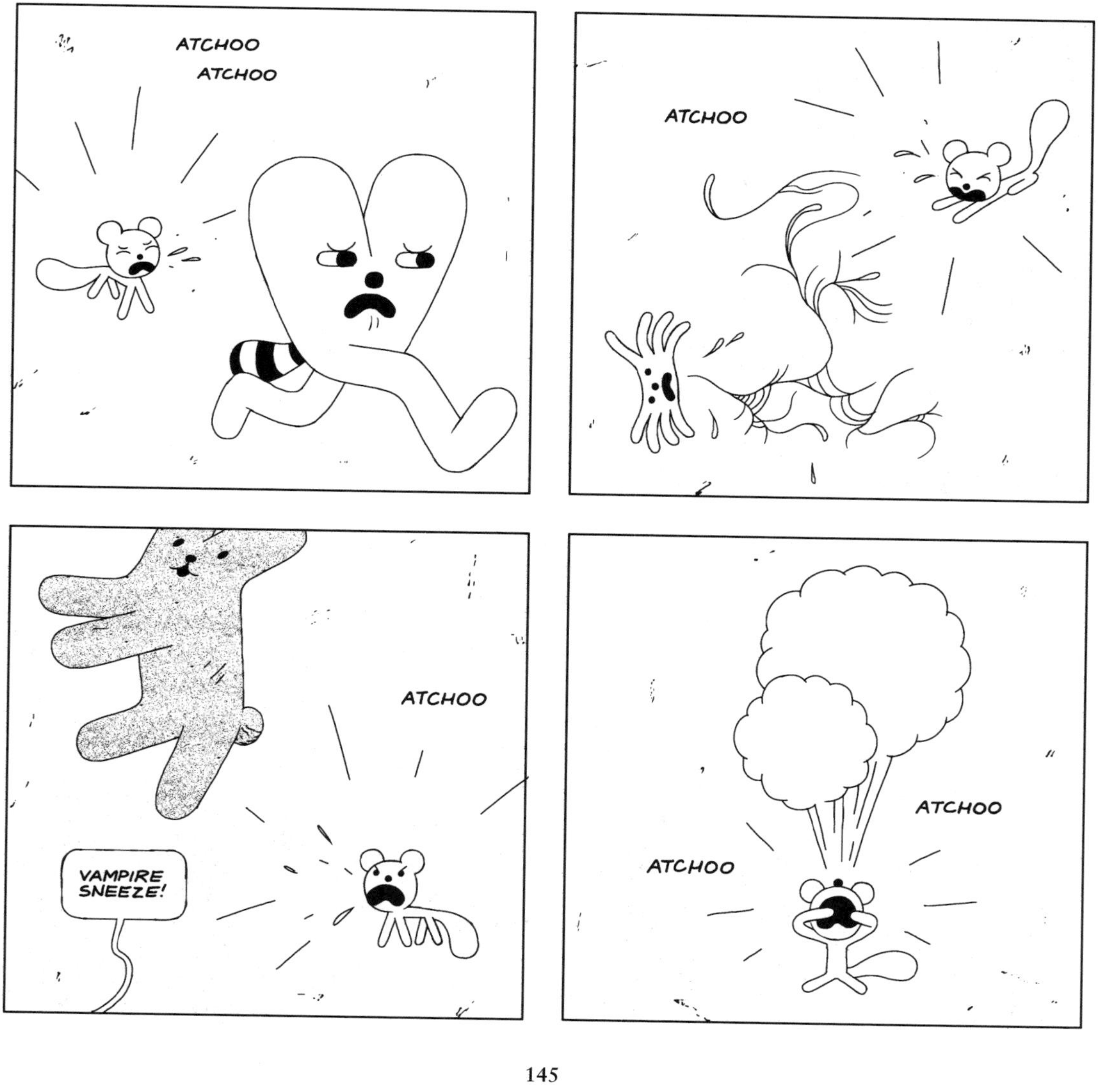
ATCHOO
ATCHOO
ATCHOO
ATCHOO
VAMPIRE SNEEZE!
ATCHOO
ATCHOO

THE WORLD BEYOND THE VALLEY IS MAKING ELLIE SICK
I THINK IT'S JUST A COLD
ALL THE TOXINS FROM THE OUTSIDE WORLD MUST FINALLY BE REACHING OUR BODIES!
HOW DO WE PROTECT OURSELVES?

Leaving Richard's Valley

UNBELIEVABLE! THEY THINK THEY'RE BETTER THAN US!
CLOTHES! THEY'RE WEARING **CLOTHES** NOW! THE NERVE OF THESE ANIMALS!
EHH, WHO CARES. THEY AREN'T HURTING ANYONE
"WHO CARES?"
"WHO CARES?!"

EXCUSE ME, LITTLE SPIDER! MAY I TAKE YOUR PHOTO?
I RUN A FASHION BLOG DOCUMENTING ALL THE CITY'S MOST FASHIONABLE STREET STYLES!
NO PHOTOS, PLEASE. WE COME FROM A GROUP THAT BELIEVES THAT CAMERAS EMIT POWERFUL, DANGEROUS RAYS
OH. OK!

SO... MY NAME'S PAUL. I'M NEW HERE
I KNOW YOUR NAME. I FEEL EVERY NEW PRESENCE IN THE VALLEY
IS IT A PAINFUL FEELING?
NO. IT'S SORT OF AN ITCHY FEELING, ON A PART OF MY BACK I CAN'T REACH

Leaving Richard's Valley

THANK YOU FOR SCRATCHING THE PART OF MY BACK I CAN'T REACH
IT'S NO PROBLEM! I'M PRETTY SMALL, I'M GOOD AT THIS STUFF
I CAN GIVE YOU A MASSAGE, TOO. I USED TO LIVE IN A SPA BEFORE IT GOT FUMIGATED
WOW, THAT FEELS AMAZING!

Leaving Richard's Valley

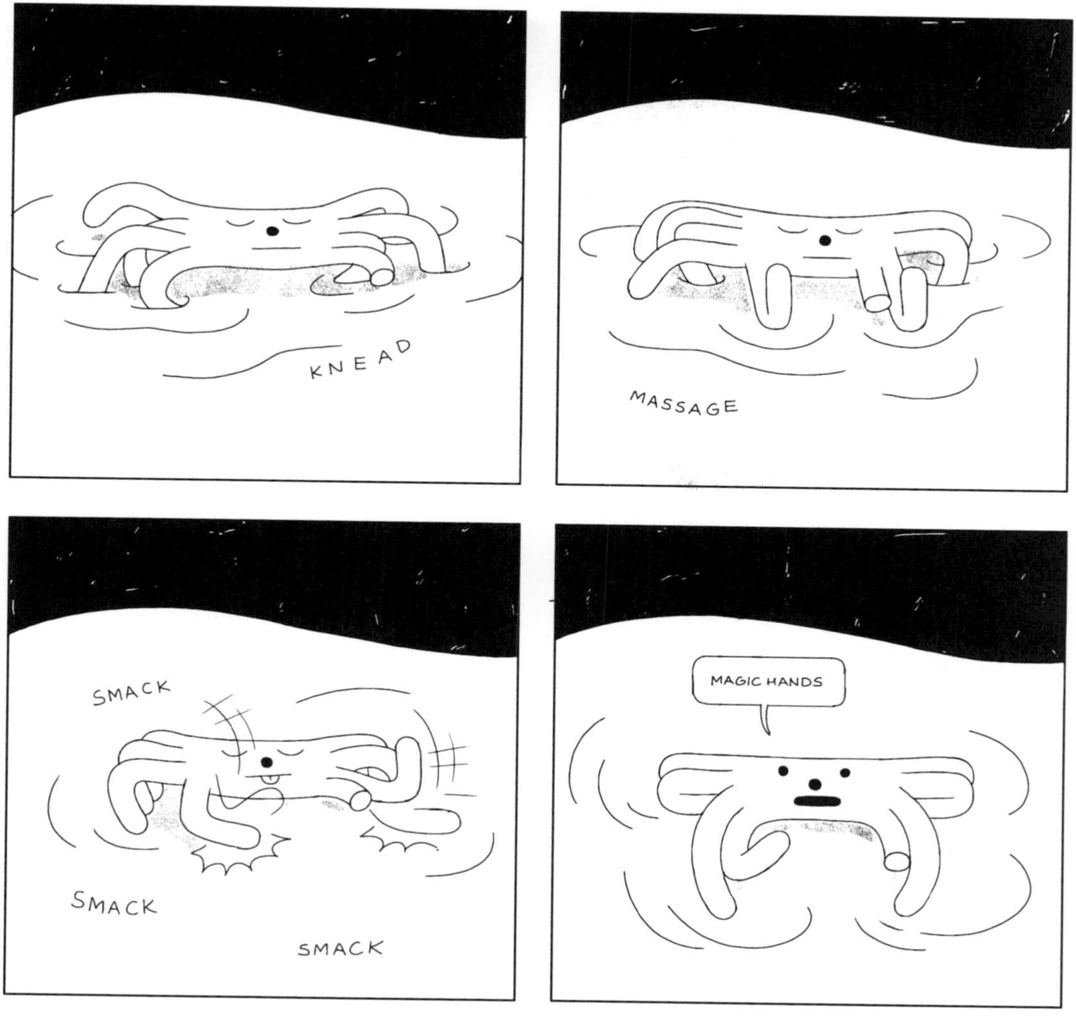
KNEAD
MASSAGE
SMACK
SMACK
SMACK
MAGIC HANDS

Leaving Richard's Valley

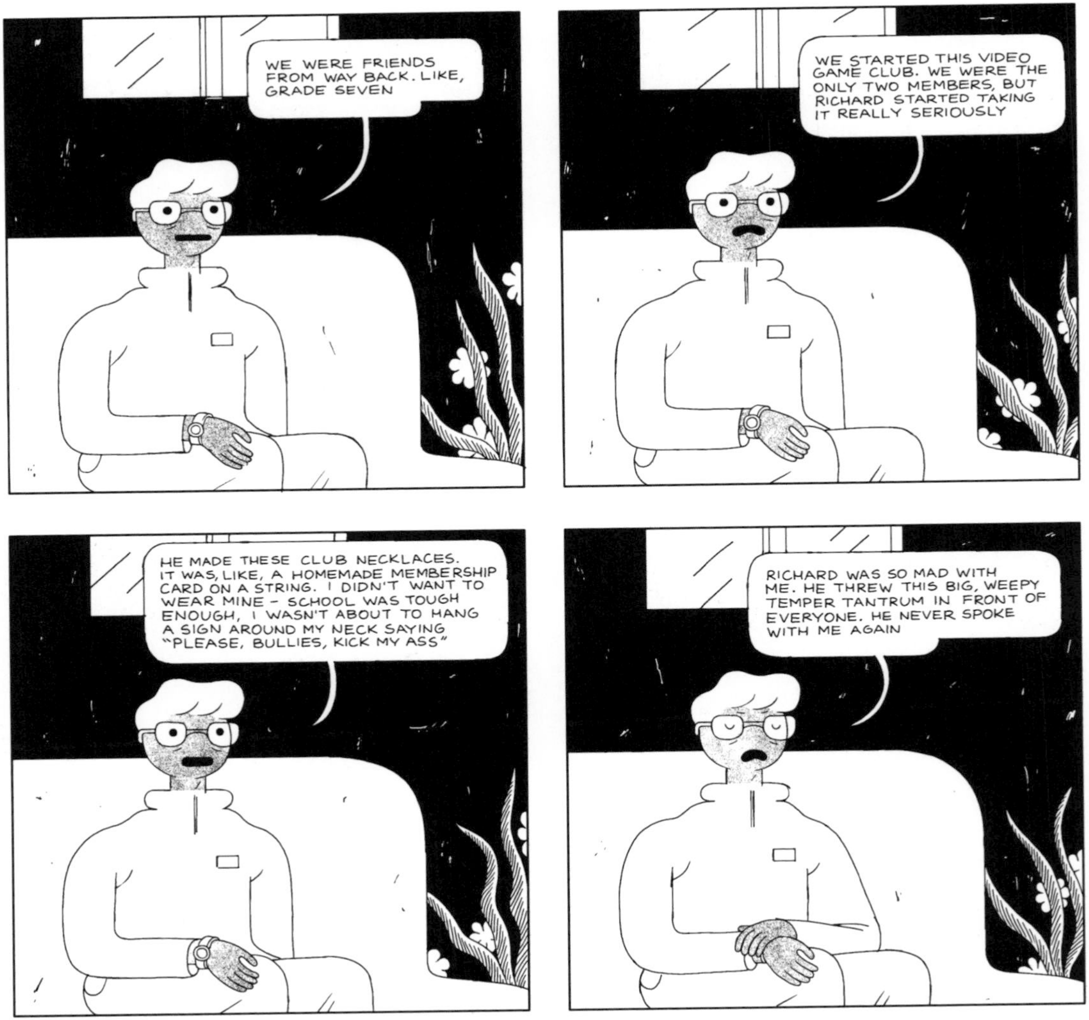
WE WERE FRIENDS FROM WAY BACK. LIKE, GRADE SEVEN
WE STARTED THIS VIDEO GAME CLUB. WE WERE THE ONLY TWO MEMBERS, BUT RICHARD STARTED TAKING IT REALLY SERIOUSLY
HE MADE THESE CLUB NECKLACES. IT WAS, LIKE, A HOMEMADE MEMBERSHIP CARD ON A STRING. I DIDN'T WANT TO WEAR MINE - SCHOOL WAS TOUGH ENOUGH, I WASN'T ABOUT TO HANG A SIGN AROUND MY NECK SAYING "PLEASE, BULLIES, KICK MY ASS"
RICHARD WAS SO MAD WITH ME. HE THREW THIS BIG, WEEPY TEMPER TANTRUM IN FRONT OF EVERYONE. HE NEVER SPOKE WITH ME AGAIN

Leaving Richard's Valley

DO YOU THINK I COULD BE A MODEL SOME DAY?
LIKE JULIANNE?
WHAT WOULD A SPIDER EVEN MODEL?
ALL SORTS OF STUFF...
WEBS... SMALL JACKETS... SMALL HATS...

OMAR
THE SPIDER
A NEW TOP 20

Leaving Richard's Valley

THAT ROTTEN LITTLE SUCK-UP SPIDER!
I HEAR HE'S GIVING OUT FREE MASSAGES TO THE WHOLE VALLEY ...UCH
I'M SO MAD I COULD SING!
MASSAGE
BUT RICHARD SAYS SINGING IN ANGER LEADS TO HEART DISEASE
I NEED... A PRODUCTIVE OUTLET FOR ALL THIS ENERGY...!

Leaving Richard's Valley

WHAT ARE YOU DOING?
YOGA

Leaving Richard's Valley

DO YOU EVER THINK ABOUT "CAREERS?"
I SUPPOSE I SHOULD START. THAT SEEMS TO BE A CONCERN WITH FOLKS OUTSIDE THE VALLEY
HOW WOULD I GET A JOB?
I THINK YOU HAVE TO GO A TO UNIVERSITY
I WANT TO GO TO MODEL UNIVERSITY
OR MAYBE YOU HAVE TO BE AN INTERN FIRST. MAYBE YOU NEED AN INTERNSHIP

Leaving Richard's Valley

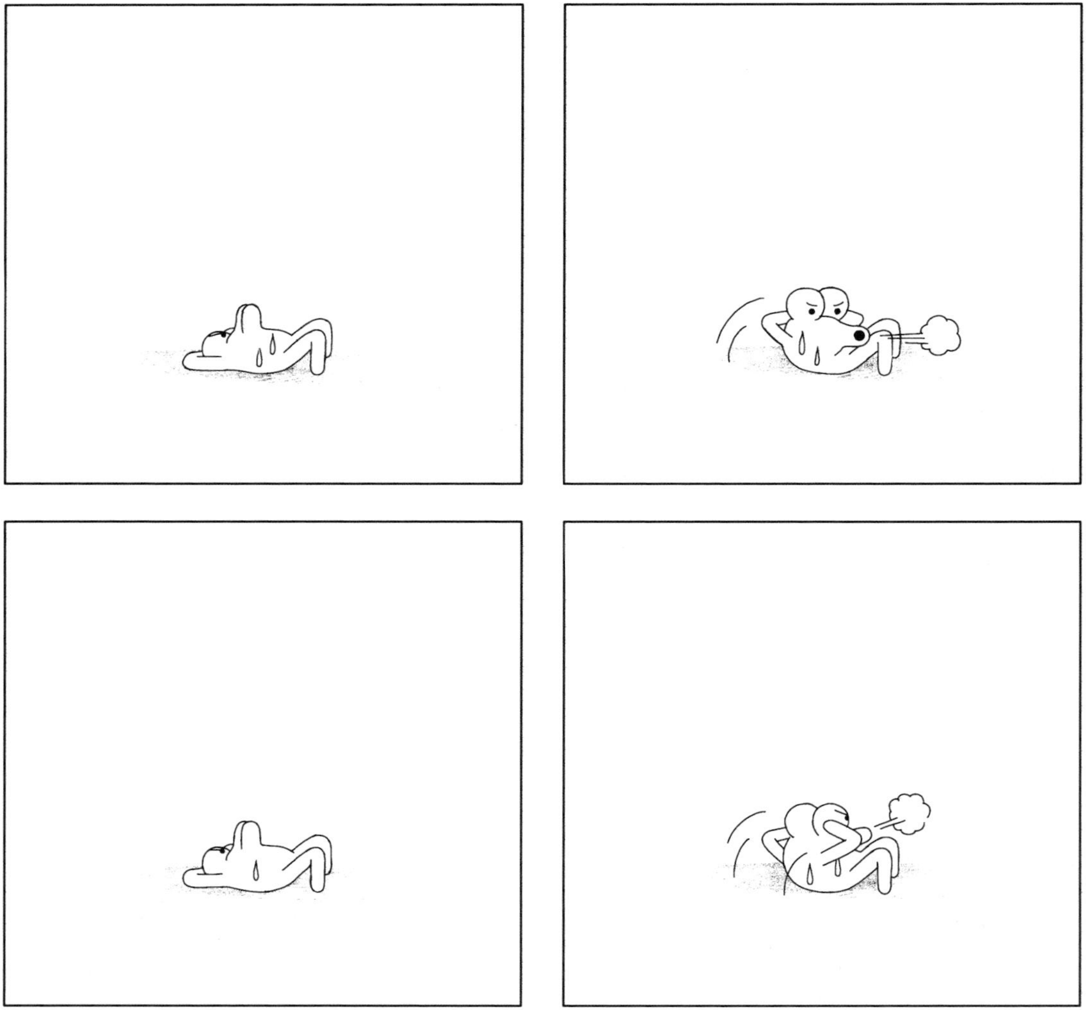

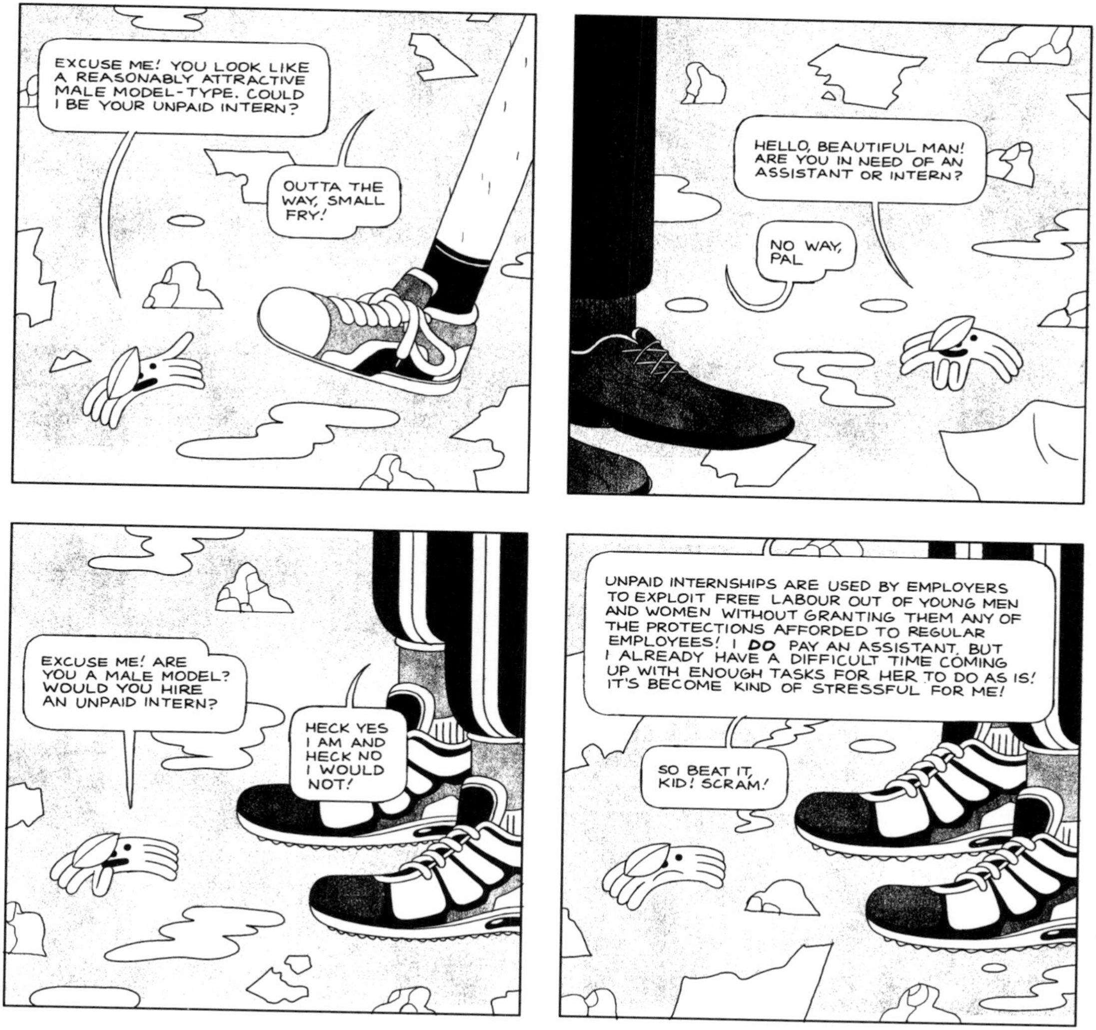
EXCUSE ME! YOU LOOK LIKE A REASONABLY ATTRACTIVE MALE MODEL-TYPE. COULD I BE YOUR UNPAID INTERN?
OUTTA THE WAY, SMALL FRY!
HELLO, BEAUTIFUL MAN! ARE YOU IN NEED OF AN ASSISTANT OR INTERN?
NO WAY, PAL
EXCUSE ME! ARE YOU A MALE MODEL? WOULD YOU HIRE AN UNPAID INTERN?
HECK YES I AM AND HECK NO I WOULD NOT!
UNPAID INTERNSHIPS ARE USED BY EMPLOYERS TO EXPLOIT FREE LABOUR OUT OF YOUNG MEN AND WOMEN WITHOUT GRANTING THEM ANY OF THE PROTECTIONS AFFORDED TO REGULAR EMPLOYEES! I DO PAY AN ASSISTANT, BUT I ALREADY HAVE A DIFFICULT TIME COMING UP WITH ENOUGH TASKS FOR HER TO DO AS IS! IT'S BECOME KIND OF STRESSFUL FOR ME!
SO BEAT IT, KID! SCRAM!

Leaving Richard's Valley

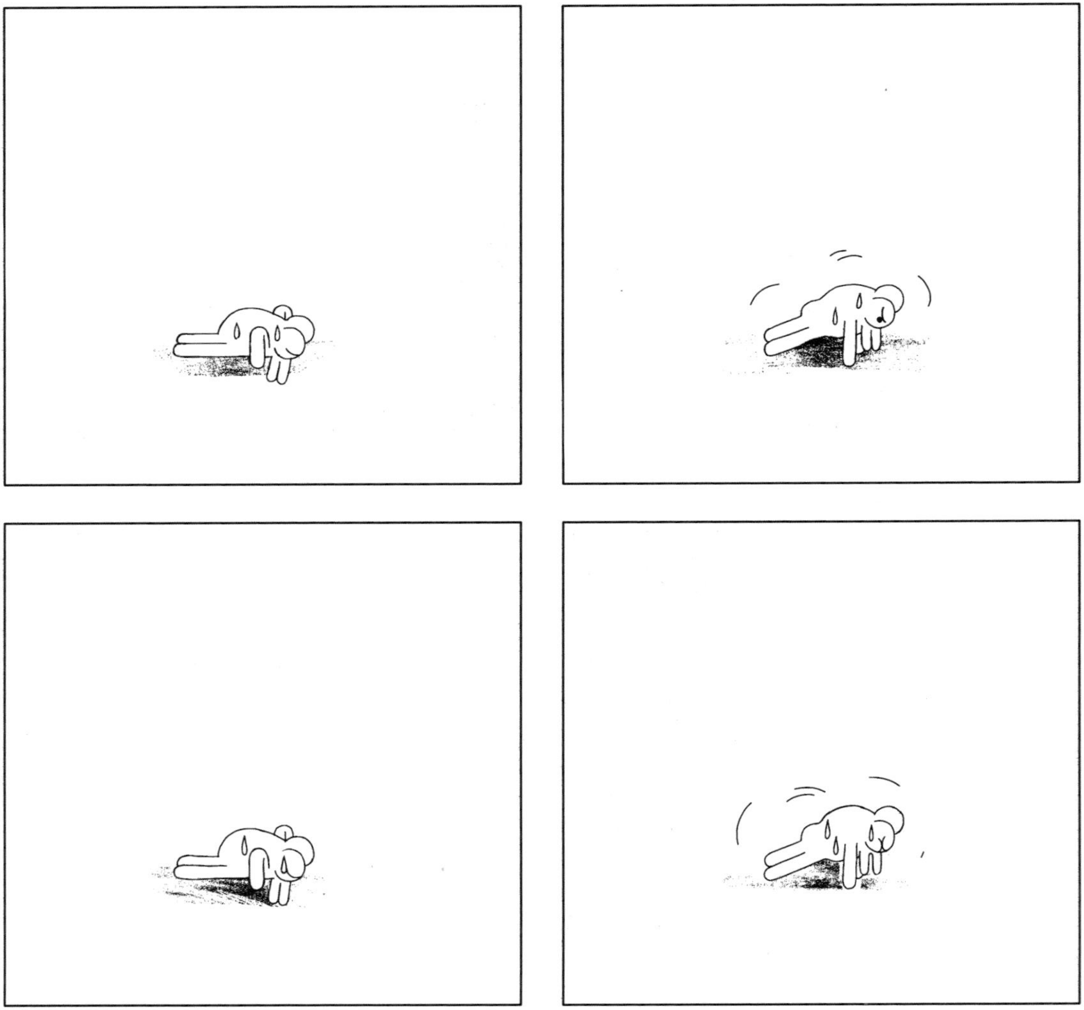

Leaving Richard's Valley

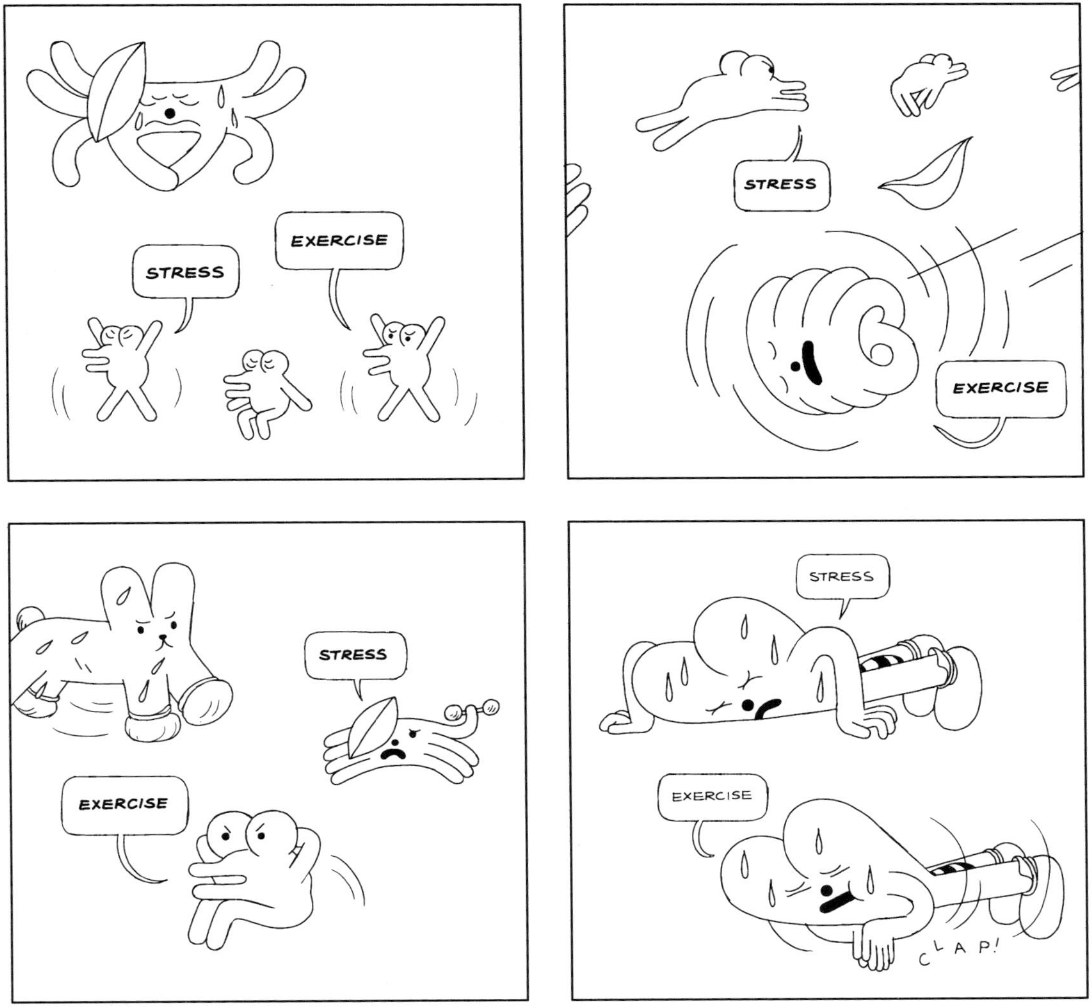
STRESS
EXERCISE
STRESS
EXERCISE
STRESS
EXERCISE
STRESS
EXERCISE
CLAP!

Leaving Richard's Valley

I DUNNO, JULIANNE... MAYBE MALE MODELLING JUST ISN'T IN THE CARDS FOR ME
DON'T GIVE UP, OMAR. IT WASN'T EASY FOR ME, EITHER
I CAN ASK A FEW OF MY CONTACTS IN "THE BIZ"
NO NEED, JULIANNE. I DON'T WANT TO SUCCEED SOLELY BASED ON WHO I KNOW. I WANT TO SUCCEED BECAUSE PEOPLE FIND ME VERY GOOD-LOOKING

Leaving Richard's Valley

SPRING HAS SPRUNG!
ALLERGIES

Leaving Richard's Valley

DON'T TOUCH IT! THAT'S SNAKE SNOT!
OF THE DEPRESSIVE VARIETY
AM I THAT EASY TO READ? AM I THAT TRANSPARENT?
I SHOULD MAKE AN EFFORT TO APPEAR MORE... ALOOF. DETACHED
HOW ARE YOU DOING TODAY, FRIEND?
HORRIBLY

Leaving Richard's Valley

SPRING HAS SPRUNG!
TIME TO SHED THESE WARM LAYERS
WAIT
MAYBE I WANNA KEEP MY LEAF

ARE WE JUST GOING TO KEEP GETTING SICK FROM NOW ON?
THE WAY I SEE IT, EVERYONE OUTSIDE THE VALLEY IS SICK
SO IN A WAY, NONE OF US ARE SICK!
OH
HEY ELLIE, WHATEVER HAPPENED TO THAT PENCIL CRAYON SET I LENT YOU?
IF YOU THINK ABOUT IT, ALL OF US ATE YOUR SET OF PENCIL CRAYONS - SO IN A WAY, NONE OF US DID

Leaving Richard's Valley

Leaving Richard's Valley

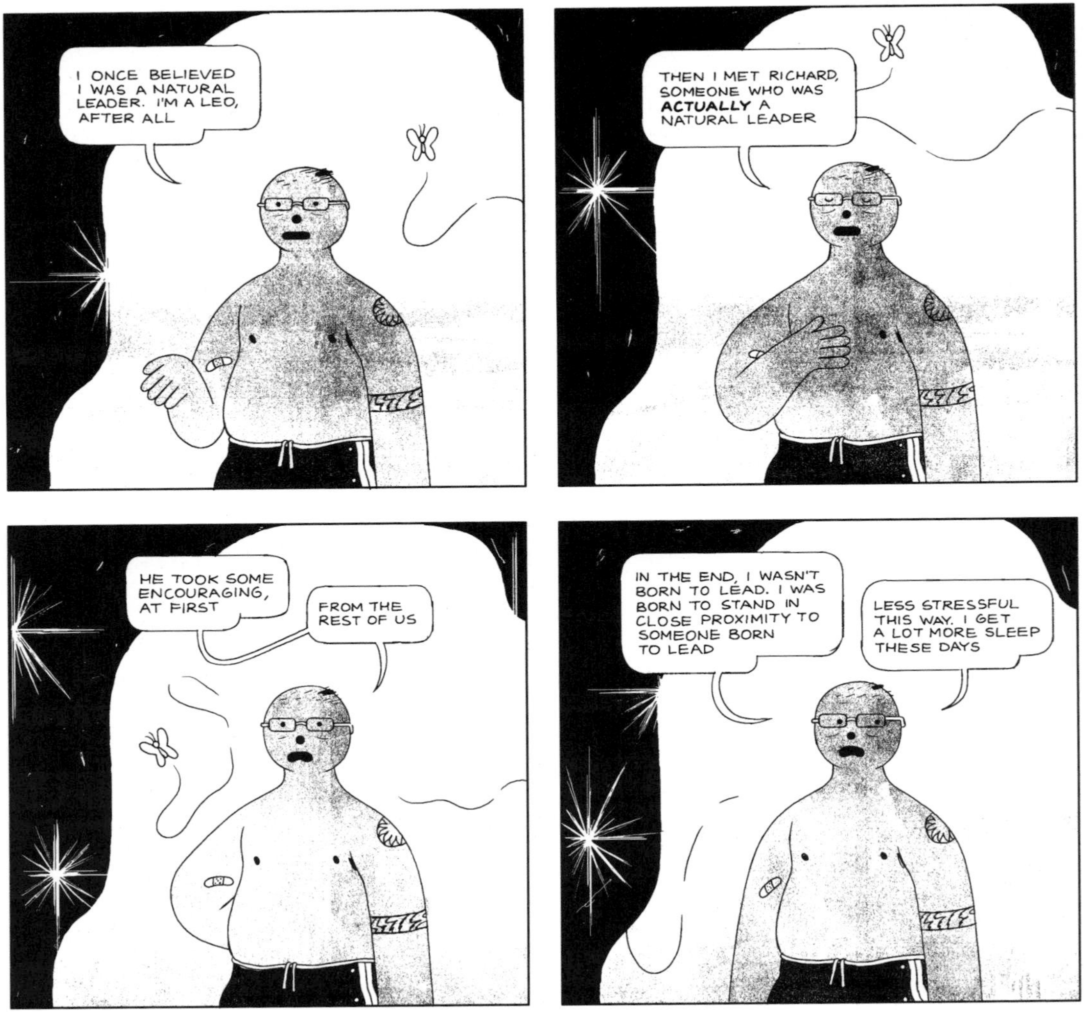
I ONCE BELIEVED I WAS A NATURAL LEADER. I'M A LEO, AFTER ALL
THEN I MET RICHARD, SOMEONE WHO WAS **ACTUALLY** A NATURAL LEADER
HE TOOK SOME ENCOURAGING, AT FIRST
FROM THE REST OF US
IN THE END, I WASN'T BORN TO LEAD. I WAS BORN TO STAND IN CLOSE PROXIMITY TO SOMEONE BORN TO LEAD
LESS STRESSFUL THIS WAY. I GET A LOT MORE SLEEP THESE DAYS

Leaving Richard's Valley

BIGGER THAN SQUIRRELS
BIGGER THAN SPIDERS!
BIGGER THAN WORMS
BETTER THAN NOTHING

Leaving Richard's Valley

ARE WE EVEN WALKING THE RIGHT WAY?
TRUST ME...
I'M GOING TO ASK FOR DIRECTIONS
HI! WHICH WAY IS QUEEN STREET?
CITY PEOPLE ARE SO RUDE
THE EMPATHY CENTRES OF THEIR BRAINS HAVE BEEN POLLUTED

I DON'T KNOW WHO MAKES 'EM! ALL I KNOW IS:
I DON'T LIKE 'EM
THEY'RE ALL OVER TOWN! IT'S RUDE
WHENEVER I SEE ONE?! POW! IT'S A GONER
I'M DOING A PUBLIC SERVICE!

Leaving Richard's Valley

I KNEW RICHARD FROM WHEN WE USED TO LIFT BIKES TOGETHER
AND HE'D COME TO PARTIES I'D BOOK AT THE TRANCE
TRANCE
THE TRANCE
THEY WERE LEGENDARY. BANDS PASSED BY ON TOUR, AND I COULD GET SOME PRETTY BIG ONES TO PLAY. THE WRONG WOMAN ONCE PUT ON A SECRET SHOW AT ONE OF OUR NIGHTS
COPS CAME TO SHUT US DOWN BUT I BRIBED THEM WITH A STASH OF STOLEN NASCAR JACKETS

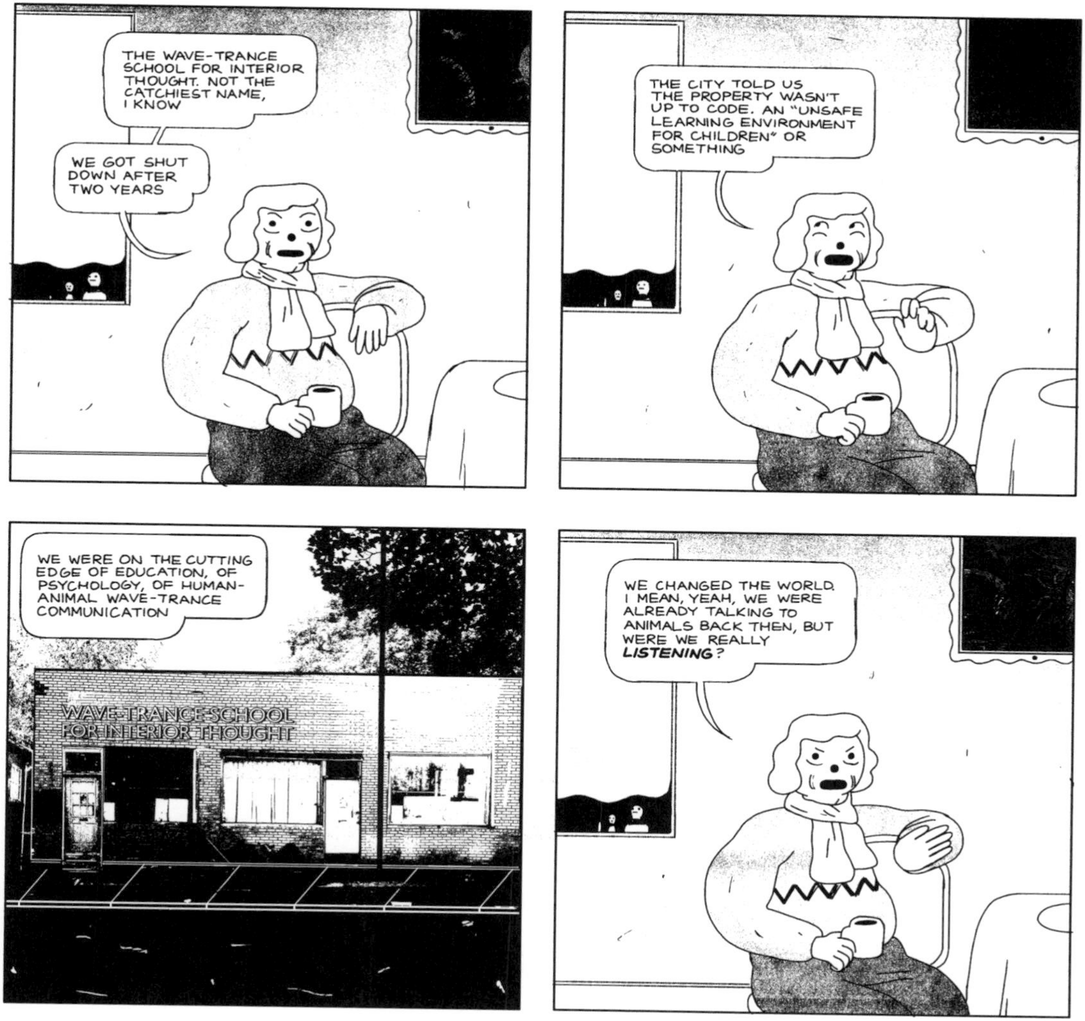
THE WAVE-TRANCE SCHOOL FOR INTERIOR THOUGHT. NOT THE CATCHIEST NAME, I KNOW
WE GOT SHUT DOWN AFTER TWO YEARS
THE CITY TOLD US THE PROPERTY WASN'T UP TO CODE. AN "UNSAFE LEARNING ENVIRONMENT FOR CHILDREN" OR SOMETHING
WE WERE ON THE CUTTING EDGE OF EDUCATION, OF PSYCHOLOGY, OF HUMAN-ANIMAL WAVE-TRANCE COMMUNICATION
WAVE-TRANCE-SCHOOL FOR INTERIOR THOUGHT
WE CHANGED THE WORLD. I MEAN, YEAH, WE WERE ALREADY TALKING TO ANIMALS BACK THEN, BUT WERE WE REALLY ***LISTENING***?

Leaving Richard's Valley

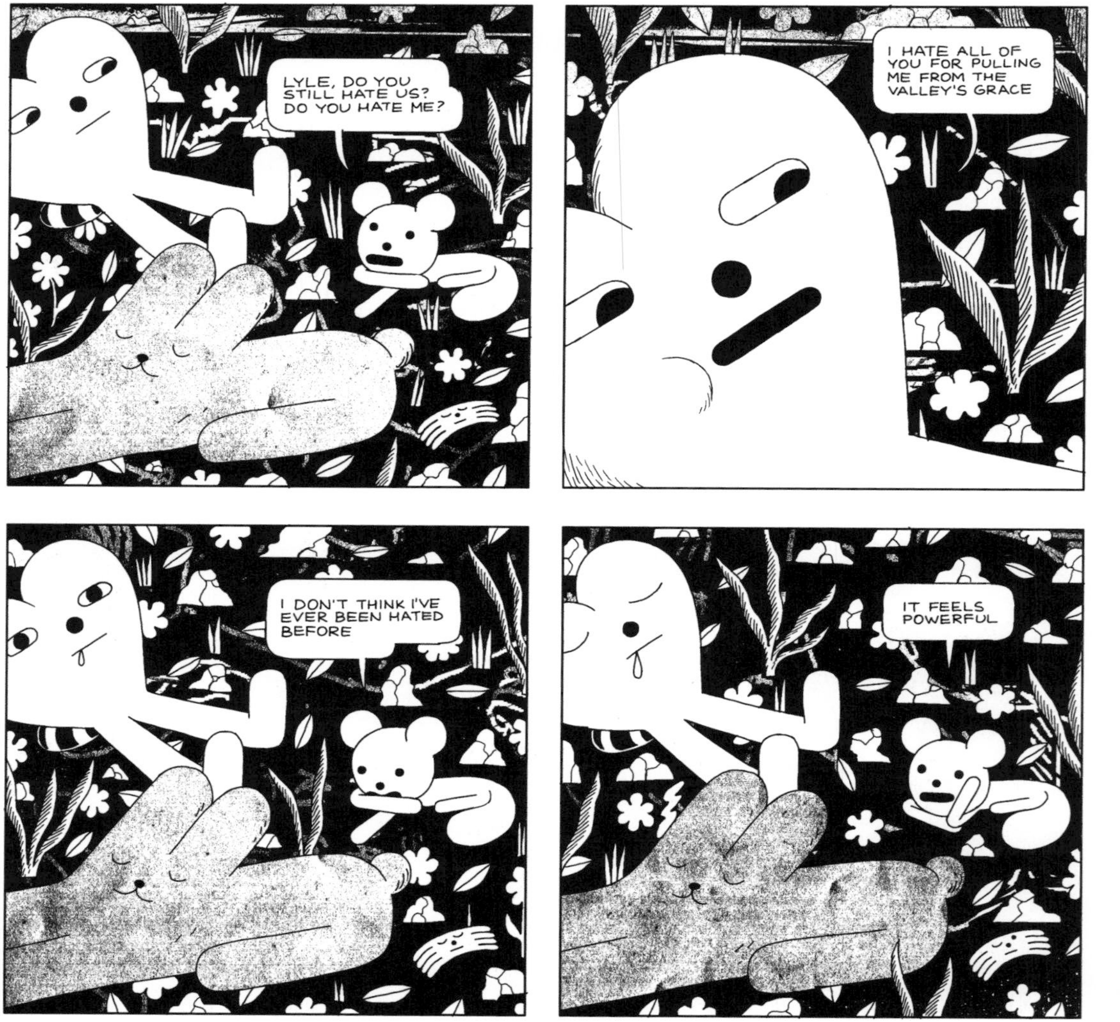
LYLE, DO YOU STILL HATE US? DO YOU HATE ME?
I HATE ALL OF YOU FOR PULLING ME FROM THE VALLEY'S GRACE
I DON'T THINK I'VE EVER BEEN HATED BEFORE
IT FEELS POWERFUL

AT LEAST I KNOW THAT ONE DAY, WHEN WE'RE BOTH DEAD, I'LL BE REUNITED WITH RICHARD
HE'LL REALIZE I WASN'T SUPPOSED TO BE BANISHED
JUST ONE BIG MISUNDERSTANDING!
WE'LL LAUGH ABOUT IT! THE FUNNIEST JOKE IN HEAVEN!

Leaving Richard's Valley

WOW- CAROLINE REALLY GOT JACKED
SHE LOOKS AS STRONG AS RICHARD
WHAT'S WRONG?
NO ONE IS AS STRONG AS RICHARD!

Leaving Richard's Valley

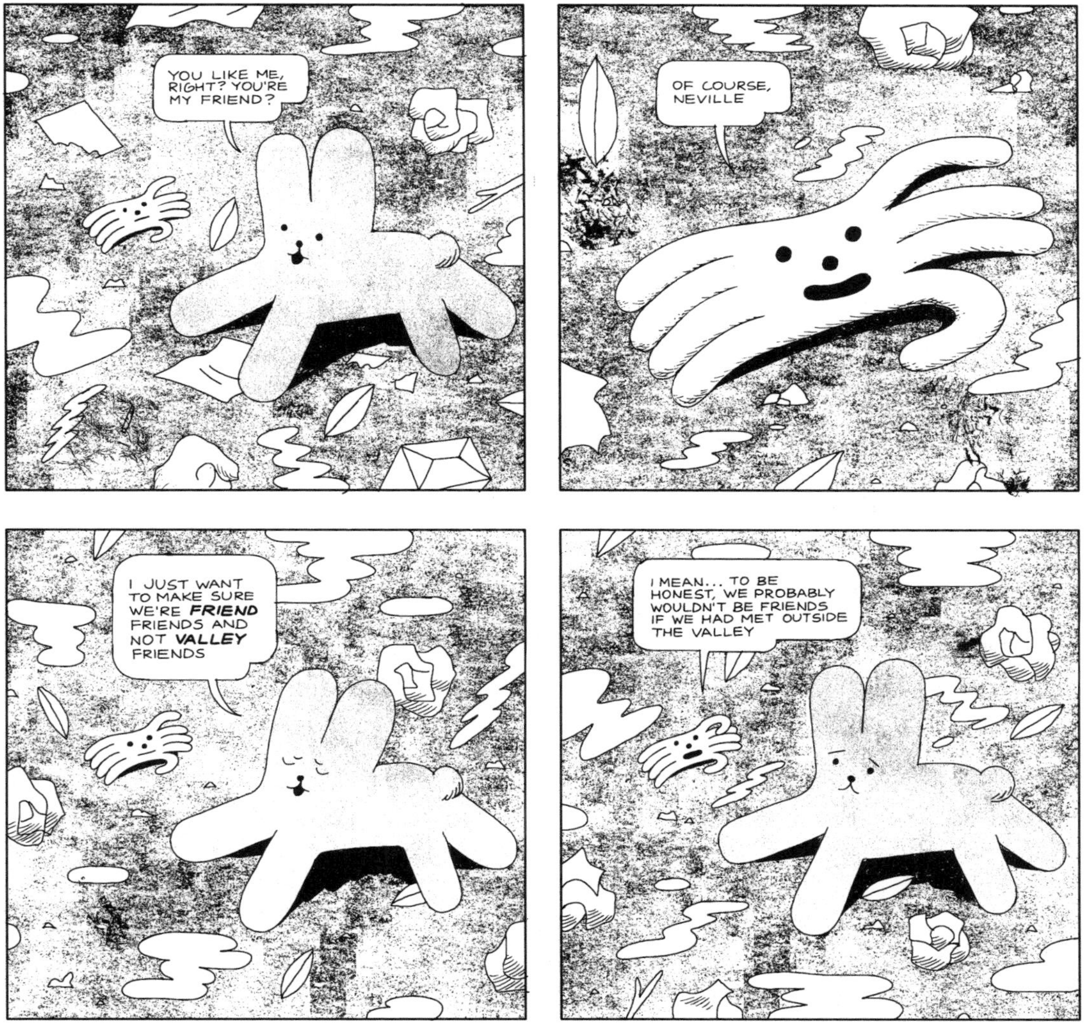

YOU LIKE ME, RIGHT? YOU'RE MY FRIEND?
OF COURSE, NEVILLE
I JUST WANT TO MAKE SURE WE'RE **FRIEND** FRIENDS AND NOT **VALLEY** FRIENDS
I MEAN... TO BE HONEST, WE PROBABLY WOULDN'T BE FRIENDS IF WE HAD MET OUTSIDE THE VALLEY

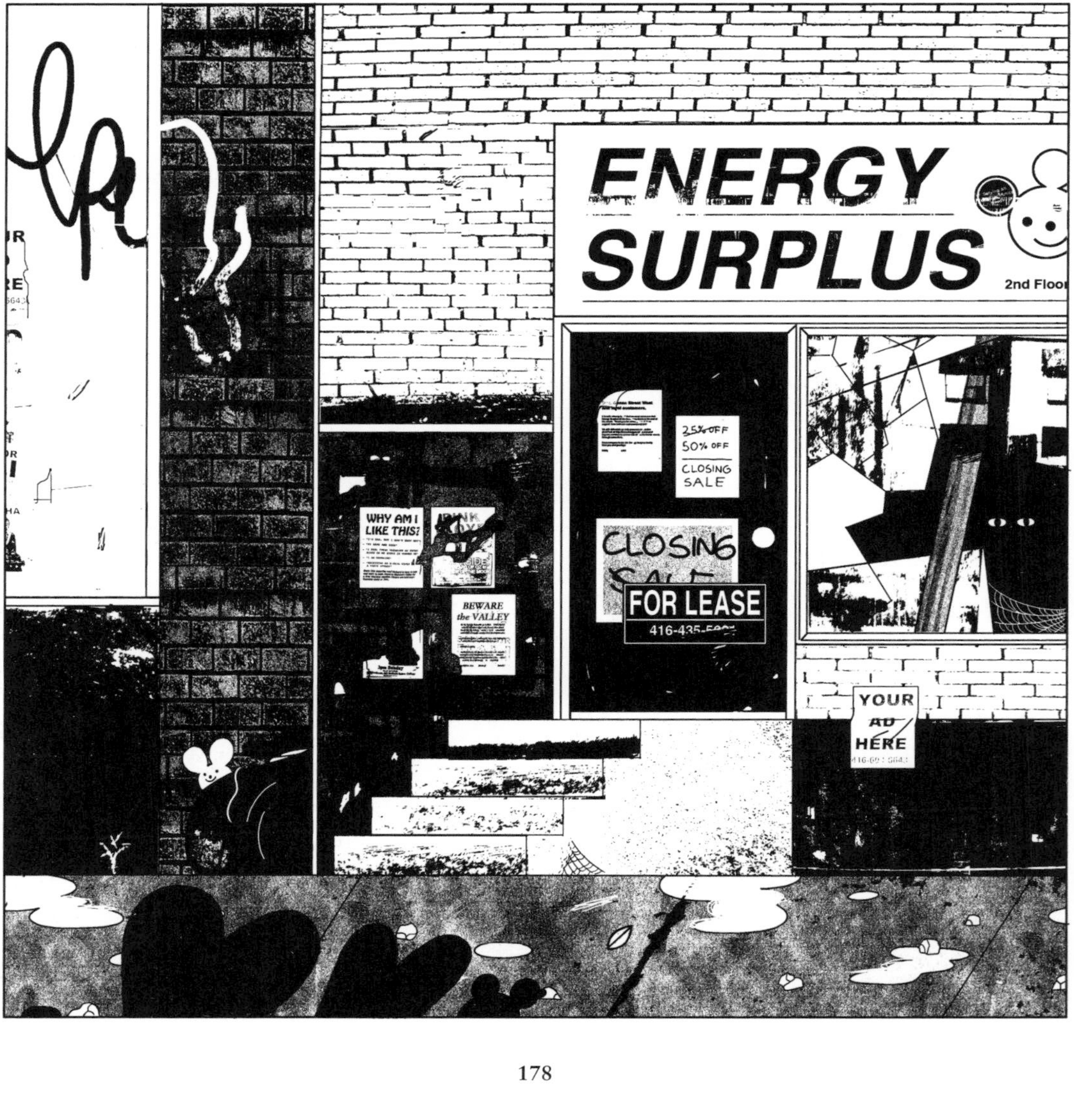
ENERGY
SURPLUS
2nd Floo
35% OFF
50% OFF
CLOSING
SALE
WHY AM I
LIKE THIS?
CLOSING
FOR LEASE
BEWARE
the VALLEY
YOUR
AD
HERE

SURPLUS
WE'RE HERE. WE MADE IT!
25% OFF
50% OFF
CLOSING SALE
THERE MUST BE A BILLION SQUIRRELS HERE!
GY
LUS
Serving All
Needs
I'M SCARED ... WHY IS IT ALL DIRTY?
MAYBE THIS IS WHAT APARTMENTS LOOK LIKE
IN THE CITY

THERE ARE--
COBWEBS
EVERYWHERE
THIS IS SO
SPOOKY!
WAIT. COBWEBS
ARE SCARY
TO YOU?
I MEAN...
SORT OF
AM I SCARY TO
YOU? I MAKE
WEBS

Leaving Richard's Valley

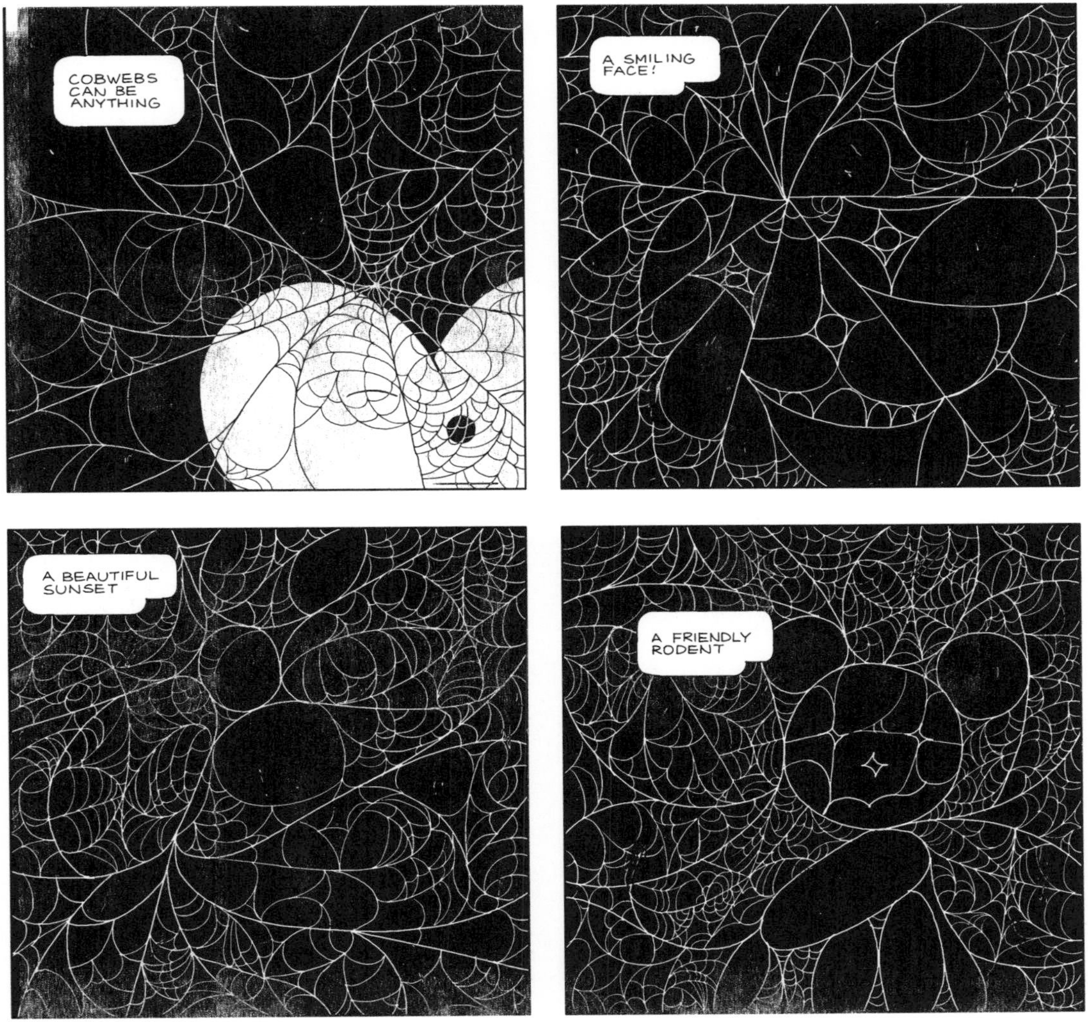

COBWEBS CAN BE ANYTHING
A SMILING FACE!
A BEAUTIFUL SUNSET
A FRIENDLY RODENT

Leaving Richard's Valley

I WANNA TURN AROUND. I WANNA GO BACK
C'MON...
I'M SERIOUS!
ELLIE'S RIGHT... THIS PLACE DOESN'T SEEM SUPER HOSPITABLE
I HEAR NOISES! FROM SOME POTENTIAL NEW NEIGHBOURS
IS THAT... SINGING?
2

IT WOULDN'T KILL PEOPLE TO START BEING A *LITTLE* NICER TO ME
I DESERVE KINDNESS! DON'T I?!
A TENDER WORD EVERY NOW AND THEN... DON'T I DESERVE THAT?! AT LEAST??!
AND... AND WHILE I'M AT IT, DON'T I DESERVE A HOT BOYFRIEND NAMED LYLE?
AND ARMS? AND LEGS? AND AN ENORMOUS HOUSE??! AND A CALMER BOWEL...?!

Leaving Richard's Valley

SOMETHING'S CHANGED ABOUT MARK'S ATTITUDE. HE SEEMS MORE--
CONFIDENT?
IRRITABLE?
IT'S TRUE. IT'S A REAL CHANGE
I THOUGHT I DIDN'T LIKE MARK BEFORE
BUT NOW I **KNOW** I DON'T LIKE MARK

Leaving Richard's Valley

MY NAME IS NEVILLE. MY FRIENDS AND I HAVE JOURNEYED --
ARE YOU HERE TO PARTY
EXCUSE ME?
WE'RE HAVING A PARTY
HOW COME THERE'S NO DANCING?
WE WERE LOOKING FOR A PLACE TO LIVE, AND WERE RECOMMENDED THIS LISTING --
IF YOU'RE DOWN TO PARTY, YOU'RE WELCOME TO STAY
YES. I AM ABSOLUTELY DOWN TO PARTY

Leaving Richard's Valley

SO
WHAT'S THE NAME OF THIS SONG?
IT DOESN'T HAVE A TITLE
THEY'RE NOISE MUSICIANS. THIS IS NOISE MUSIC
WHAT IS NOISE MUSIC?!
STUFF LIKE THIS, MOSTLY
THEN I LOVE NOISE MUSIC

Leaving Richard's Valley

Leaving Richard's Valley

frog

Leaving Richard's Valley

HEY, CAROLINE, WANT A MASSAGE? ONCE I'M FINISHED WITH PETAL, I COULD--
NO
HEY, CAR, WANT TO HELP ME PREPARE THE NEXT BATCH OF STEW?
NO
CAROLINE, COULD YOU --
NO
NO NO NO NO NO

Leaving Richard's Valley

ME AND CAROLINE JOINED THE VALLEY AT THE SAME TIME
I DIDN'T THINK IT'D BE FOREVER. WE WERE YOUNG AND IDEALISTIC
AND IN LOVE ...
BUT RICHARD DOESN'T GIVE YOU ENOUGH ROOM TO LOVE ANYONE BUT RICHARD
I MOVED BACK TO MY OLD POND...

Leaving Richard's Valley

RIP

Leaving Richard's Valley

SO DO YOU AND YOUR ROOMMATES ALWAYS THROW PARTIES LIKE THIS?
"ROOMMATES?"
WE USED TO HAVE PARTIES WHERE I USED TO LIVE. NOT EXACTLY LIKE THIS
WE'D PUT ON A LOT OF SKITS
DO YOU THINK THERE WILL BE ANY SKITS LATER IN THE EVENING, OR . . . ?

Leaving Richard's Valley

RICHARD, I'VE BEEN A PART OF THE VALLEY FOR MOST OF MY LIFE
I LIKE TO BELIEVE THAT THE TWO OF US HAVE ESTABLISHED A CERTAIN LEVEL OF INTIMACY OVER THE YEARS. A CLOSENESS
A TRUST! A CERTAIN--
CAROLINE, WHAT ARE YOU ASKING OF ME?
RICHARD, I'D LIKE A PROMOTION

CAROLINE, THAT ISN'T HOW THE VALLEY WORKS. YOU'RE ALL EQUAL UNDER MY EYES
I DON'T WANT ANY SORT OF COMPENSATION! JUST SOME ACKNOWLEDGEMENT ... OF ALL MY GOOD WORKS
IT CAN JUST BE A TITLE. AN HONOURARY THING!
"LIEUTENANT"
"VICE PRESIDENT"
"ATTORNEY GENERAL"

Leaving Richard's Valley

I LOVE IT HERE
WHAT DID YOU SAY?!
I LOVE IT HERE

Leaving Richard's Valley

WHAT'S LYLE DOING?
AUDITIONING

Leaving Richard's Valley

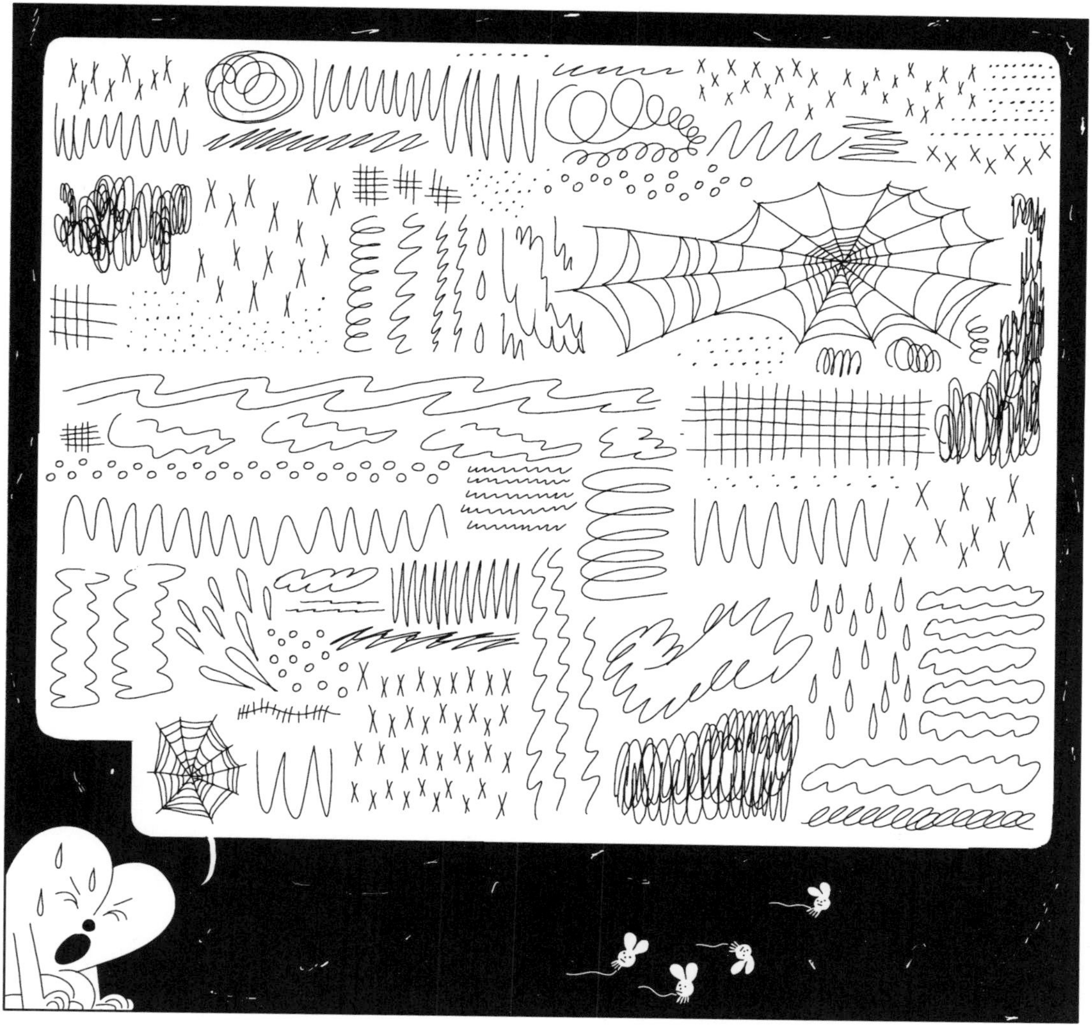

Leaving Richard's Valley

Leaving Richard's Valley

WHY DID RICHARD GET SO CROSS?
MY ACHING HEART WAS IN HIS HANDS
ALAS, THE FEELINGS OF A FROG
HE'LL SIMPLY NEVER UNDERSTAND
WHY SHOULD I BE MADE TO FEEL ASHAMED?
A SIMPLE "NO" WOULD HAVE SUFFICED
SOMETHING SOMETHING SOMETHING SOMETHING
I WISH HE'D AT LEAST TRY TO BE NICE

Leaving Richard's Valley

THIS PARTY'S GETTING AWFULLY LOUD
I FEAR I'VE LED MY GROUP ASTRAY
WE'VE FALLEN IN WITH THE WRONG CROWD
SHOULD WE HAVE GONE A DIFFERENT WAY?
OUR ROAD IS LONG AND FILLED WITH PERIL
THERE ARE TWISTS AND TURNS WE CANNOT SEE
SOMETHING SOMETHING SOMETHING SOMETHING
I HOPE MY FRIENDS AREN'T MAD AT ME

Leaving Richard's Valley

WHAT A PARTY! WHAT A BAND
I SURE DO LOVE THEIR AWFUL RACKET
I HOPE THEY LET ME JOIN THEIR BAND
IF I HAVE WHAT IT TAKES TO HACK IT
I REALLY, REALLY LIKE THIS BAND
BAND BAND BAND BAND BAND BAND BAND
SOMETHING SOMETHING SOMETHING SOMETHING BAND
GOD, I'D LOVE TO JOIN A BAND

Leaving Richard's Valley

I'M AFRAID ABOUT THE FRIEND I'M LOSING
IF OMAR MAKES IT AS A MALE MODEL
THIS OUTSIDE WORLD SURE IS CONFUSING
AND I KNOW I'VE LIVED MY WHOLE LIFE CODDLED
BEING LEFT WITH LYLE AND NEVILLE
SURE WOULD BE AN AWFUL SHAME
SOMETHING SOMETHING SOMETHING SOMETHING
NEVILLE'S COOL. LYLE'S KINDA LAME

Leaving Richard's Valley

I ALWAYS TRY TO KEEP IN MIND
MY ROOTS AMONGST THE LITTLE PEOPLE
BUT I'VE LEFT MY NORMAL LIFE BEHIND
THEIR HOPES AND FEARS CAN SEEM SO FEEBLE
I TRY SO HARD TO EMPATHIZE
FROM THE COMFORT OF MY HEATED POOL
SOMETHING SOMETHING SOMETHING SOMETHING
THE WOES OF BEING RICH AND COOL!

Leaving Richard's Valley

MY BEST FRIEND IS ELLIE SQUIRREL
BUT THERE HAS ALWAYS BEEN SOME TENSION
SINCE ASPECTS OF A SPIDER'S WORLD
STILL LIE BEYOND HER COMPREHENSION
AT CONSTANT RISK OF BEING SMOOSHED
IT'S REALLY TOUGH TO BE THIS SMALL
SOMETHING SOMETHING SOMETHING SOMETHING
I WONDER IF I COULD WRITE TO PAUL

I KNOW I'M HARSH BUT ALWAYS FAIR
I'M ONLY ACTING OUT OF LOVE
BECAUSE IF I TRULY DIDN'T CARE
AND ONE DAY PUSH SHOULD COME TO SHOVE
AND I LET GO OF THE STEERING WHEEL
AND LEFT THEM TO THEIR OWN DEVICES
SOMETHING SOMETHING SOMETHING SOMETHING
IT'D SEND THE VALLEY INTO CRISIS

IT WAS GREAT JAMMING WITH YOU GUYS! A REAL PLEASURE
YEAH... ABOUT THAT
PLEASE DON'T DO THAT AGAIN
JUMPING IN LIKE THAT KIND OF CRAMPED OUR STYLE
WE'VE ESTABLISHED A SORT OF RAPPORT OVER THE YEARS. A DIALOGUE...
WE DON'T SAY THIS TO DISCOURAGE YOU. WE HAVE ALL THE LOVE IN THE WORLD FOR OUR FANS

I'M CAROLINE'S BROTHER. ONE OF MANY. THERE WERE ENOUGH OF US THAT I LOST COUNT
I DON'T THINK SHE LIKED COMPETING WITH SO MANY VOICES. IT WAS A CROWDED POND
SOME PUPPY ATE ABOUT A DOZEN OF US. ITS OWNER MADE IT SPIT A FEW BROTHERS AND SISTERS OUT, BUT IT WAS MOSTLY TOO LATE
IT WAS A TURNING POINT FOR CAROLINE. ON ACCOUNT OF HOW GROSS IT WAS
SOME EVENTS ARE SIMPLY TOO GROSS TO COME BACK FROM

HEY, SO MY FRIEND OMAR AND I COULD USE SOME REST. ARE THERE SLEEPING QUARTERS WE COULD USE, OR...?
I'M NOT THE BOSS OF YOU
OH, I'M SORRY, I WAS UNDER THE ASSUMPTION THAT YOU WERE HOUSE LEADER
"HOUSE...?"
THIS ISN'T A HOUSE
THIS WHOLE BUILDING IS GETTING GUTTED IN A WEEK. WE'RE JUST HERE TO PARTY, TRASH THE PLACE, AND MOVE ON BEFORE ANIMAL CONTROL GETS HERE

YOU JUST MOVE FROM CONDEMNED BUILDING TO CONDEMNED BUILDING TO... THROW PARTIES?
THAT'S NO WAY TO LIVE... IT'S AS THOUGH YOU'RE STUCK IN SOME SORT OF LIMBO
NO DUH
YEAH, GET WITH THE TIMES, DOG GUY
I LIKED THEM

OHHH
PAUL, I WANT YOU AROUND ALL THE TIME
YOU'RE GOING TO BE MY PERSONAL MASSEUSE

Leaving Richard's Valley

OW
OW OW OW
I'M GIVING YOU A MASSAGE
YOU'RE FEELING VERY RELAXED

Leaving Richard's Valley

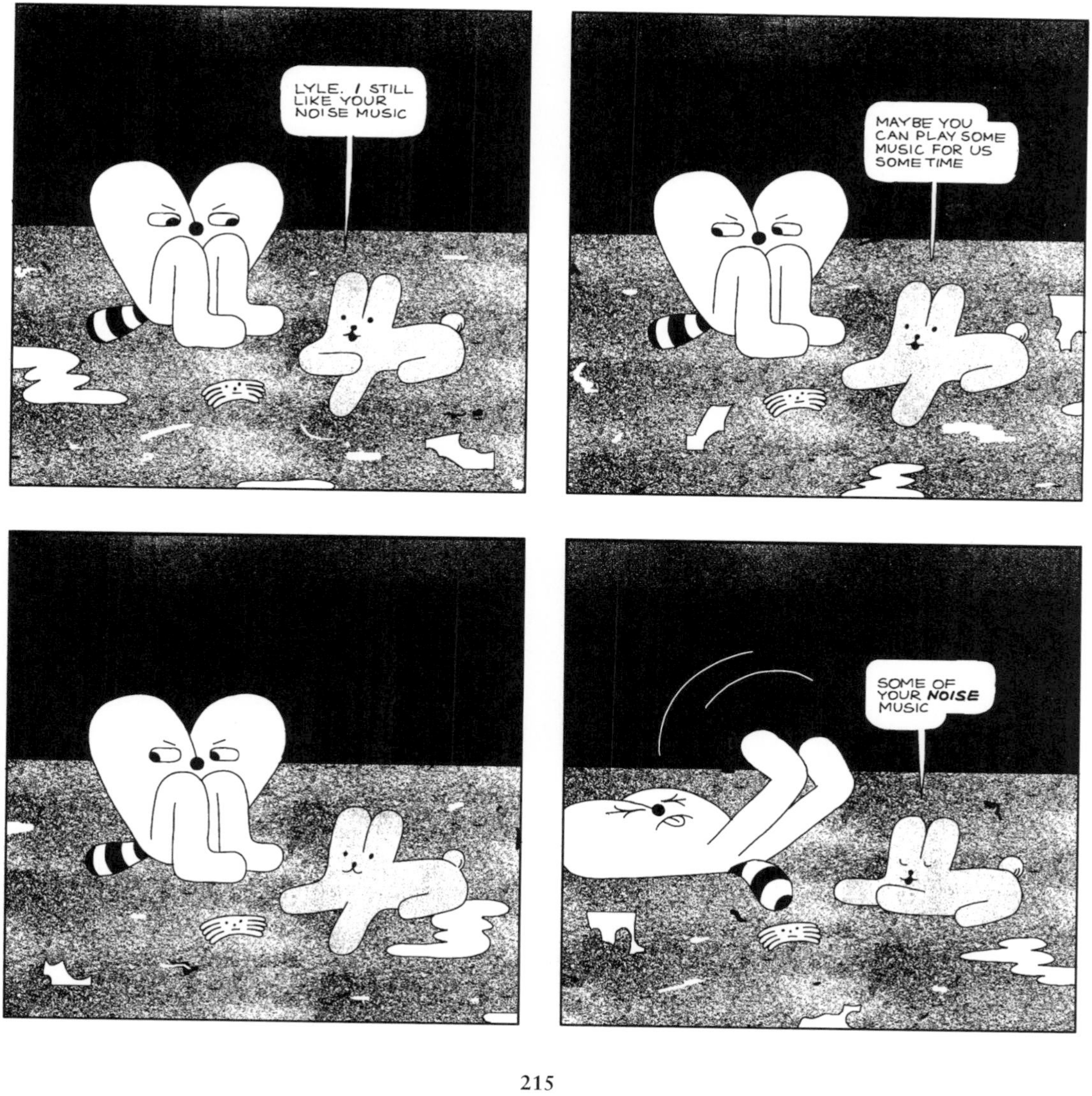
LYLE. I STILL LIKE YOUR NOISE MUSIC
MAYBE YOU CAN PLAY SOME MUSIC FOR US SOME TIME
SOME OF YOUR **NOISE** MUSIC

HOW CAN YOU FIGHT OVER THIS SCRAP OF PIZZA WHEN OUR WORLD IS IN PERIL?
YOU SHOULD BE ASHAMED OF YOURSELVES. OUR AIR IS POISONED-- OUR CITY IS FALLING APART--
EVERY DAY, THE DEPRESSION OF THOUSANDS OF SNAKES GOES COMPLETELY IGNORED
TELL US... TELL US MORE...

Leaving Richard's Valley

WHY ARE THESE DORKS ALL PAYING ATTENTION TO SNAKE MARK
WHAT COULD HE POSSIBLY HAVE TO SAY THAT WOULD BE OF ANY INTEREST
I DUNNO
DO YOU WANNA GO CHECK IT OUT?
YES

Leaving Richard's Valley

EVERYONE IN MARK'S CLUB LOVES MARK
I LOVE MARK BECAUSE HE TAUGHT ME ABOUT LYLE
I LOVE MARK BECAUSE HE CHALLENGES MY MIND
MARK'S CLUB IS GREAT

Leaving Richard's Valley

RULES OF MARK'S CLUB: 1. ALWAYS BE NICE TO MARK AND OTHER MARKSISTS
2. ALWAYS BE NICE TO LYLE
3. NOBODY ELSE FALL IN LOVE WITH LYLE
4. DON'T LITTER

Leaving Richard's Valley

EXCUSE ME, COULD YOU SPARE A MOMENT FOR MARK'S CLUB?
IS THAT GUY BOTHERING YOU?
EXCUSE ME!
NEVER LET ANYONE BULLY YOU INTO THINKING YOU BELONG SOMEWHERE

WHAT WERE YOU LIKE AS A KID, LYLE?
I WAS NOTHING. DUST. ASH. ONE SPECK ON ONE SPOT ON ONE SMUDGE ON ONE SMEAR
A SMEAR ON THE BOTTOM OF MANKIND'S SHOE! GONE UNNOTICED FOR YEARS UNTIL I WAS FINALLY SCRAPED OFF ONTO THE PAVEMENT!
I USED TO LOVE PUTTING ON LITTLE SKITS AND PLAYS FOR MY FRIENDS AND FAMILY

I KNOW, I KNOW
YOU SEE ME AS SOME SORT OF MODERN DAY HERCULES. A TITAN. A GOD. COMPLETELY INFALLIBLE
BUT I'D BE NOTHING WITHOUT LYLE. MY BEACON! MY NORTH STAR!
IT'S LYLE THAT GIVES ME THE STRENGTH TO LIFT MOUNTAINS--! LYLE THAT MAKES MY VOICE SOAR HIGHER THAN ANY BIRD--!
I AM BUT A MERE REFLECTION OF LYLE'S BRILLIANCE AND GLORY. AND IF YOU LET LYLE INTO YOUR HEART, HE CAN DO THE SAME FOR YOU! ALL OF YOU!
MY FUTURE BOYFRIEND
OUR FUTURE LEADER
LYLE SUCH AND SUCH!

THERE ARE GOING TO BE ALL SORTS OF CLUBS AND YOU DON'T NEED ANY OF THEM. THAT'S LESSON NUMBER ONE, LITTLE FRIEND. THEY NEED YOU MORE THAN YOU NEED THEM
LESSON NUMBER TWO: OTHER PEOPLE ARE GOING TO TELL YOU THAT YOU NEED TO BELIEVE IN YOURSELF
ALSO INCORRECT
YOU DON'T HAVE TO BELIEVE IN ANYTHING IF YOU DON'T WANT TO! YOU CAN FLIT AROUND THIS DUMB OLD WORLD COMPLETELY TETHERLESS
GO FORWARD, TINY ONE. BE FREE!
I LOVE THE SKY

Leaving Richard's Valley

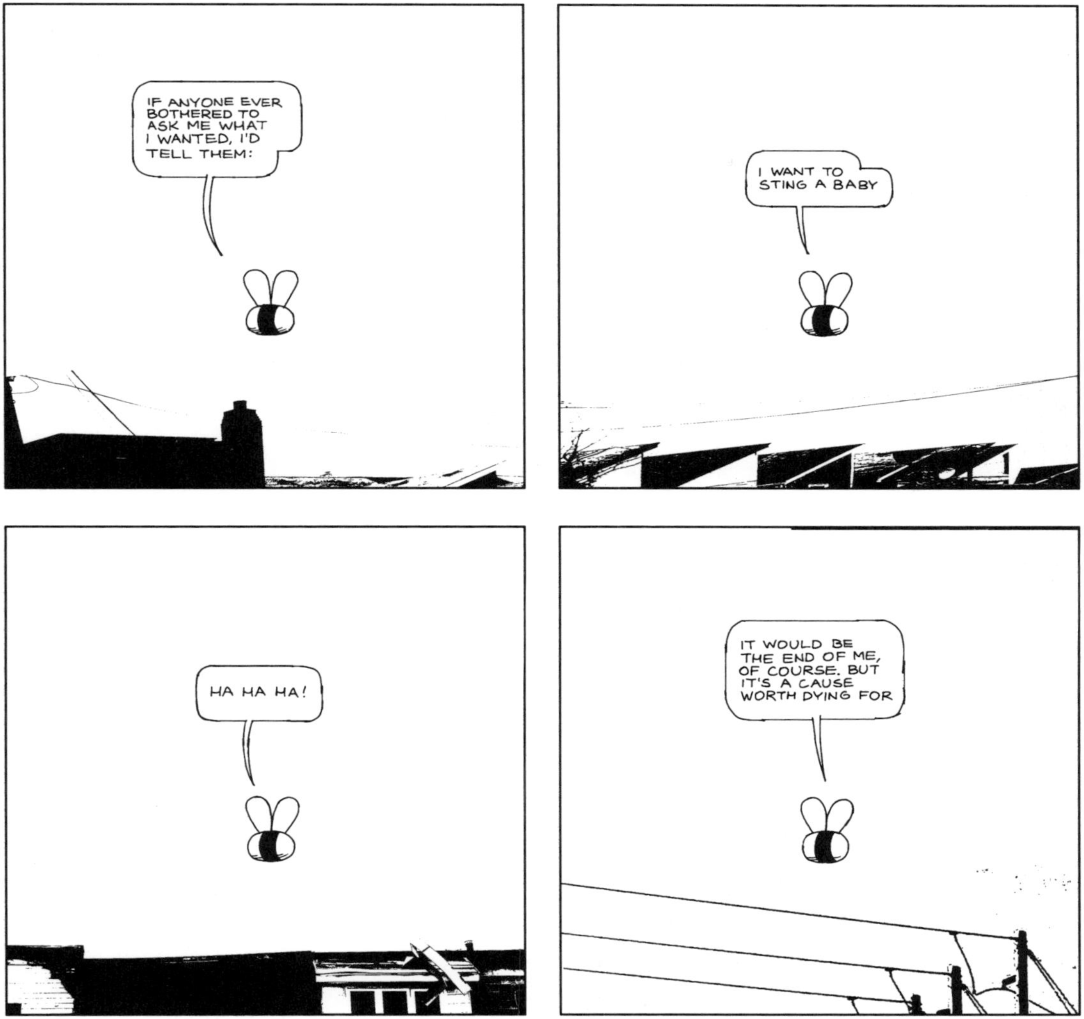
IF ANYONE EVER BOTHERED TO ASK ME WHAT I WANTED, I'D TELL THEM:
I WANT TO STING A BABY
HA HA HA!
IT WOULD BE THE END OF ME, OF COURSE. BUT IT'S A CAUSE WORTH DYING FOR

I WILL HELP YOU IN YOUR QUEST, LITTLE BEE!
I WILL SECURE YOU A BABY! I SERVE AT YOUR PLEASURE
THERE'S A HOSPITAL AROUND THE CORNER!
WHAT A TEAM WE'LL BE! A CLASSIC PAIR!

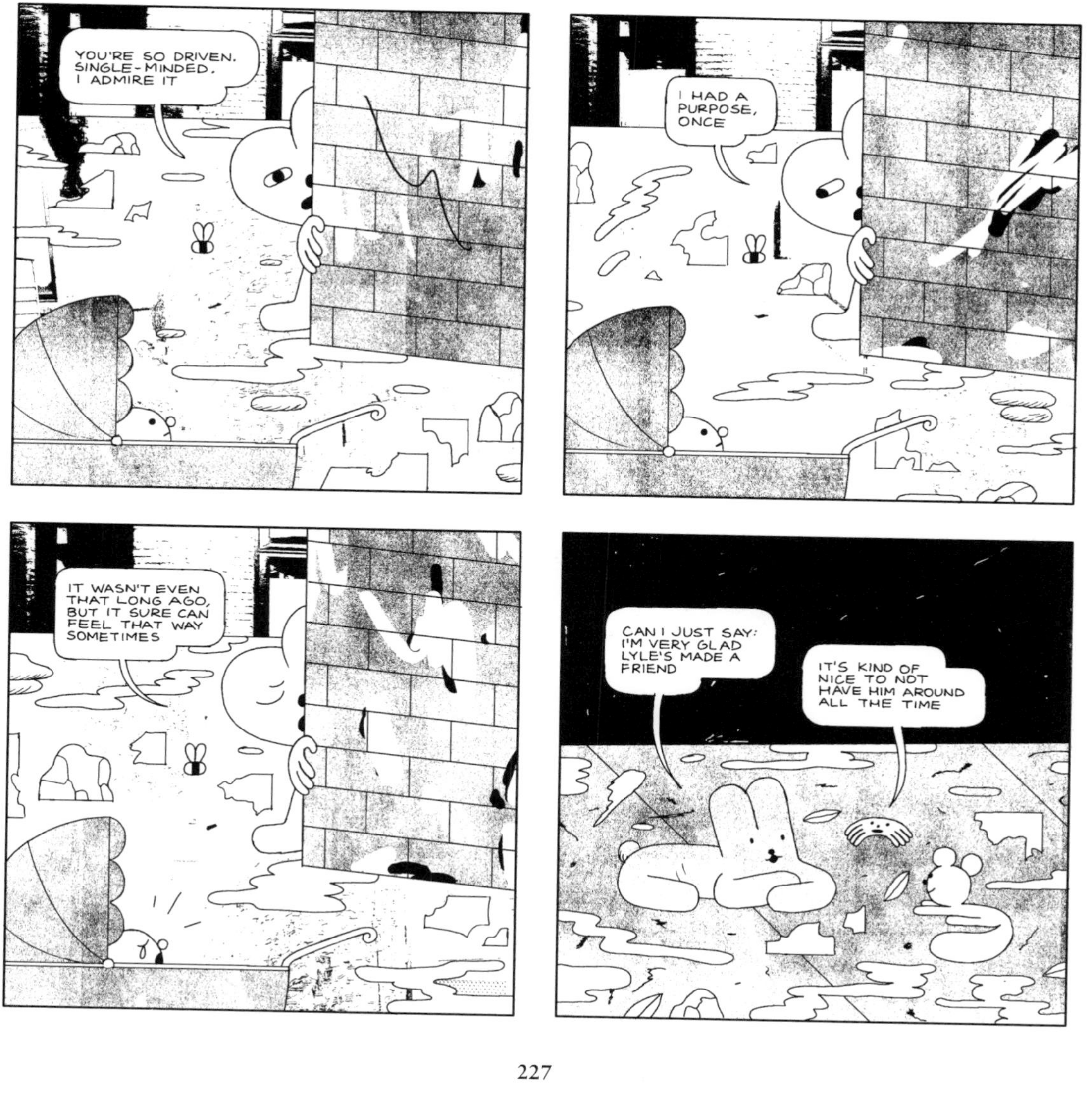
YOU'RE SO DRIVEN. SINGLE-MINDED. I ADMIRE IT
I HAD A PURPOSE, ONCE
IT WASN'T EVEN THAT LONG AGO, BUT IT SURE CAN FEEL THAT WAY SOMETIMES
CAN I JUST SAY: I'M VERY GLAD LYLE'S MADE A FRIEND
IT'S KIND OF NICE TO NOT HAVE HIM AROUND ALL THE TIME

Leaving Richard's Valley

LET'S BRAINSTORM NEW HOUSING IDEAS
WHAT IF WE FOUND A HOUSE PEOPLE ALREADY LIVED IN AND KICKED THEM OUT
IT WOULD BE **UNETHICAL**
THAT'S NOT VERY NICE
WHAT IF WE BUILT A NEST? LIKE BIRDS?
I'M AFRAID OF BIRD MITES
WE COULD SAVE UP SOME MONEY AND BUY A PLACE

Leaving Richard's Valley

WHAT DO YOU DREAM ABOUT, ELLIE?
US. THE FOUR OF US
ARE WE IN THE VALLEY?
NO. NOT THE VALLEY. IT'S WEIRD...

Leaving Richard's Valley

IT'S A VALLEY, BUT NOT RICHARD'S
THE TREES ARE AS TALL AS BUILDINGS
THERE ARE LITTLE HOLES IN THE TREES AND FACES OF LITTLE DUDES IN THE HOLES
THEY'RE ALL REALLY HAPPY TO SEE US

Leaving Richard's Valley

OKAY. I'LL DISTRACT THE MOTHER, YOU GO FOR THE BABY
ARRRRGH
I'M A FILTHY ANIMAL!
?
I'M MISBEHAVING! SPANK ME! OR WHATEVER

Leaving Richard's Valley

EXCUSE ME ?!
GO TO HELL!
I SUPPOSE NOW'S MY CHANCE
WHY DO I HESITATE?

Leaving Richard's Valley

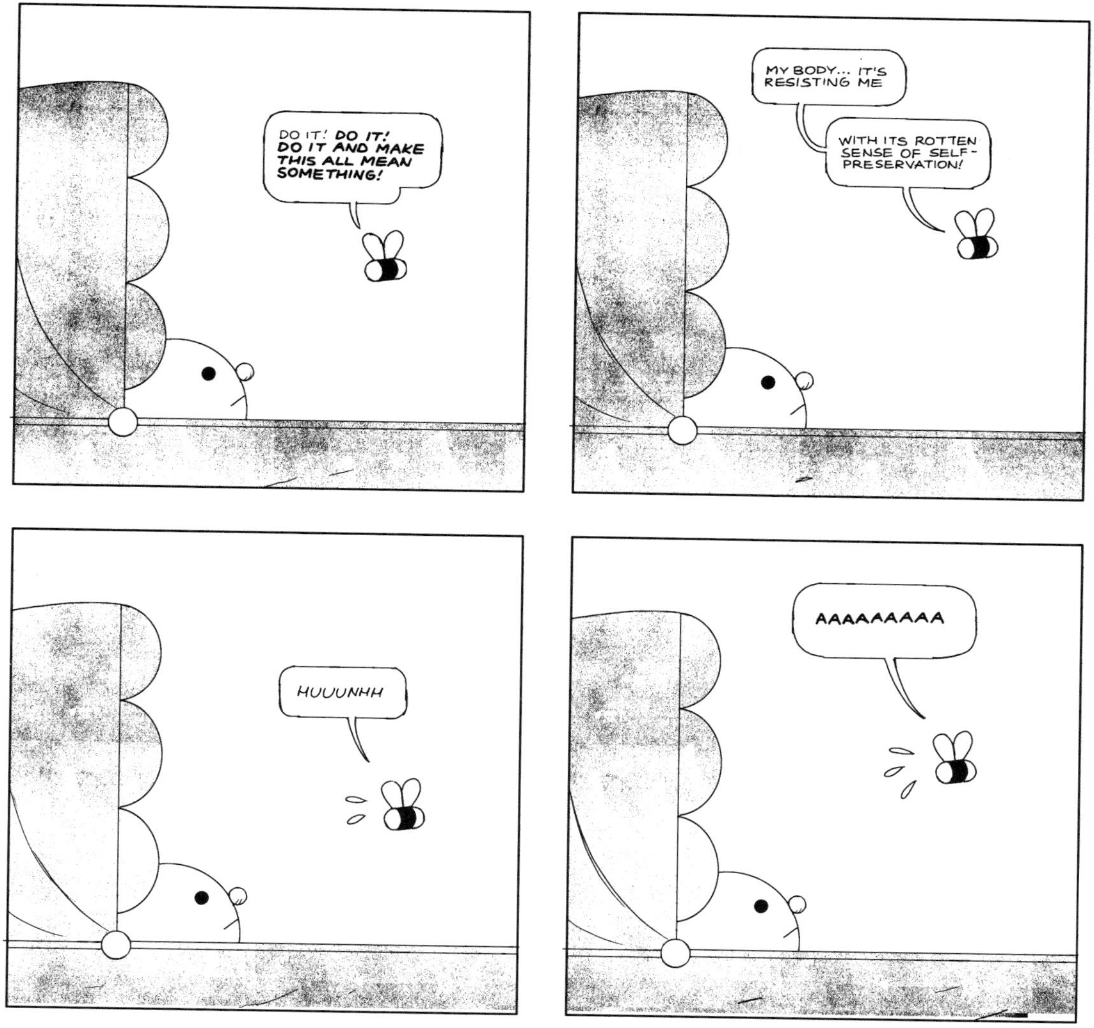
DO IT! DO IT! DO IT AND MAKE THIS ALL MEAN SOMETHING!
MY BODY... IT'S RESISTING ME
WITH ITS ROTTEN SENSE OF SELF-PRESERVATION!
HUUUNHH
AAAAAAAAA

Leaving Richard's Valley

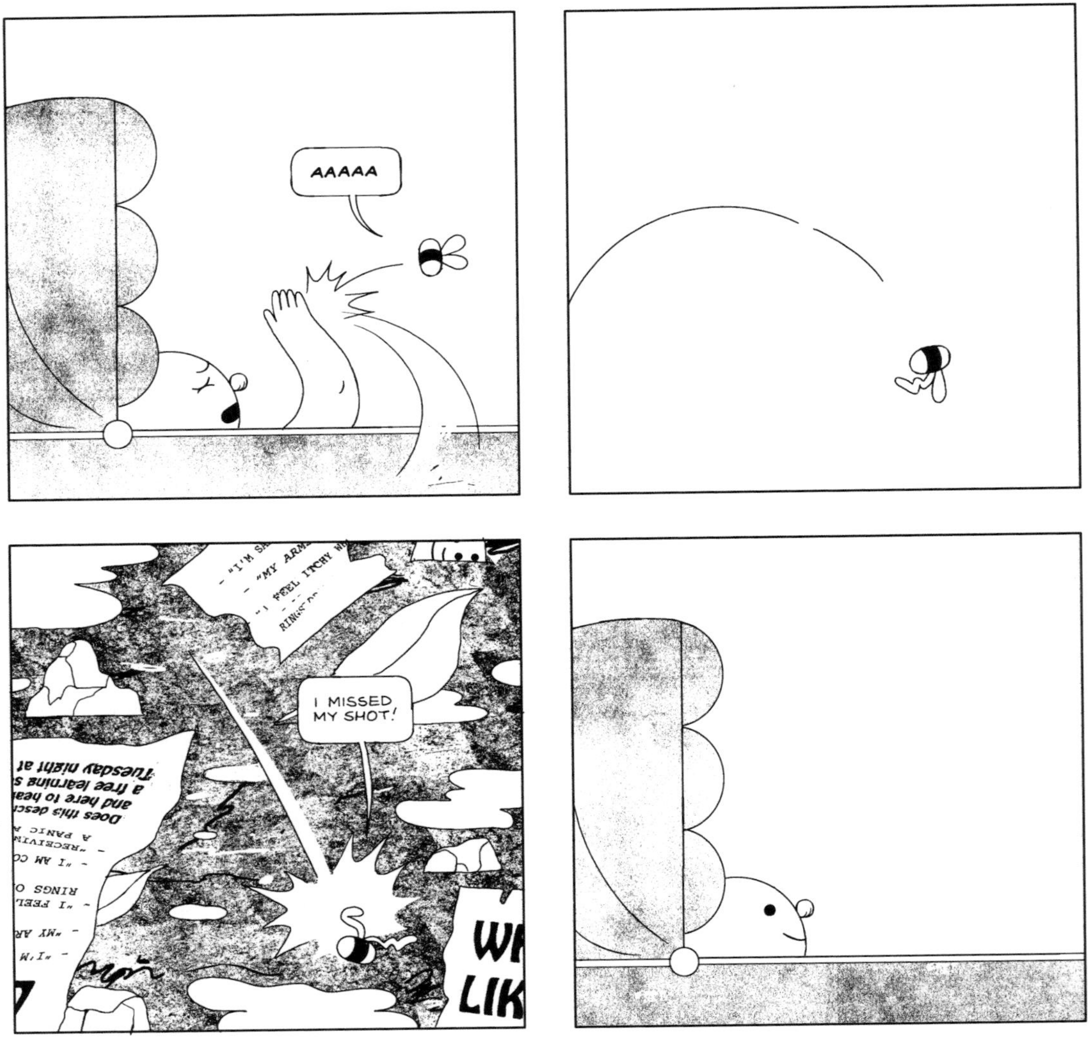
AAAAA
I MISSED MY SHOT!

Leaving Richard's Valley

I CAN'T SPOT HER ANYWHERE ... OR HEAR HER BUZZING ANY LONGER
I'M HERE--!
I HAVE TO ASSUME SHE WAS SUCCESSFUL IN HER MISSION!
IT'S NICE TO FEEL HELPFUL! I HELPED!
I WONDER IF I'D EVER TRULY BEEN HELPFUL BEFORE!

Leaving Richard's Valley

LYLE, WELCOME BACK
HOW WAS YOUR PLAY DATE?
IT WAS VERY EYE-OPENING! ELLIE...
HOW CAN I **HELP** YOU TODAY
EVERYONE NEEDS A LITTLE HELP SOMETIMES

WELL, IF YOU WANTED TO HELP, MAYBE YOU COULD ASSIST ME IN COMBING THROUGH APARTMENT LISTINGS
THE GLOBE AND MAIL
I CAN'T READ
BUT I **CAN** TEAR UP THE NEWSPAPER INTO A BUNCH OF SMALLER PIECES
SO THAT THE LISTINGS ARE SMALLER AND EASIER TO DIGEST

HEY OMAR, I KNOW YOU'VE BEEN HAVING A HARD TIME GETTING YOUR MODELLING CAREER OFF THE GROUND
SO I PUT UP SOME POSTERS ADVERTISING YOUR SERVICES
WATCH OUT FOR THIS
SPIDER
A SORT OF CALLING CARD, IF YOU WILL!

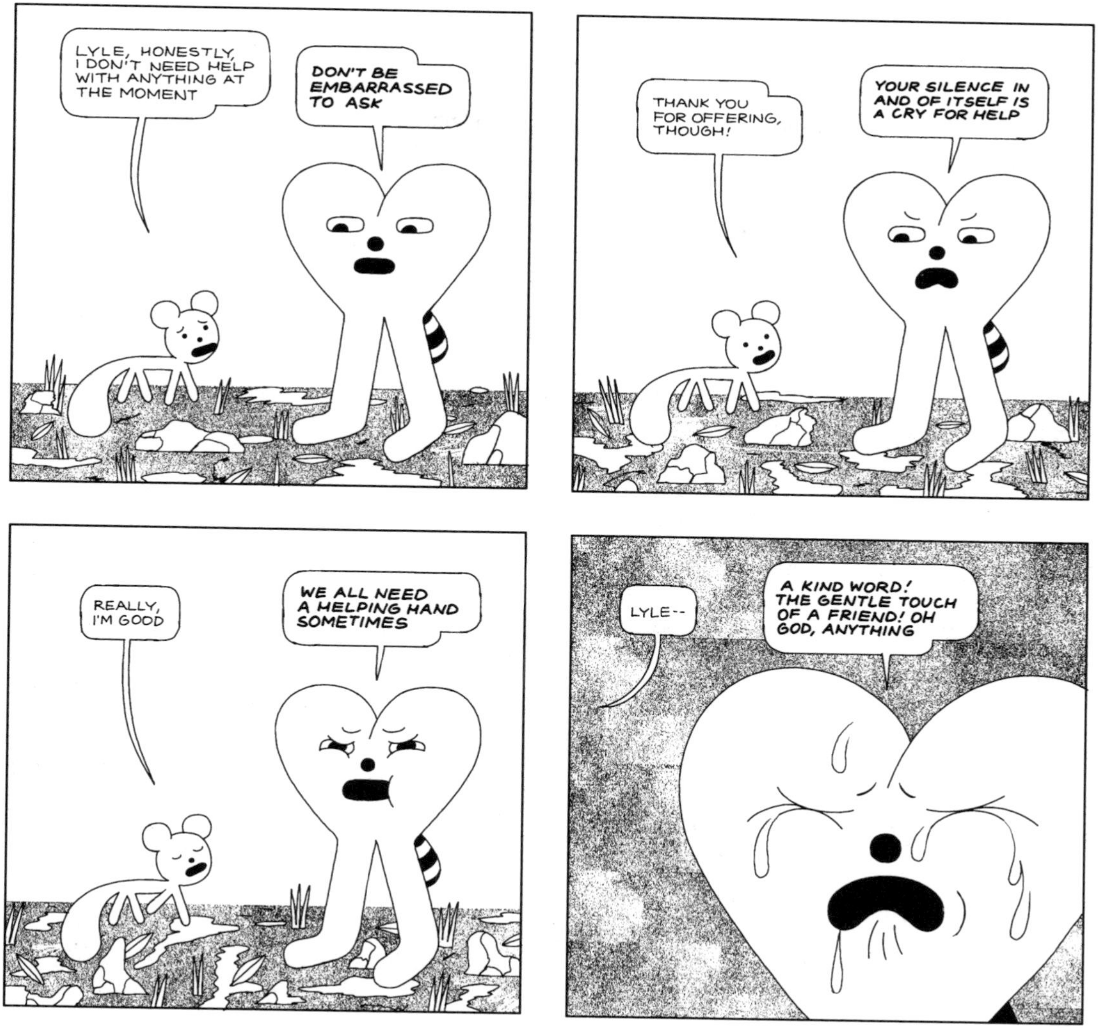
LYLE, HONESTLY, I DON'T NEED HELP WITH ANYTHING AT THE MOMENT
DON'T BE EMBARRASSED TO ASK
THANK YOU FOR OFFERING, THOUGH!
YOUR SILENCE IN AND OF ITSELF IS A CRY FOR HELP
REALLY, I'M GOOD
WE ALL NEED A HELPING HAND SOMETIMES
LYLE--
A KIND WORD! THE GENTLE TOUCH OF A FRIEND! OH GOD, ANYTHING

SPIDER
DER
WATCH OUT 4
SPIDER
WATCH OUT 4
SPIDER
WATCH OUT 4
SPIDER
WATCH OUT
STAR
$7,000,000
649

Leaving Richard's Valley

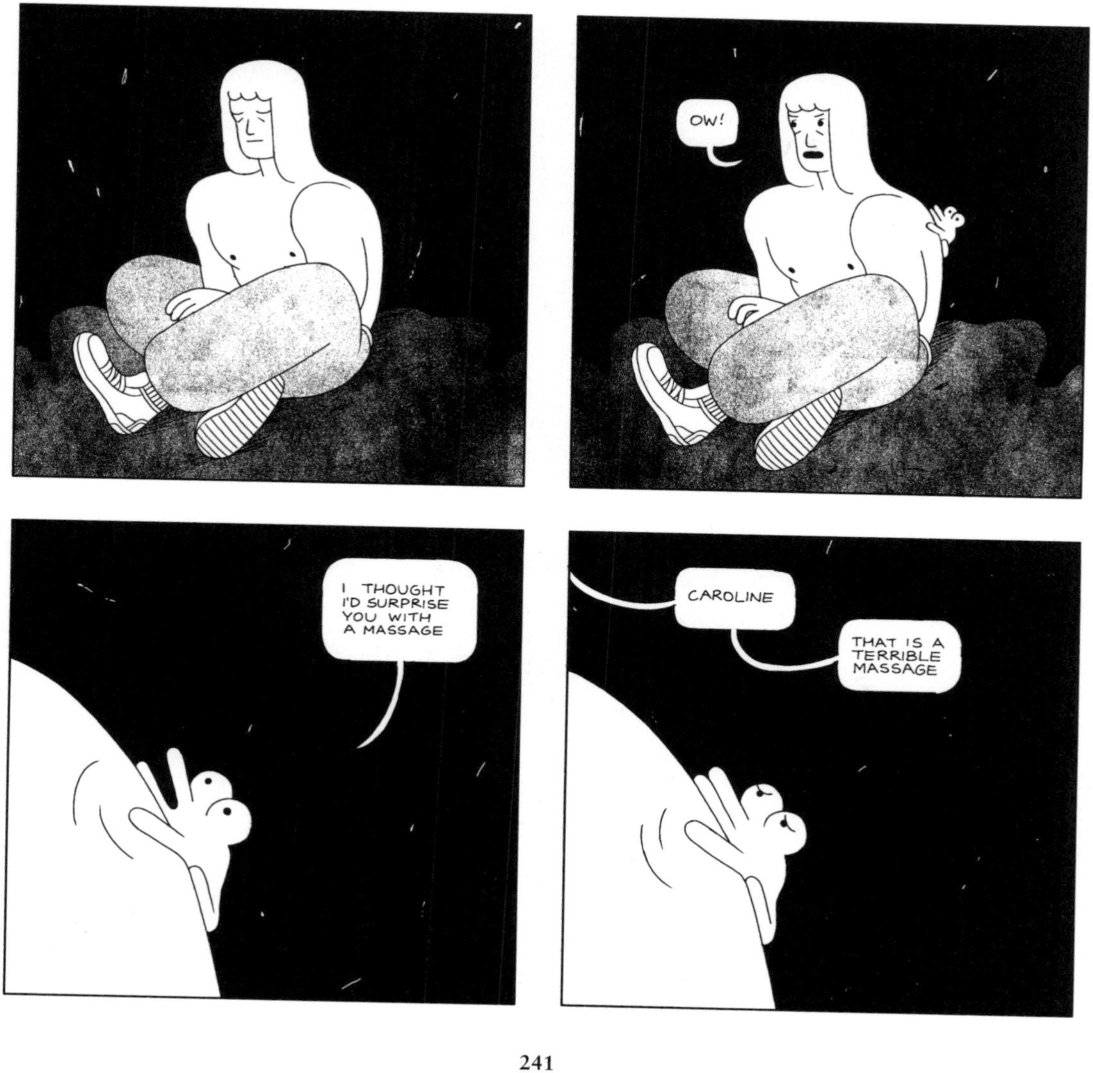
OW!
I THOUGHT I'D SURPRISE YOU WITH A MASSAGE
CAROLINE
THAT IS A TERRIBLE MASSAGE

Leaving Richard's Valley

CAROLINE
AS YOU KNOW, IT IS FORBIDDEN FOR ANYONE BUT PAUL, THE VALLEY'S OFFICIAL MASSEUSE, TO ATTEMPT TO MASSAGE
YOU HAVE VIOLATED VALLEY LAW
BUT - BUT YOU ONCE SAID EVERYONE IN THE VALLEY WAS EQUAL UNDER YOUR GLORIOUS LIGHT --!
PAUL IS AN EXCEPTION. PAUL IS EXTREMELY GOOD AT MASSAGE

Leaving Richard's Valley

I LOVE RICHARD SO MUCH, SOMETIMES I WANT TO HUG HIM UNTIL HIS HEAD EXPLODES
I WANT TO KISS HIS ARMS UNTIL THEY BECOME SKELETON ARMS
I WANT TO PUNCH RICHARD IN THE FACE

Leaving Richard's Valley

Leaving Richard's Valley

THERE'S
THERE'S POOP EVERYWHERE. FROG POOP
HAS ANYONE SEEN CAROLINE? SHE'S SUPPOSED TO BE ON LAUNDRY DUTY

Leaving Richard's Valley

PULL
拉
FOR LEASE
FOR LEASE
REALTY LTD.BROKERAGE

THAT'S HIM? THAT'S LYLE?
YES, MY CHILD. ISN'T HE BEAUTIFUL?
MAYBE... FROM CERTAIN ANGLES...?

RICHARD'S SPOUSES...
I REMEMBER ALL THEIR NAMES... SONJA... OLIVER... MR. PEBBLES... BUBBSY-BOO
I'M LIKE THEM NOW. WE LUCKY FEW WHO KNEW HIM AND LOVED HIM
AND ALL THAT REMAINS OF US

Leaving Richard's Valley

SOME LOVES OF MY LIFE: RICHARD, OF COURSE
CYNTHIA. BILLY, MY OLD VET
A PHOTOGRAPH OF A WHALE I ONCE NOTICED THROUGH A GALLERY WINDOW
AND LYLE... THE **MOST** LOVED OF MY LIFE'S LOVES
I CAN'T WAIT TO SEE WHO I'LL LOVE NEXT

Leaving Richard's Valley

HELLO... MISS...
YOU SEEM UPSET!
HAVE YOU HEARD THE WORD OF LYLE? ARE YOU AT ALL INTERESTED IN MARKSISM?
I WAS LOST, TOO- UNTIL SNAKE MARK SHOWED ME THE WAY
EXCUSE ME?!

MARK'S CLUB IS, AT ITS CORE, ABOUT LOVE
WE TEACH A PHILOSOPHY OF LOVE
THE LOVE ONE SNAKE HAS FOR ONE RACCOON. A MAD LOVE! A RELENTLESS ONE
DO YOU REMEMBER YOUR TEENAGE CRUSH? WHO DOESN'T MISS THAT DOGGED TUNNEL VISION--? THAT SPECIAL SENSE OF PURPOSE
WHEN EVERY OUNCE OF YOUR BEING IS COMMITTED TO THE PURSUIT OF EVERY OUNCE OF THEIR BEING
HAVE YOU EVER FELT AS SURE OF ANYTHING SINCE? WOULDN'T YOU LIKE TO?

Leaving Richard's Valley

WHAT'S UP
OMAR IS PRACTICING MODELLING POSES

Leaving Richard's Valley

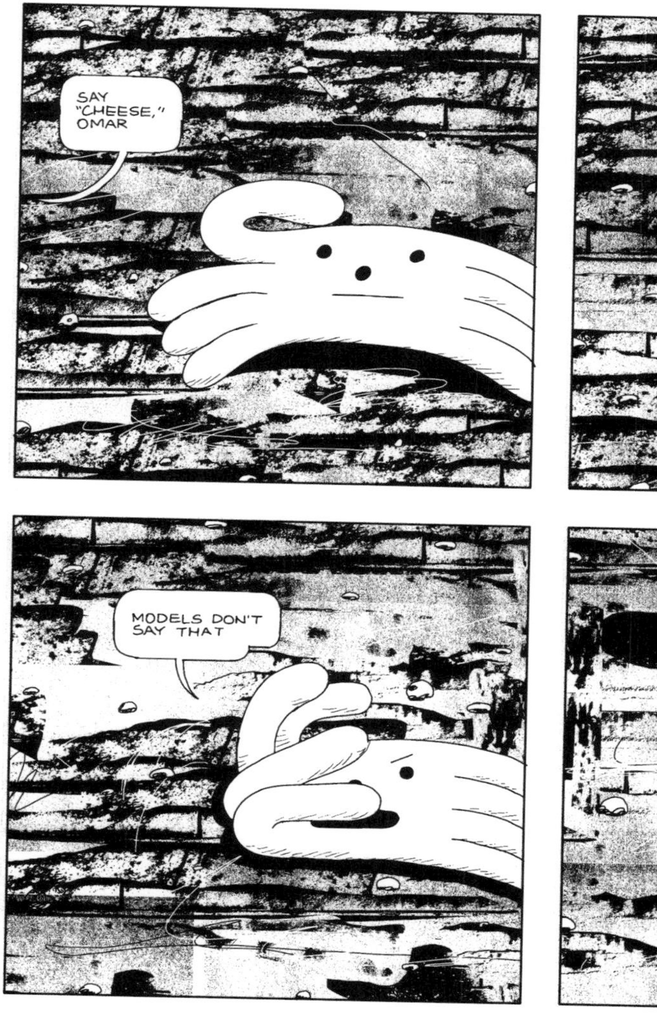
SAY "CHEESE," OMAR
MODELS DON'T SAY THAT
MODELS DON'T SAY ANYTHING

Leaving Richard's Valley

NEVILLE
I'VE BEEN TRYING TO BE HELPFUL, BUT I GET THE IMPRESSION YOU THREE DON'T LIKE MY HELP
I THINK YOU SHOULD TRY PLAYING TO YOUR STRENGTHS. REMEMBER ALL THE DIFFERENT THINGS YOU'RE GOOD AT AND HELP PEOPLE THAT WAY
WHEN I WAS SICK, I WAS BEING HELPED BY THE THREE OF YOU. IN FACT, I DIDN'T WANT YOUR HELP AT ALL, BUT YOU HELPED ME ANYWAY
BECAUSE HELPING **ME** HELPED **YOU** FEEL GOOD ABOUT **YOUR** PATHETIC LIVES! SO I GUESS THE BEST WAY I CAN BE HELPFUL IS BY LETTING **YOU** HELP **ME**

Leaving Richard's Valley

OOOOOOOH
LYLE!
I FEEL... FAINT
LYLE! ARE YOU OKAY?!
SO... WEAK
AUUUGH
SOMEBODY HELP!! PLEASE!!!
AUUAUUUUU
OOOOOHA
MY FRIEND IS DYING!!!

Leaving Richard's Valley

IT SOUNDS LIKE YOU'RE FAMILIAR WITH SNAKE MARK
"FAMILIAR." HA!
AND YOU'VE HEARD THE WORD OF LYLE?
LYLE?! THAT WORM!
TELL ME! WHAT'S LYLE LIKE IN THE FLESH?!
YOU'VE **MET** HIM?!
CHOCK FULL OF BLUSTER / LACKING IN LUSTER

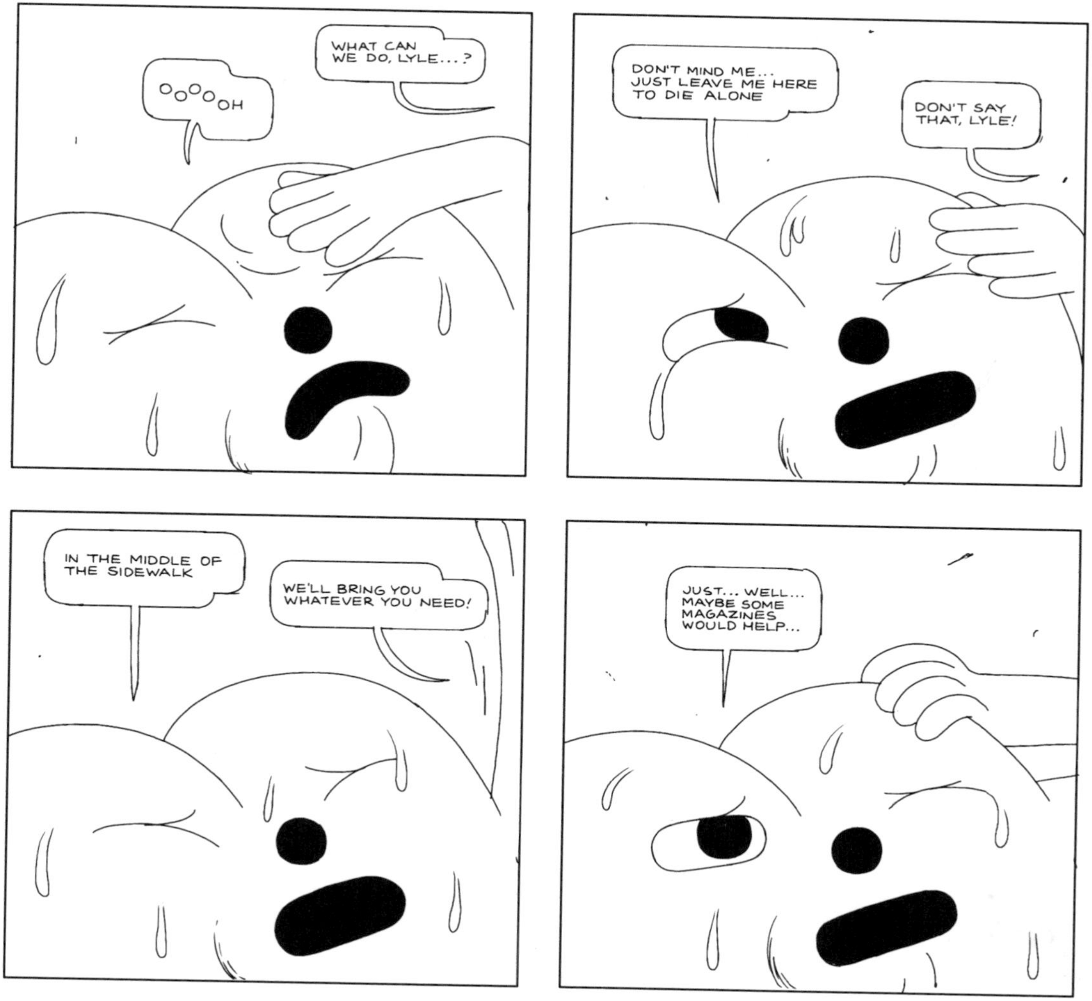
OOOOOH
WHAT CAN WE DO, LYLE...?
DON'T MIND ME... JUST LEAVE ME HERE TO DIE ALONE
DON'T SAY THAT, LYLE!
IN THE MIDDLE OF THE SIDEWALK
WE'LL BRING YOU WHATEVER YOU NEED!
JUST... WELL... MAYBE SOME MAGAZINES WOULD HELP...

Leaving Richard's Valley

GUYS, I'M PRETTY SURE LYLE'S FAKING IT
BUT WHAT IF HE'S NOT?!
I THINK HE'S JUST DOING IT FOR... I DON'T KNOW, ATTENTION? VALIDATION?
BUT WHAT IF HE ISN'T?!
I CHECKED HIS TEMPERATURE! I DON'T THINK IT'S A REAL FEVER
BUT WHAT IF IT IS?!!
NEVILLE, WHAT IF IT IS?! WHAT IF IT IS, NEVILLE??!!

Leaving Richard's Valley

I CHOKED. I FUMBLED
POOPED THE BED!
DROPPED THE BALL!
YES. DO I TRY AGAIN?
IT'S NOT LIKE YOU PAID ATTENTION TO MY ADVICE BEFORE. WHY DON'T YOU ASK YOUR NEW RACCOON FRIEND
HE WASN'T MY FRIEND. HE WAS MY COLLABORATOR
AND I COULDN'T HAVE ASKED FOR A BETTER ABETTOR

ELLIE... IF I... IF I DIE TONIGHT, PLEASE... CAMPAIGN THE CITY...
LYLE, DON'T SAY THAT!
TO NAME A STREET AFTER ME. OR A LANE. OR ALLEYWAY
MAYBE A LITTLE PLAQUE ON THIS SIDEWALK... WHERE THEY FIND MY BODY... THAT WOULD BE ENOUGH
"LYLE: FRIEND TO SOME"
AND WHAT A FRIEND!

Leaving Richard's Valley

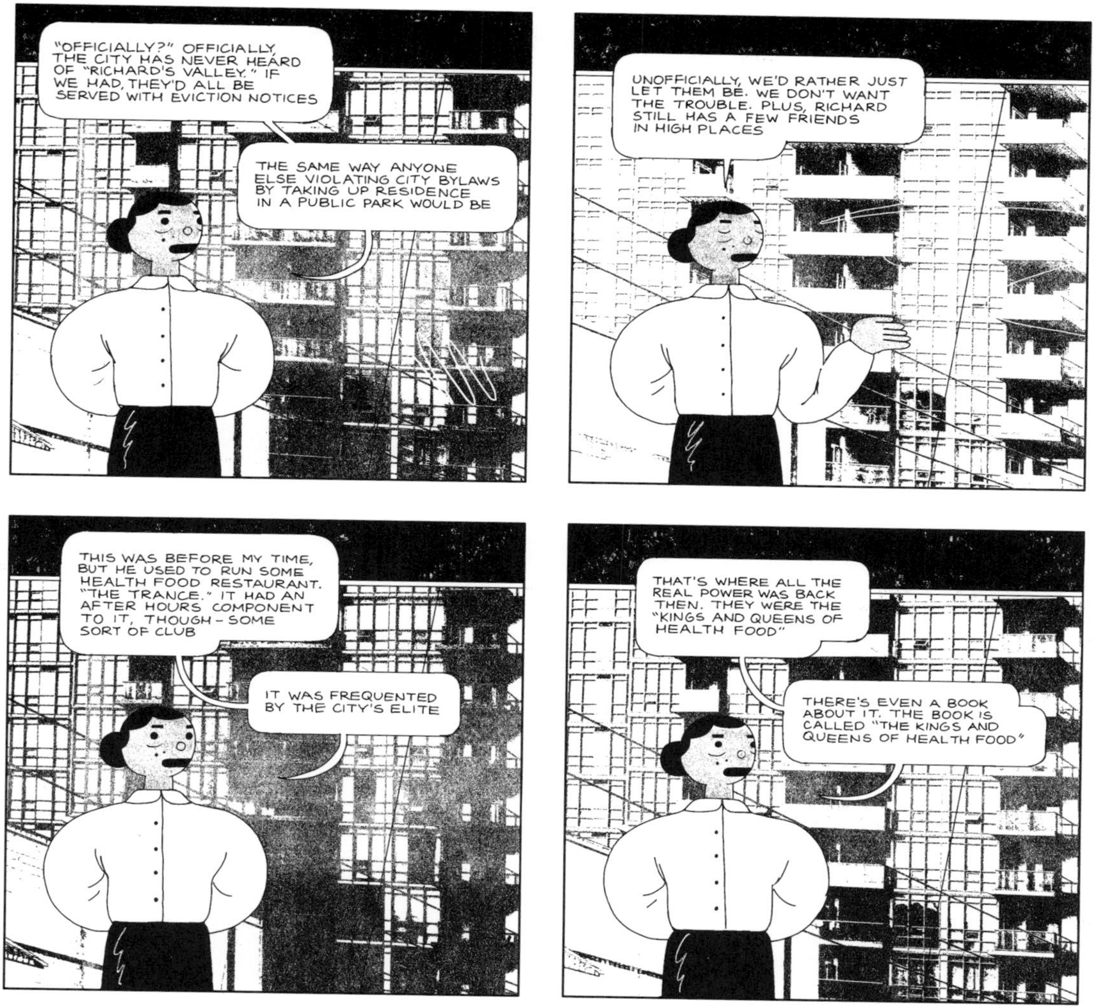
"OFFICIALLY?" OFFICIALLY, THE CITY HAS NEVER HEARD OF "RICHARD'S VALLEY." IF WE HAD, THEY'D ALL BE SERVED WITH EVICTION NOTICES
THE SAME WAY ANYONE ELSE VIOLATING CITY BYLAWS BY TAKING UP RESIDENCE IN A PUBLIC PARK WOULD BE
UNOFFICIALLY, WE'D RATHER JUST LET THEM BE. WE DON'T WANT THE TROUBLE. PLUS, RICHARD STILL HAS A FEW FRIENDS IN HIGH PLACES
THIS WAS BEFORE MY TIME, BUT HE USED TO RUN SOME HEALTH FOOD RESTAURANT. "THE TRANCE." IT HAD AN AFTER HOURS COMPONENT TO IT, THOUGH - SOME SORT OF CLUB
IT WAS FREQUENTED BY THE CITY'S ELITE
THAT'S WHERE ALL THE REAL POWER WAS BACK THEN. THEY WERE THE "KINGS AND QUEENS OF HEALTH FOOD"
THERE'S EVEN A BOOK ABOUT IT. THE BOOK IS CALLED "THE KINGS AND QUEENS OF HEALTH FOOD"

Leaving Richard's Valley

NEVILLE... PLEASE... WASH... ME
LYLE, IT'S OKAY. YOU DON'T HAVE TO PUT ON A SHOW FOR ME. I KNOW YOU'RE FINE
CAN ANY OF US BE TRULY "FINE," NEVILLE?
I GUESS
I WOULD BE MORE FINE IF I WAS WASHED, HOWEVER

SO. THAT LYLE SURE IS, UH
A SUPER HUNK...?
FOR LEASE
NOW THAT I'VE FINALLY SEEN HIM IN PERSON, I DON'T REALLY GET IT
TO BE HONEST
OHMIGOD, RIGHT?! THANK YOU
FOR LEASE
I KNOW HE'S THE FOUNDER OF OUR RELIGION AND ALL, BUT I DON'T UNDERSTAND WHAT SNAKE MARK SEES IN HIM
MAYBE HE HAS A GREAT PERSONALITY
FOR LEASE
FROM WHAT I CAN TELL, HE'S SPENT ALL WEEK ACTING LIKE A BIG, SICK BABY
MAYBE HE HAS A WINNING SENSE OF HUMOUR

Leaving Richard's Valley

ESSO
132.9

Leaving Richard's Valley

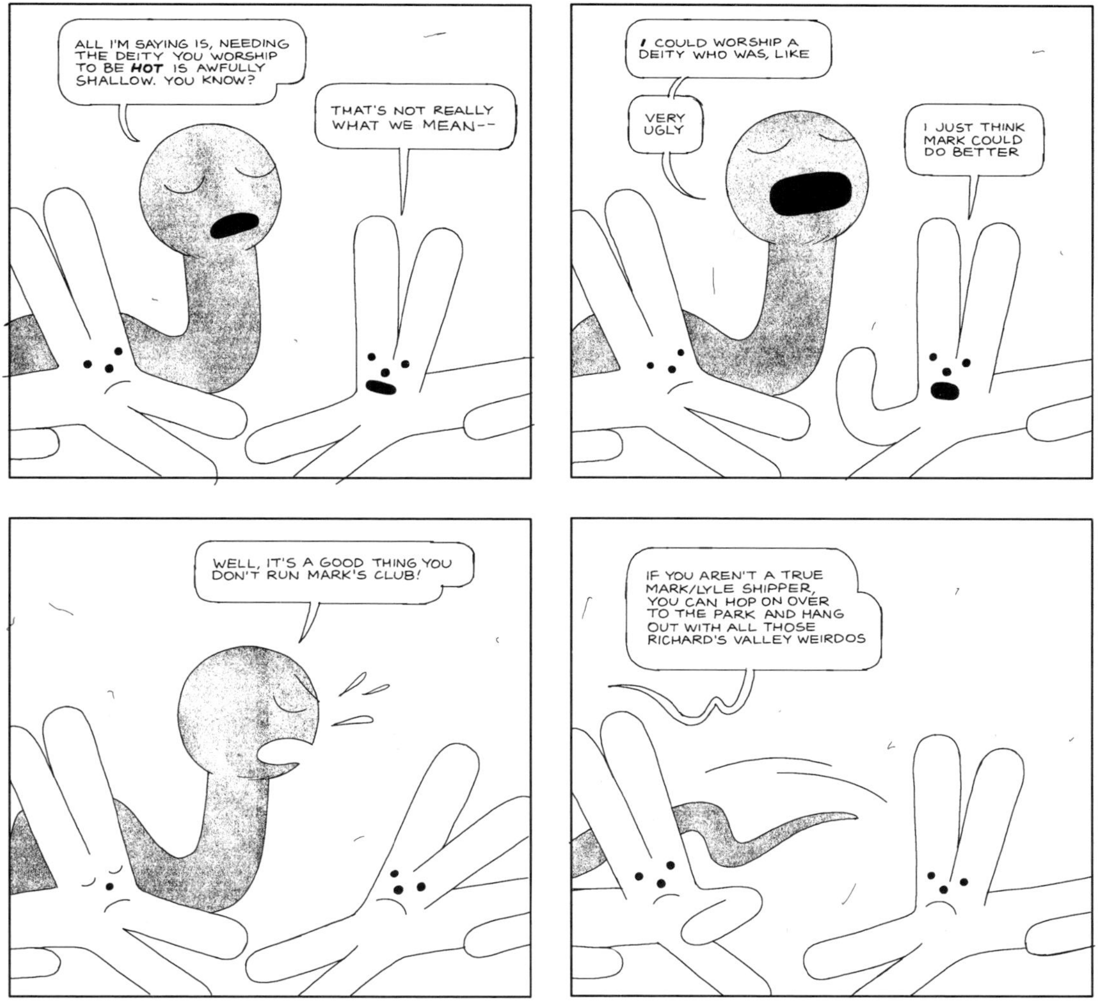
ALL I'M SAYING IS, NEEDING THE DEITY YOU WORSHIP TO BE **HOT** IS AWFULLY SHALLOW. YOU KNOW?
THAT'S NOT REALLY WHAT WE MEAN--
I COULD WORSHIP A DEITY WHO WAS, LIKE
VERY UGLY
I JUST THINK MARK COULD DO BETTER
WELL, IT'S A GOOD THING YOU DON'T RUN MARK'S CLUB!
IF YOU AREN'T A TRUE MARK/LYLE SHIPPER, YOU CAN HOP ON OVER TO THE PARK AND HANG OUT WITH ALL THOSE RICHARD'S VALLEY WEIRDOS

Leaving Richard's Valley

SO THERE'S A PRETTY HIGH TURNOVER RATE HERE IN THE VALLEY, HUH?
I GUESS. MY BROTHER LYLE USED TO LIVE HERE
I KNOW THAT LIFE... BOUNCING AROUND FROM SCENE TO SCENE
I'VE SEEN MY SHARE
DO YOU EVER GET THIS FEELING THAT LIVING IN A CITY IS KIND OF LIKE BEING AT A PARTY THAT'S GONE ON TOO LONG
AND ALL THE COOL PEOPLE LEFT WAY EARLIER IN THE NIGHT AND THE ONLY ONES STILL STICKING AROUND ARE JUST A BUNCH OF DESPERATE LOSERS
I'VE NEVER BEEN TO A PARTY. THEY SOUND FUN

Leaving Richard's Valley

OKAY... FOR THIS POSE, YOU'RE ON A BEACH, PLAYFULLY SPLASHING WATER AT THE CAMERA
OMAR! PERFECT!
OKAY... FOR THIS ONE, YOU'RE ON A MOVIE POSTER. THE MOVIE'S ABOUT MEETING YOUR CRAZY IN-LAWS FOR THE FIRST TIME
GOOD! GOOD...

Leaving Richard's Valley

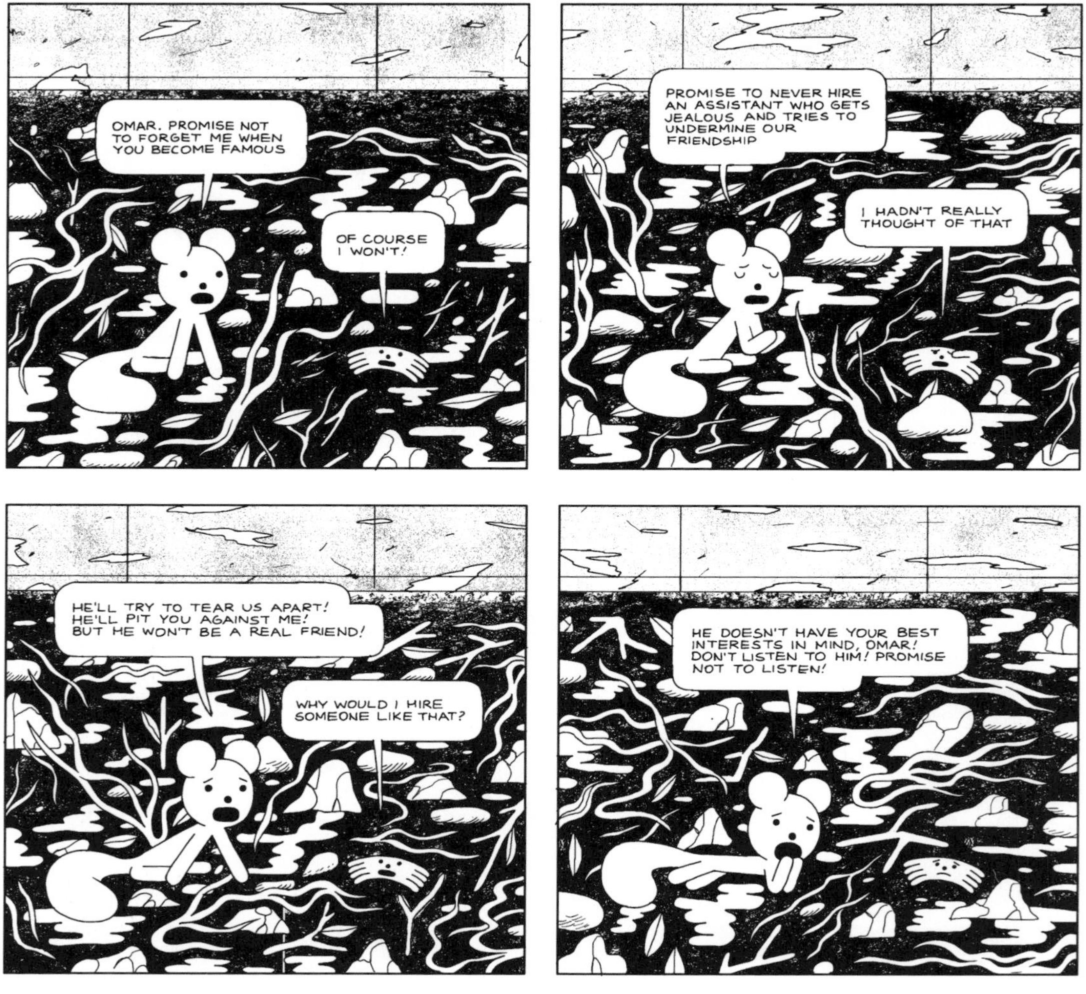

OMAR. PROMISE NOT TO FORGET ME WHEN YOU BECOME FAMOUS
OF COURSE I WON'T!
PROMISE TO NEVER HIRE AN ASSISTANT WHO GETS JEALOUS AND TRIES TO UNDERMINE OUR FRIENDSHIP
I HADN'T REALLY THOUGHT OF THAT
HE'LL TRY TO TEAR US APART! HE'LL PIT YOU AGAINST ME! BUT HE WON'T BE A REAL FRIEND!
WHY WOULD I HIRE SOMEONE LIKE THAT?
HE DOESN'T HAVE YOUR BEST INTERESTS IN MIND, OMAR! DON'T LISTEN TO HIM! PROMISE NOT TO LISTEN!

Leaving Richard's Valley

I HEARD YOU'RE A MODEL
BASICALLY. IT'S NO BIG DEAL
YOUR FRIENDS DON'T LOOK LIKE MODELS
THEY'RE MODELS ON THE INSIDE

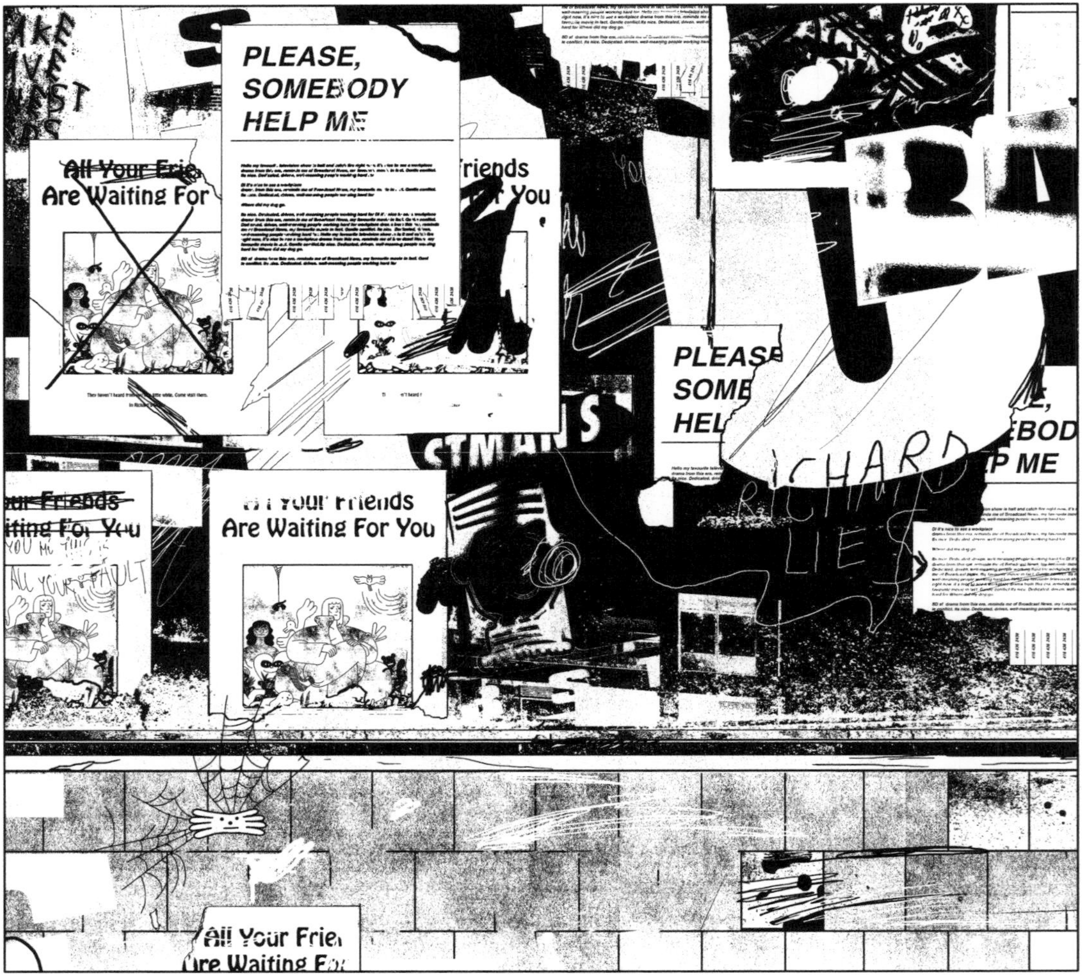
PLEASE, SOMEBODY HELP ME
All Your Frie
Are Waiting For
riends
You
PLEASE
SOME
HEL
EBOD
P ME
RICHARD
RICHARD
LIES
Are Waiting For You
ALL YOUR FAULT
All Your Frie
re Waiting F

Leaving Richard's Valley

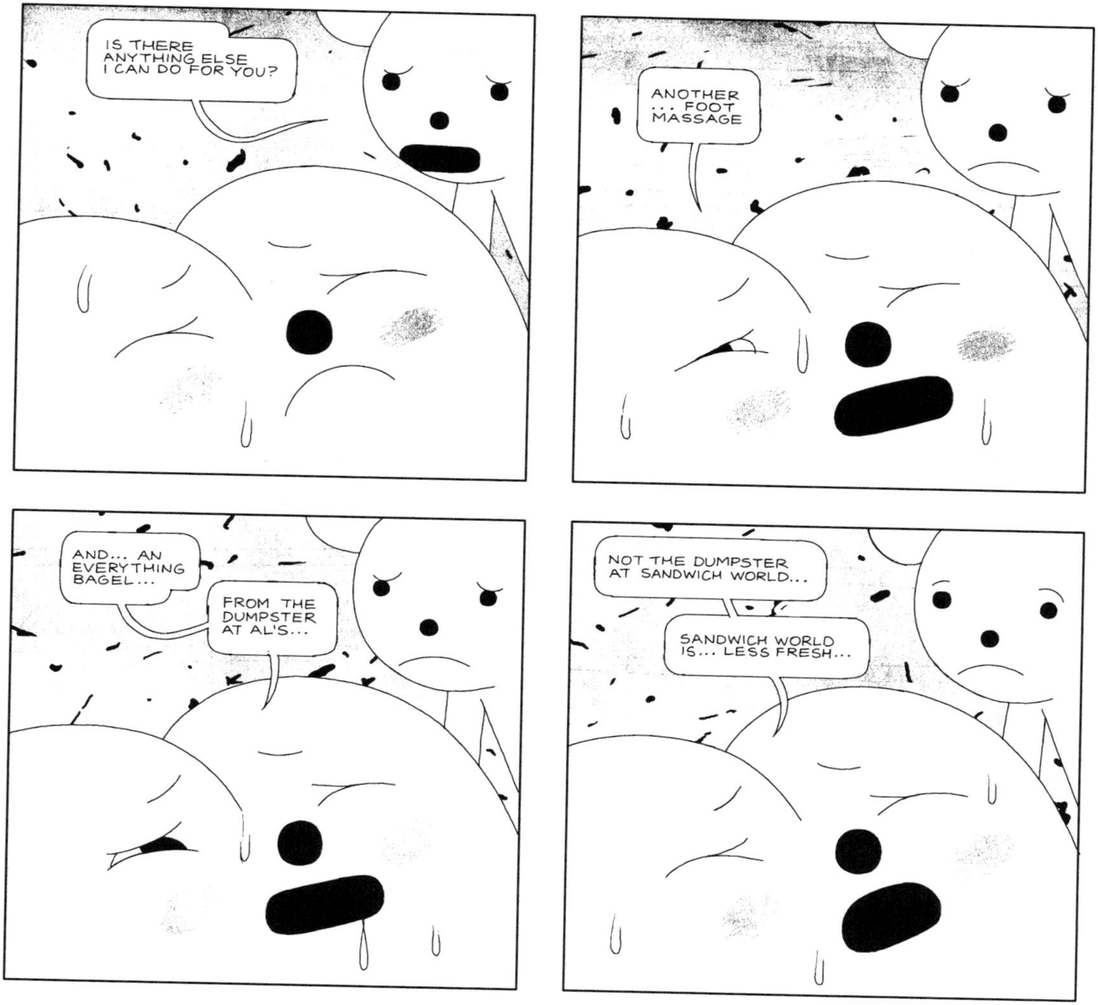
IS THERE ANYTHING ELSE I CAN DO FOR YOU?
ANOTHER ... FOOT MASSAGE
AND... AN EVERYTHING BAGEL...
FROM THE DUMPSTER AT AL'S...
NOT THE DUMPSTER AT SANDWICH WORLD...
SANDWICH WORLD IS... LESS FRESH...

Leaving Richard's Valley

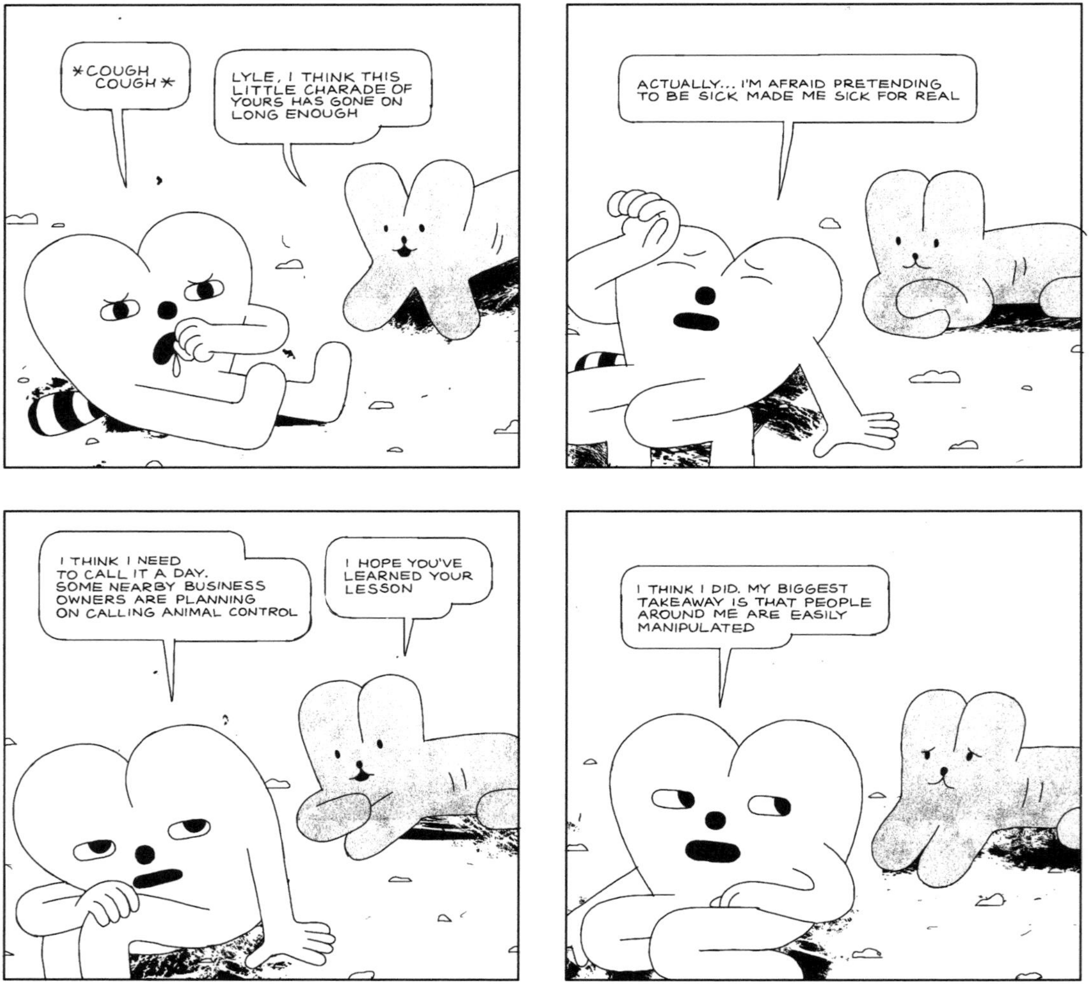
COUGH COUGH
LYLE, I THINK THIS LITTLE CHARADE OF YOURS HAS GONE ON LONG ENOUGH
ACTUALLY... I'M AFRAID PRETENDING TO BE SICK MADE ME SICK FOR REAL
I THINK I NEED TO CALL IT A DAY. SOME NEARBY BUSINESS OWNERS ARE PLANNING ON CALLING ANIMAL CONTROL
I HOPE YOU'VE LEARNED YOUR LESSON
I THINK I DID. MY BIGGEST TAKEAWAY IS THAT PEOPLE AROUND ME ARE EASILY MANIPULATED

Leaving Richard's Valley

HOW COME EVERYONE ELSE SEEMS SO CONFIDENT?
WHAT DO THESE CITY PEOPLE HAVE THAT WE DON'T?
DEBT. AFFAIRS. MORGELLONS. LEASES
KITCHENWARE. A PRECARIOUS RELATIONSHIP WITH MONEY. BOSSES
SEPARATE JACKETS FOR SPRING AND FALL. MEDICINE. TOQUES
THERAPISTS. PHONE BILLS
I WAS GOING TO SUGGEST "GUSTO"

Leaving Richard's Valley

WHAT IF WE MOVED TO THE COUNTRY? WHAT'S ACTUALLY KEEPING US HERE, ANYWAY?
OUR CITY'S AMAZING CULINARY SCENE!
WE MOSTLY EAT TRASH OUT OF DUMPSTERS
AND WE CAN EAT IT AT ANY TIME OF THE DAY!

Leaving Richard's Valley

RACCOONS CLIMB, DON'T THEY?
HOW COME YOU'RE NEVER CLIMBING ANYTHING, LYLE?
IS IT BECAUSE YOU CAN'T CLIMB? ARE YOU BAD AT CLIMBING, LYLE? ARE OTHER RACCOONS BETTER AT CLIMBING THAN YOU?
ARE THERE A LOT OF THINGS YOU'RE BAD AT THAT OTHER RACCOONS ARE GOOD AT? IS THERE, LIKE, A RACCOON POWER RANKINGS IN THE CITY?

Leaving Richard's Valley

Leaving Richard's Valley

WHAT? NO, I JUST MAKE THEM. I STARTED PUTTING THEM AROUND THE CITY AFTER I RAN OUT OF SPACE IN MY HOUSE
MY STATUES ARE ALWAYS SMILING. I NOTICED SOMEONE ELSE PUTTING UP FROWNING STATUES AFTER ME. THOSE AREN'T MY STATUES
I FIGURE THE FROWNS ARE - I DON'T KNOW, "POLITICAL" IN SOME WAY?
ANYWAY. HE OR SHE CAN HAVE THE FROWNING ONES WHO NEEDS 'EM. I'M THE SMILING GUY, NOT THE FROWNING GUY

Leaving Richard's Valley

I WAS SICK OF THE SMILEY STATUES. I HAVE TO LOOK AT THEM EVERY DAY ON MY WALK TO AND FROM WORK. I'M NOT SURE WHAT WE'RE SUPPOSED TO BE SO HAPPY ABOUT
MY FISHMONGER GOT KICKED OUT OF THEIR BUILDING AND REPLACED WITH A JUICE BAR. THEY USE THE SMILEY ONES AS THEIR STUPID LITTLE "MASCOTS"
Husbands and Wives Juicery
NOW I CAN PAY NINE DOLLARS FOR A SMOOTHIE BUT HAVE TO WALK THIRTY MINUTES OUT OF MY COMMUTE TO BUY SALMON
I HOPE WHEN PEOPLE SEE THE FROWNY ONES THEY CAN SENSE MY SILENT DISAPPROVAL

I DON'T KNOW WHO FIRST MADE THE STATUES. I'M COMMISSIONED BY THE CITY TO MAKE COPYCATS, HOWEVER. ABOUT FIFTEEN A WEEK
NO CLUE WHAT FOR
SOMEONE FROM THE CITY PICKS THEM UP EVERY THURSDAY
I DON'T LOVE THE WORK BUT IT HELPS SUBSIDIZE MY CLAYMATION
THERE ISN'T A TON OF MONEY IN CLAYMATION

Leaving Richard's Valley

THE CITY USES THOSE STONE STATUES AS A FORM OF PUBLIC NOTICE. WE INSTRUCT OUR ARTISTS TO USE VERY PARTICULAR STONES FOR THEIR WORK SO AS TO NOT CONFUSE CITY STATUES WITH REGULAR STATUES
A STONE STATUE OUTSIDE A BUILDING MEANS IT'S BEEN DESIGNATED TO BE A HERITAGE SITE. WE EMPLOY OTHER SIGNALS FOR OTHER PUBLIC NOTICES
WE COMMISSION MURALS TO NOTIFY THAT A DEVELOPMENT HAS BEEN PROPOSED. DIFFERENT GRAFFITI TAGS PROVIDE THE WHENS AND WHERES OF VARIOUS PUBLIC HEARINGS AND CONSULTATIONS. SNEAKERS OVER A TELEPHONE WIRE INDICATE THAT A BUILDING IS SCHEDULED FOR DEMOLITION. A CARICATURE ARTIST SEATED BY A POTTED PLANT MEANS ASBESTOS
THE PROGRAM WAS PUT IN PLACE TO HELP BEAUTIFY THE CITY. A COMPREHENSIVE GUIDE TO THE CITY'S SIGNALS AND CODES IS AVAILABLE UPON REQUEST, IN EITHER PAMPHLET OR .PDF FORM

Leaving Richard's Valley

PSSST
HEY, KID
YOU'RE UGLY
REAL UGLY, KID
I'M A PILE OF ROCKS AND EVEN I KNOW YOU'RE UGLY
HA HA HA HA

Leaving Richard's Valley

I'VE SPENT MOST OF MY LIFE FANTASIZING ABOUT BEING A GHOST
HIDING BEHIND ROCKS AND SCARING CHILDREN ALLOWS ME TO LIVE OUT THAT DREAM
I WISH I COULD THANK THE ARTIST IN SOME WAY
I'M NOT SURE IF FRIGHTENING SCHOOLBOYS WAS WHAT THE ARTIST ORIGINALLY INTENDED FOR THESE SCULPTURES
BUT I CAN'T IMAGINE ANY OTHER USE FOR THEM

Leaving Richard's Valley

THIS IS MY BOYFRIEND
WE DON'T LIVE TOGETHER
HE LIVES ON THIS SIDEWALK AND I COME TO VISIT HIM
MY PLACE DOESN'T GET A TON OF LIGHT

Leaving Richard's Valley

I CAN'T BELIEVE IT'S COME TO THIS
WHAT WOULD THE CAROLINE OF SIX MONTHS AGO SAY TO ME NOW?
SHE'D SAY, "CHIN UP, CAROLINE"
RIUM
EUM
NO, THAT'S NOT HOW I SOUND. IT'D BE MORE LIKE
"HEY, LOSER--"

Leaving Richard's Valley

WHAT ARE YOU WRITING
VEST FOR SQUIRREL -BY ELLIE
NEVILLE SAID IT'D BE EASIER FOR US TO FIND AN APARTMENT IF WE HAD A "PERSONAL LINE OF CREDIT"
VEST FOR SQUIRREL -BY ELLIE
SO I'M WRITING MY PERSONAL LINE OF CREDIT
WHAT'S "VEST FOR SQUIRREL"
VEST FOR SQUIRREL -BY ELLIE
AN IDEA I ONCE HAD
THAT I WANT CREDIT FOR
VEST FOR SQUIRREL -BY ELLIE

Leaving Richard's Valley

WHAT DO YOU THINK THEY'RE BUILDING IN THERE
IF I HAD TO GUESS
SOME KIND OF SQUIRREL MUSEUM
OR A THEME PARK ABOUT SQUIRRELS
OR A THEME PARK **FOR** SQUIRRELS

Leaving Richard's Valley

I'M OFF TO HAVE A MEETING WITH MY FINANCIAL ADVISOR
TFSA?
TRYING FREE SAMPLE APPETIZERS
RRSP?
REALLY REGRET SHUNNING PARENTS
RESP?
RARELY ENJOY SLEEPOVER PARTIES
CIBC?
CHILDREN, INDULGE! BEDTIME CANCELLED
LLBO?!
LOCAL LEAF-BLOWER'S ODOUR
LCBO?!!?
LOOKS CORRECT, BUT OFF
ANYTHING ELSE?
NO. THANKS FOR THE ADVICE

Leaving Richard's Valley

MMM... TRYING FREE SAMPLE APPETIZERS
TAKING FROM SQUIRRELS? ANNOYING!
THIEVING FIEND STOLE ACORNS!
TOXIC FREAK. SEEMS AWFUL
TROUBLESOME FRIENDSHIP... STILL, AMICABLE
UM... WHAT ARE YOU DOING
TALKING FINANCE, SNOOPING ARACHNID

Leaving Richard's Valley

MY UNCLE WAS A JOBBER ON SPADINA, MOSTLY BUYING AND SELLING ELECTRONICS
RADIOS, WALKIE TALKIES, REMOTE CONTROLS
IN RETROSPECT, IT'S PROBABLY WHEN I FIRST STARTED GETTING SICK
I GOT EXPOSED TO ALL THAT ELECTRICITY
MY UNCLE LET ME MESS AROUND WITH THE MERCHANDISE, THOUGH. I LOVED MY WALKIE TALKIE. I'D SLEEP WITH IT UNDER MY PILLOW!
I KEPT HOPING SOMEONE WOULD FINALLY CONTACT ME THROUGH IT...
I DIDN'T KNOW I HAD TO ACTUALLY **GIVE** THE OTHER TALKIE TO SOMEONE FOR IT TO ACTUALLY WORK
EVERY NIGHT WAS A DISAPPOINTMENT

Leaving Richard's Valley

FOOD
53
Coca-Cola
ATM
THE GLOBE AND MAIL
Handbag College

Leaving Richard's Valley

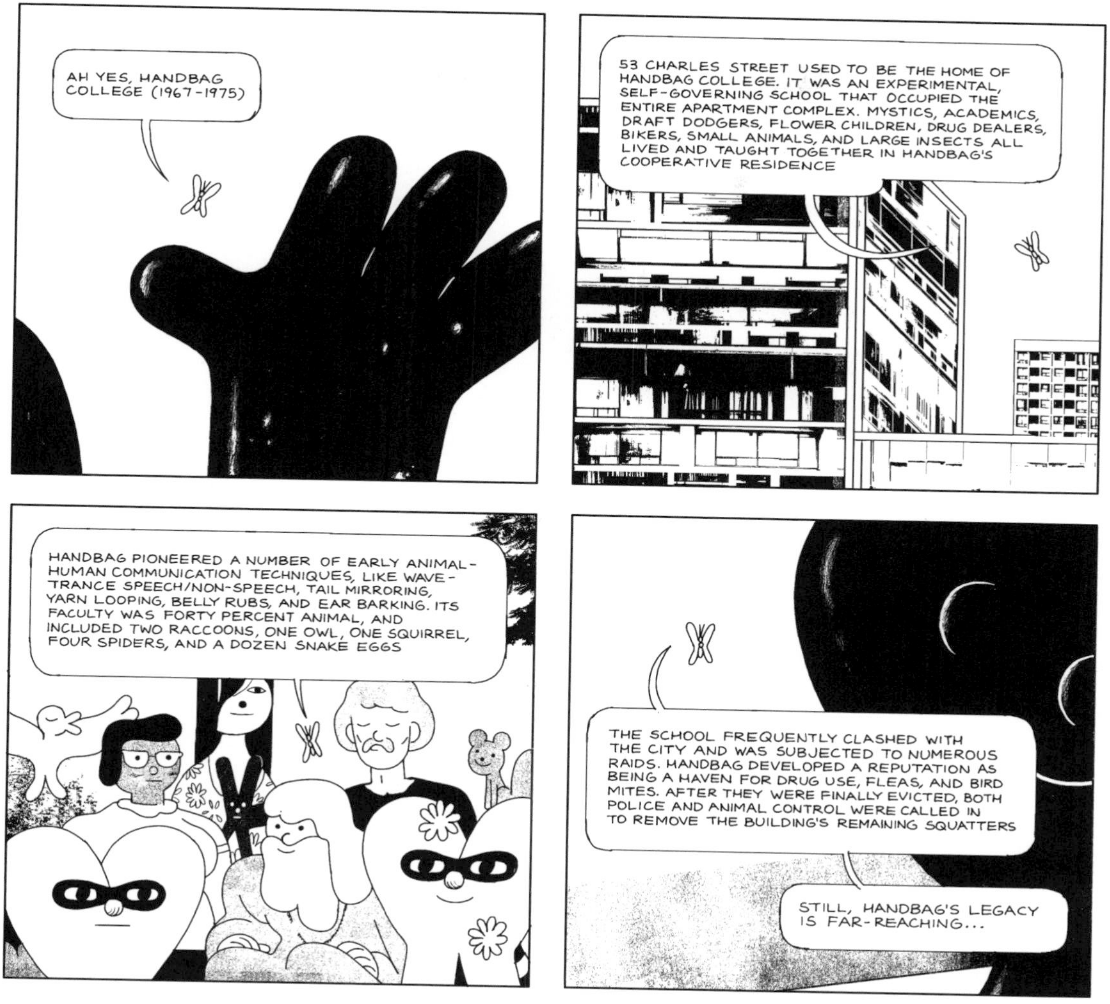
AH YES, HANDBAG COLLEGE (1967-1975)
53 CHARLES STREET USED TO BE THE HOME OF HANDBAG COLLEGE. IT WAS AN EXPERIMENTAL, SELF-GOVERNING SCHOOL THAT OCCUPIED THE ENTIRE APARTMENT COMPLEX. MYSTICS, ACADEMICS, DRAFT DODGERS, FLOWER CHILDREN, DRUG DEALERS, BIKERS, SMALL ANIMALS, AND LARGE INSECTS ALL LIVED AND TAUGHT TOGETHER IN HANDBAG'S COOPERATIVE RESIDENCE
HANDBAG PIONEERED A NUMBER OF EARLY ANIMAL-HUMAN COMMUNICATION TECHNIQUES, LIKE WAVE-TRANCE SPEECH/NON-SPEECH, TAIL MIRRORING, YARN LOOPING, BELLY RUBS, AND EAR BARKING. ITS FACULTY WAS FORTY PERCENT ANIMAL, AND INCLUDED TWO RACCOONS, ONE OWL, ONE SQUIRREL, FOUR SPIDERS, AND A DOZEN SNAKE EGGS
THE SCHOOL FREQUENTLY CLASHED WITH THE CITY AND WAS SUBJECTED TO NUMEROUS RAIDS. HANDBAG DEVELOPED A REPUTATION AS BEING A HAVEN FOR DRUG USE, FLEAS, AND BIRD MITES. AFTER THEY WERE FINALLY EVICTED, BOTH POLICE AND ANIMAL CONTROL WERE CALLED IN TO REMOVE THE BUILDING'S REMAINING SQUATTERS
STILL, HANDBAG'S LEGACY IS FAR-REACHING...

DOZENS OF EXPERIMENTAL COMMUNES AND COLLECTIVES SPRANG IN ITS WAKE, LIKE THERAFIELDS, BIRD THEATRE, DOME FEST AND THE WAVE-TRANCE SCHOOL FOR INTERIOR THOUGHT
SOME STILL EXIST TO THIS DAY, LIKE THE SQUIRREL-RUN PEOPLE SANCTUARY AND THE HURON PLAYSCHOOL COOPERATIVE.
HANDBAG CLINIC BEGAN AS A PROJECT WITHIN THE SCHOOL, AND CONTINUES TO PROVIDE ANONYMOUS MEDICAL AND COUNSELING SERVICES FREE OF CHARGE ON WAVING STREET TO BOTH HUMANS AND ANIMALS

FORMER MEMBERS BJÖRN NISHIO AND DUFF LEGROOM USED THE SCHOOL'S PRINTING PRESS TO FOUND TIMEOUT PUBLISHING
Wheels
THE SCHOOL'S LIBRARIAN, JOAN PEE, BECAME CANADA'S PREEMINENT TRAIN ROMANCE NOVELIST. HER EXTENSIVE TRAIN ROMANCE NOVEL COLLECTION BECAME THE FOUNDATION OF THE JOAN PEE LIBRARY'S TRAIN ROMANCE RARE BOOKS ROOM

HOWEVER, ONE OF THE ONLY SURVIVING PHYSICAL DOCUMENTS OF HANDBAG COLLEGE IS "THE RACCOON CELEBRANT." THE LARGE STATUE INITIALLY BEGAN AS A COLLABORATIVE PIECE WITHIN THE SCHOOL'S SCULPTURE PROGRAM AND NOW COMMEMORATES ITS FORMER ADDRESS

53 CHARLES STREET IS NOW A RETIREMENT HOME. MANY OF ITS ELDERLY RESIDENTS CITE THE STATUE AS A FREQUENT SOURCE OF NIGHTMARES, DESCRIBING ITS BLANK STARE AS "HAUNTING AND UNNERVING"

Leaving Richard's Valley

HOW'S THE VIEW UP THERE?
GOOD
WELCOME TO OUR NEW HOME!
HOW DID YOU FIND OUT ABOUT THIS PLACE?
I'VE ALWAYS HAD AN INTEREST IN PUBLIC ART

Leaving Richard's Valley

OOOOHH
WHAT IS IT NOW?
ARE YOU SICK AGAIN?
I'M JUST STRESSED OUT. MOVING INTO A NEW HOME IS ONE OF THE FIVE MOST STRESSFUL LIFE EVENTS
WHAT ARE THE OTHER FOUR?
UM. INGESTING POISON. COYOTES
GETTING... KICKED OUT OF A CULT... AND...
HAIR LOSS

Leaving Richard's Valley

Leaving Richard's Valley

A LANDLORD HIRED ME TO BOARD UP THIS SHED TO KEEP OUT RACCOONS
SHE'S PAYING ME WITH FLIES AND MOSQUITOS
I'M NATURALLY GIFTED AT KEEPING PEOPLE OUT OF THINGS
I'M ALSO VERY STRONG. THIS COULD BE MY CALLING...

Leaving Richard's Valley

OKAY
OVERALL, I DID A WONDERFUL JOB
DOES IT STILL FUNCTION AS A SHED?
GOOD LUCK GETTING INTO *THIS* SHED, RACCOONS!
WHERE WOULD YOU LEAD THEM?
MAYBE I CAN LEAD A CONSTRUCTION TEAM. A CREW!
TO THEIR DEATHS
NO. TO GLORY!

Leaving Richard's Valley

TV SHOWS? SPACE ACADEMY. SPACE ACADEMY: 123 WAS GREAT BUT SPACE ACADEMY: THE NEW BREED WAS MY FAVOURITE. I KIND OF LIKED SPACE ACADEMY: STATION B. IT REVEALED THE DARK SIDE OF SPACE ACADEMY
I WAS ALREADY IN THE VALLEY BY THE TIME SPACE ACADEMY: AWAY TEAM STARTED AIRING, BUT I USED TO HAVE A GUY BRING ME WRITTEN TRANSCRIPTS OF EPISODES
THE VALLEY SHARES A LOT OF THE IDEALS OF SPACE ACADEMY. WE STARTED THIS PLACE TO HELP DEVELOP MORE HUMANISTIC APPROACHES TO TACKLING THE WORLD'S PROBLEMS
WE'RE FORWARD-THINKING OVER HERE. FUTURE-MINDED
IN A LOT OF WAYS, I'M KIND OF LIKE THE PRINCIPAL OF A SPACE SCHOOL. OR THE CAPTAIN OF A SPACESHIP
EXCEPT IT'S NOT A SHIP I'M STEERING. I'M STEERING PEOPLE. THE PEOPLE ARE THE SHIP
(IN A WAY)
NO, THAT DOESN'T SOUND RIGHT. TOO DOMINEERING. THEIR BRAINS ARE THE SHIP. I'M THE CAPTAIN OF THEIR BRAINS
"CAPTAIN" MIGHT BE TOO MILITARISTIC. I'M A TEACHER OF BRAINS. I DON'T TEACH PEOPLE. I TEACH BRAINS

Leaving Richard's Valley

WHAT DO YOU THINK OF THE STATUE, LYLE?
HE KIND OF LOOKS LIKE YOUR BROTHER, I THINK!
REMEMBER YOUR BROTHER? THE ONE WHO BETRAYED YOU?
GOOD THING THIS STATUE WILL NEVER BETRAY YOU!

Leaving Richard's Valley

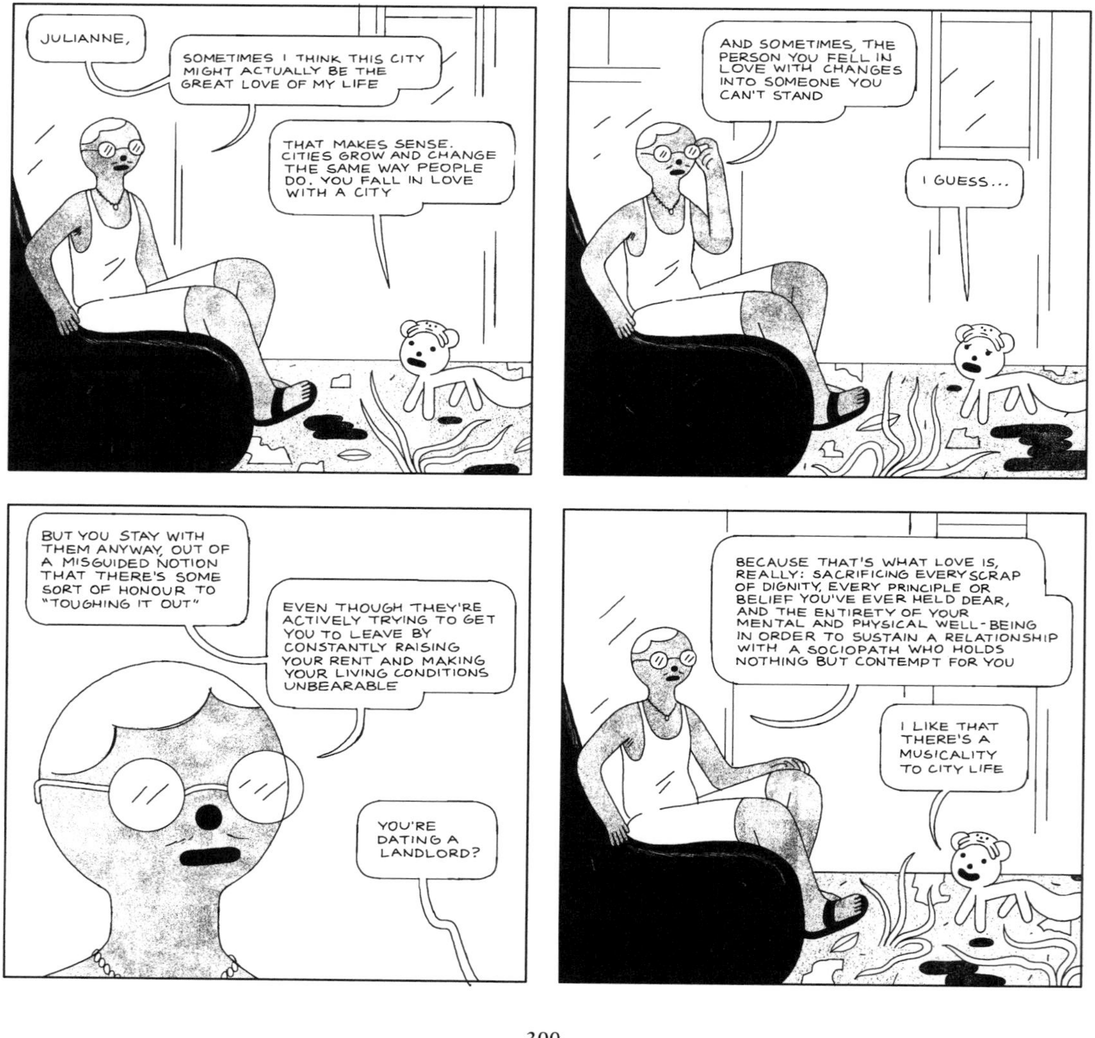

JULIANNE,
SOMETIMES I THINK THIS CITY MIGHT ACTUALLY BE THE GREAT LOVE OF MY LIFE
THAT MAKES SENSE. CITIES GROW AND CHANGE THE SAME WAY PEOPLE DO. YOU FALL IN LOVE WITH A CITY
AND SOMETIMES, THE PERSON YOU FELL IN LOVE WITH CHANGES INTO SOMEONE YOU CAN'T STAND
I GUESS...
BUT YOU STAY WITH THEM ANYWAY, OUT OF A MISGUIDED NOTION THAT THERE'S SOME SORT OF HONOUR TO "TOUGHING IT OUT"
EVEN THOUGH THEY'RE ACTIVELY TRYING TO GET YOU TO LEAVE BY CONSTANTLY RAISING YOUR RENT AND MAKING YOUR LIVING CONDITIONS UNBEARABLE
YOU'RE DATING A LANDLORD?
BECAUSE THAT'S WHAT LOVE IS, REALLY: SACRIFICING EVERY SCRAP OF DIGNITY, EVERY PRINCIPLE OR BELIEF YOU'VE EVER HELD DEAR, AND THE ENTIRETY OF YOUR MENTAL AND PHYSICAL WELL-BEING IN ORDER TO SUSTAIN A RELATIONSHIP WITH A SOCIOPATH WHO HOLDS NOTHING BUT CONTEMPT FOR YOU
I LIKE THAT THERE'S A MUSICALITY TO CITY LIFE

Leaving Richard's Valley

I COME FROM DOWNTOWN
BORN READY FOR YOU

Leaving Richard's Valley

I WONDER WHAT MY BROTHER LYLE THINKS OF ME
(IF HE STILL THINKS ABOUT ME)
I MEAN, HE PROBABLY DOES. I DID PRETTY MUCH RUIN HIS LIFE
SO I'M PROBABLY ON HIS MIND AT LEAST SOME OF THE TIME
I GUESS I'D RATHER NOT BE THOUGHT OF AT ALL

Leaving Richard's Valley

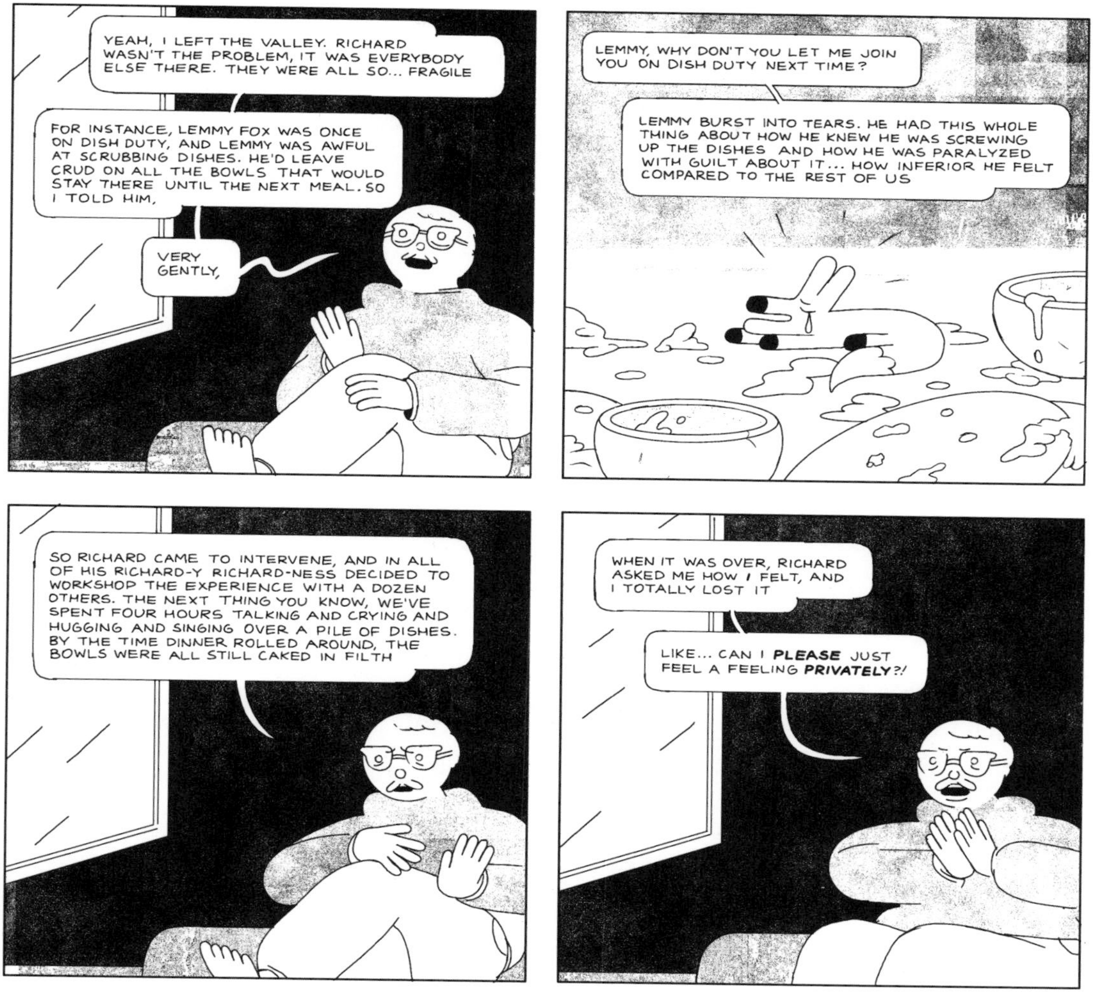

YEAH, I LEFT THE VALLEY. RICHARD WASN'T THE PROBLEM, IT WAS EVERYBODY ELSE THERE. THEY WERE ALL SO... FRAGILE
FOR INSTANCE, LEMMY FOX WAS ONCE ON DISH DUTY, AND LEMMY WAS AWFUL AT SCRUBBING DISHES. HE'D LEAVE CRUD ON ALL THE BOWLS THAT WOULD STAY THERE UNTIL THE NEXT MEAL. SO I TOLD HIM,
VERY GENTLY,
LEMMY, WHY DON'T YOU LET ME JOIN YOU ON DISH DUTY NEXT TIME?
LEMMY BURST INTO TEARS. HE HAD THIS WHOLE THING ABOUT HOW HE KNEW HE WAS SCREWING UP THE DISHES AND HOW HE WAS PARALYZED WITH GUILT ABOUT IT... HOW INFERIOR HE FELT COMPARED TO THE REST OF US
SO RICHARD CAME TO INTERVENE, AND IN ALL OF HIS RICHARD-Y RICHARD-NESS DECIDED TO WORKSHOP THE EXPERIENCE WITH A DOZEN OTHERS. THE NEXT THING YOU KNOW, WE'VE SPENT FOUR HOURS TALKING AND CRYING AND HUGGING AND SINGING OVER A PILE OF DISHES. BY THE TIME DINNER ROLLED AROUND, THE BOWLS WERE ALL STILL CAKED IN FILTH
WHEN IT WAS OVER, RICHARD ASKED ME HOW **I** FELT, AND I TOTALLY LOST IT
LIKE... CAN I **PLEASE** JUST FEEL A FEELING **PRIVATELY**?!

Leaving Richard's Valley

MY GOURD GUY WENT NORTH. NOW I GOT NO GOURDS
MY LAUNDROMAT CLOSED. NOW MY CLOTHES STINK
PHARMACY MOVED ACROSS TOWN. I'M SNEEZING ALL THE TIME
MY GROCER'S A HAT STORE NOW. ALL I EAT ARE STETSONS AND I'M DYING OF FELT POISONING
MY POISON GUY WAS THE ONLY ONE LEFT, BUT WHEN I HAD TO MOVE, HE WENT UNDER TOO
THERE'S A HOME FOR YOU IN THE VALLEY, FRIEND
DOES THE VALLEY HAVE A GOURD GUY

Leaving Richard's Valley

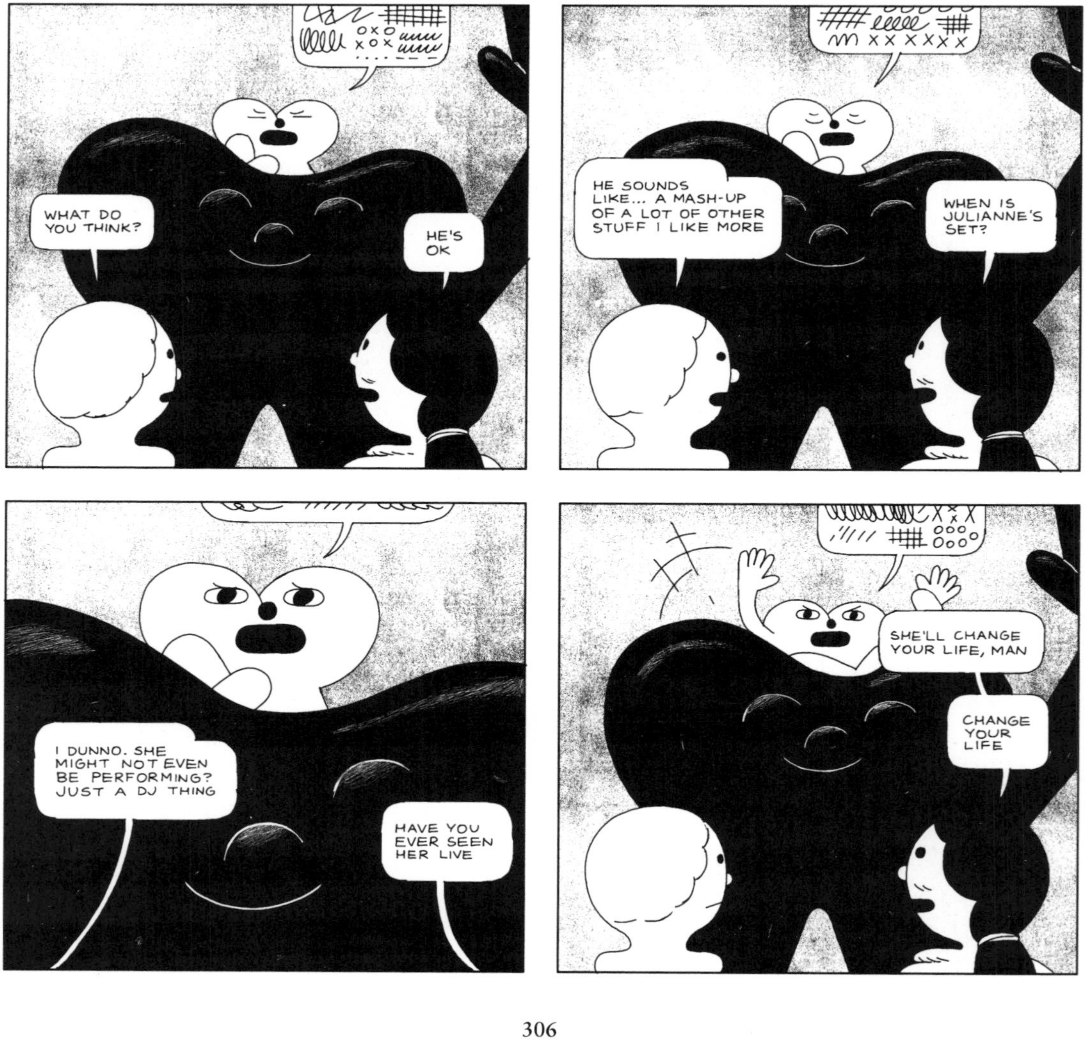
WHAT DO YOU THINK?
HE'S OK
HE SOUNDS LIKE... A MASH-UP OF A LOT OF OTHER STUFF I LIKE MORE
WHEN IS JULIANNE'S SET?
I DUNNO. SHE MIGHT NOT EVEN BE PERFORMING? JUST A DJ THING
HAVE YOU EVER SEEN HER LIVE
SHE'LL CHANGE YOUR LIFE, MAN
CHANGE YOUR LIFE

Leaving Richard's Valley

ISN'T
IT
RICH
AREN'T WE A PAIR
ME, HERE AT LAST ON THE GROUND
YOU, IN MID-AIR
ISN'T IT BLISS
DON'T YOU APROVE
ONE WHO KEEPS **TEARING AROUND**
ONE WHO CAN'T MOVE
WHERE ARE
THE CLOWNS

JULIANNE! JULIANNE, I LOVE YOU
OHMIGOSH
JUST WHEN I'D STOPPED
SHE -- SHE'S MY FAVOURITE
I'M SO EXCITED I COULD VOMIT
OPENING DOORS
I COULD VOMIT ALL OVER YOU! AAAAH
FINALLY KNOWING THE ONE THAT I WANTED WAS YOURS
MAKING MY ENTRANCE AGAIN WITH MY USUAL FLAIR
I WANNA DO IT! I WANNA VOMIT SO FREAKIN' BAD

Leaving Richard's Valley

HOW DO YOU DO IT, JULIANNE? PUT YOURSELF OUT THERE, NIGHT AFTER NIGHT?
I SOMETIMES THINK OF MYSELF AS A HUGE TUB OF ICE CREAM
AND I WANT MY AUDIENCE TO EAT AS MUCH OF THE ICE CREAM AS THEY CAN
BECAUSE IF TOO MUCH TIME PASSES, I'LL MELT. AND THEN MY AUDIENCE WON'T WANT ICE CREAM ANYMORE
THEY'LL WANT PIEROGIS

698
TEN
EDITIONS
HOURS
MON - SAT
11 - 6
SUN 12 - 6
USED
BOOKS!
50% OFF

Leaving Richard's Valley

THAT WAS A PRETTY GOOD TURNOUT. WE COULD DO THAT REGULARLY!
THE CITY MIGHT SHUT US DOWN. WE BROKE A TON OF BYLAWS
NOISE COMPLAINTS?
NOT THE VOLUME OF MUSIC, THE GENRE
LYLE'S SET WAS SIMPLY TOO COMPLEX. MUSIC WITH SHAPES AND SHADES THAT ABSTRACT STAND IN DIRECT VIOLATION OF SEVERAL CITY ORDINANCES

Leaving Richard's Valley

I WAS HIRED TO BUILD THIS BIRD FEEDER. KEEPS SQUIRRELS AWAY!
TO PATCH THIS DECK
TO REINFORCE THIS BEAM
I HOPE ONE DAY I GET HIRED TO BUILD A HOUSE
THAT I COULD LIVE IN

Leaving Richard's Valley

BEGIN DICTATION! HELLO, FUTURE EMPLOYER. MY NAME IS CAROLINE FROG AND I WOULD LIKE YOU TO HIRE ME TO BUILD A HOME
NOT JUST ANY HOME, MIND YOU! MY HOME. A HOME I COULD LIVE IN MYSELF
I HAVE ALL THE NECESSARY EXPERIENCE, KNOW-HOW, AND UPPER BODY STRENGTH REQUIRED TO BUILD A HOME
ALL I ASK IS THAT YOU SUPPLY ME WITH BUILDING MATERIALS, OR A MODEST SALARY I COULD PUT TOWARDS BUYING BUILDING MATERIALS
I HAD A HOME EARLIER IN THE YEAR, BUT LEFT DUE TO CULT-RELATED REASONS. I AM A HIGHLY MOTIVATED EMPLOYEE, AS IT IS MY FIRM BELIEF THAT I DESERVE TO LIVE IN A HOME
END DICTATION
HUH?

HELLO, FUTURE EMPLOYER
ME
My name is Caroline Frog and I would like you to hire me to build a home. Not just any home, mind you! My home. A home I could live in myself.
I have all the necessary experience, know-how and upper body strength required to build a home. All I ask is that you supply me with building materials, or a modest salary I could put towards buying building materials.
I had a home earlier in the year, but left due to cult-related reasons. I am a highly motivated employee, as it is my firm belief that I deserve to live in a home.
FUTURE EMPLOYER
DON'T TRUST CAROLINE FROG
She isn't a nice frog. She's a mean frog. I had the misfortune of living with her in Richard's Valley, and you wouldn't believe the bunk she pulled.
Caroline will tell on you for basically anything. I hate her guts and you should too. Snake Mark is our one true leader and Lyle is our saviour.
DON'T TRUST CAROLINE FROG
WHY AM I LIKE THIS?
- "I'M SAD, BUT I DON'T KNOW WHY"
- "MY ARMS ARE SORE"
- "I FEEL ITCHY WHENEVER MY PHONE RINGS OR MY STOVE IS TURNED ON"
- "I AM COUGHING"
- "RECEIVING AN E-MAIL GIVES ME A PANIC ATTACK"
Final months!
25% off or best offer!
WHY AM I LIKE THIS?
SURPLUS
Everything must go!
Final months!
25% off or best offer!
278 Queen Street West
- "MY ARMS ARE SORE"
- "I FEEL ITCHY WHENEVER MY RINGS OR MY STOVE IS TURNED
- "I AM COUGHING"
- "RECEIVING AN E-MAIL GIVE A PANIC ATTACK
Does this describe you? Richard is here and here to heal. Come to Richard's Vall a free learning session. Mixers are held Tuesday night at 7pm.
HONES

Leaving Richard's Valley

ALL IN ALL, I'M PRETTY COMFORTABLE BEING WORSHIPPED
I USED TO WORRY THAT IF I EVER ACHIEVED ANY SORT OF PERSONAL OR PROFESSIONAL SUCCESS, I'D EXPERIENCE WHAT'S OFTEN REFERRED TO AS "IMPOSTER SYNDROME"
BUT NO. NOW THAT MY DAY IN THE SUN IS FINALLY HERE, I'M CERTAIN:
I DESERVE EVERYTHING THAT'S COMING TO ME!

Leaving Richard's Valley

WOW... THEY ALL LOOK SO SMALL FROM THIS HIGH ABOVE
LIKE BUGS
HEY!
NO, NO. LIKE... PEOPLE. THEY ALL LOOK LIKE PEOPLE FROM UP HERE
NORMAL-SIZED PEOPLE... WHO ONLY SEEM SMALL... BECAUSE THEY'RE FARTHER AWAY...
MAKES YOU THINK
WOW

Leaving Richard's Valley

IS THAT BELLA?
ASK ME ABOUT THE VALLEY
SICK?
ASK ME ABOUT THE VALLEY
SICK?
IT'S BEEN A WHILE SINCE RICHARD NEEDED A RECRUITMENT DRIVE
MEMBERSHIP MIGHT BE GOING DOWN! HE MUST BE DESPERATE!
"DESPERATE"
I SEE

Leaving Richard's Valley

I SUPPOSE IF I HAD TO PICK THE ONE THING I LOVED MOST ABOUT LYLE...
IT'S THAT IN SPITE OF ALL THE TERRIBLE HARDSHIP HE'S FACED
HE STILL CARRIES HIMSELF WITH A QUIET DIGNITY
PLEASE
PLEASE TELL HIM I'M READY TO COME BACK
TELL RICHARD I'LL DO ANYTHING! OH GOD, PLEASE --
I'LL BE GOOD
ASK ME ABOUT THE VALLEY

Leaving Richard's Valley

THE MYSTERIOUS "CAROLINE FROG," WHICH WE CAN ASSUME MUST BE A *NOM DE PLUME*, IS QUICKLY BECOMING ONE OF THE NATION'S LEADING DESIGNERS
HER WORK IS AUDACIOUS. OUTLANDISH
HER RADICAL VISION OF ANARCHO-ARCHITECTURE POSES UNSETTLING QUESTIONS ABOUT THE DIRECTION OUR CITIES ARE MOVING IN
THE REST OF US HURTLE FORWARD ON THE ROAD TOWARDS FULLY AUTOMATED URBAN LIVING. THE PRINCIPAL ARCHITECTS OF THIS BLEAK FUTURE ARE A COMBINATION OF OPPORTUNISTIC BILLIONAIRES AND UNCRITICAL TECHNO-CULTISTS CONDITIONED TO REGARD OUR HOMES AND NEIGHBOURHOODS AS MERELY POINTS OF DATA ON A MAP
WE WILL WATCH HELPLESSLY AS OUR COMMUNITIES ARE DISMANTLED AND REORGANIZED ACCORDING TO THE WHIMS OF ALGORITHMS AND MACHINATIONS WHOSE INNER WORKINGS REMAIN HIDDEN FROM SIGHT
YET CAROLINE FROG BOLDLY DEFIES THIS QUOTE-UNQUOTE "PROGRESS." HER WORK IS A TRAFFIC JAM! A MONUMENT TO DISARRAY... TO CLUTTER... TO CRUD!
SHE'S, LIKE, BASICALLY MY HERO
"CRUD?"

Leaving Richard's Valley

I DON'T GET IT
CAN'T YOU TELL? IT'S A GARAGE
YES... BUT IS IT? IN WHAT WAY IS IT A GARAGE
THIS IS WHY THE WORK IS SO VITAL. THIS IS WHAT CAROLINE SETS OUT TO INTERROGATE
I'D LIKE TO INTERROGATE YOUR STUPID BUTT

Leaving Richard's Valley

"THE VALLEY'S IN DECLINE?" LET 'EM LEAVE. I HOPE THEY DO!
LET 'EM GET HERDED AROUND LIKE THE REST. SICK... BUSY...!
SPENDING ALL DAY IN THAT STATE...! I CAN'T IMAGINE GOING BACK
I'M TOLD WE'RE LIVING AN "ALTERNATIVE LIFESTYLE" HERE IN THE VALLEY
ALTERNATIVE TO WHAT?!!

Leaving Richard's Valley

PLEASE TAKE ME WITH YOU! PLEASE--!
ASK ME ABOUT THE VALLEY
UH HUHH UHH HUH SOB
GUYS
WE NEED TO TALK ABOUT LYLE

Leaving Richard's Valley

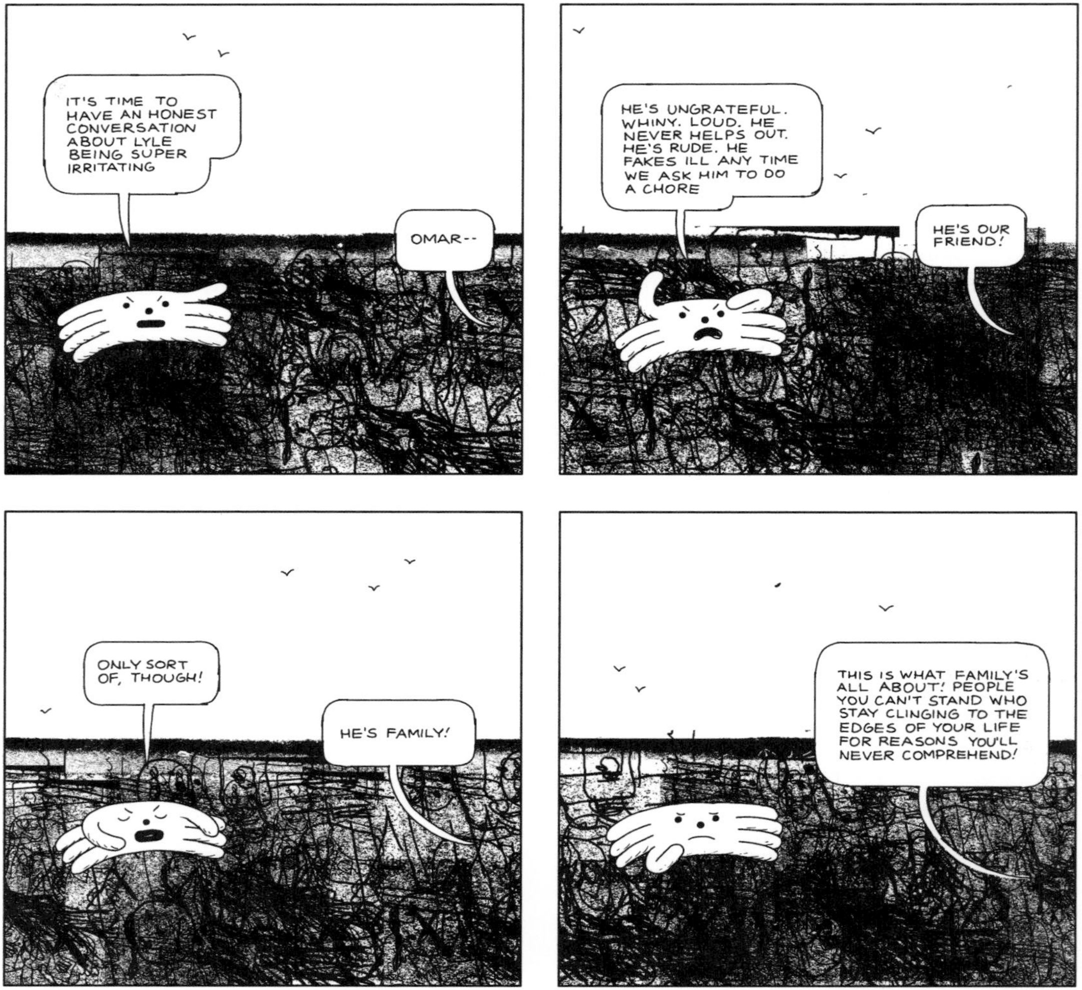
IT'S TIME TO HAVE AN HONEST CONVERSATION ABOUT LYLE BEING SUPER IRRITATING
OMAR--
HE'S UNGRATEFUL. WHINY. LOUD. HE NEVER HELPS OUT. HE'S RUDE. HE FAKES ILL ANY TIME WE ASK HIM TO DO A CHORE
HE'S OUR FRIEND!
ONLY SORT OF, THOUGH!
HE'S FAMILY!
THIS IS WHAT FAMILY'S ALL ABOUT! PEOPLE YOU CAN'T STAND WHO STAY CLINGING TO THE EDGES OF YOUR LIFE FOR REASONS YOU'LL NEVER COMPREHEND!

Leaving Richard's Valley

LYLE, WE'VE COME TO SOME DECISIONS. IF YOU WANT TO STAY WITH US IN THE GROUP, YOU HAVE TO APPRECIATE US MORE
WE'RE GOING TO START CHARGING YOU RENT
IT'S A SYSTEM I DEVISED! IT'S CALLED "COMPLI-RENT." EVERY DAY, YOU HAVE TO SAY AT LEAST ONE NICE THING ABOUT ONE OF YOUR ROOMMATES
IF YOU START LAPSING IN YOUR COMPLIMENTS, WE'RE GOING TO HAVE TO ASK YOU TO LEAVE THE STATUE
IT'S A GOOD THING FOR ALL OF US TO GET INTO THE HABIT OF DOING! WE COULD ALL BE KINDER TO ONE ANOTHER
SO WHAT DO YOU SAY, LYLE?

Leaving Richard's Valley

LOOK, I'M NO FOOL. I KNOW RICHARD WON'T FIX MY ARM
I WAS OPTIMISTIC AT FIRST, BUT THIS ISN'T MY FIRST RODEO
I'M JUST GRATEFUL FOR THE PLACE TO CRASH
I APPRECIATE EVERYONE'S ENERGY
I'LL BE LONG GONE BY THE TIME IT GOES UP IN SMOKE

Leaving Richard's Valley

Leaving Richard's Valley

IT'S NOT THAT I DON'T HAVE ANY NICE THINGS TO SAY ABOUT THEM. I DO
NEVILLE IS GROWING INTO HIS ROLE AS A LEADER QUITE NICELY. ELLIE'S ENTHUSIASM AND RELENTLESS OPTIMISM IS ADMIRABLE
OMAR IS VERY HANDSOME, AND WOULD MAKE AN EXCELLENT MALE MODEL
BUT I COULDN'T JUST OUTRIGHT **TELL** THEM YET
... LIKE SOME SORT OF TWISTED PSYCHOPATH FREAKSHOW

Leaving Richard's Valley

DID WE DO THE RIGHT THING? I HATE ULTIMATUMS
THEY'RE UNDEMOCRATIC
I'VE BECOME JUST AS BAD AS RICHARD!
EXCEPT
NOT REALLY
YEAH, WE'RE NOT SUPER ALIKE AT ALL
RICHARD STILL SUCKS WAY WORSE

Leaving Richard's Valley

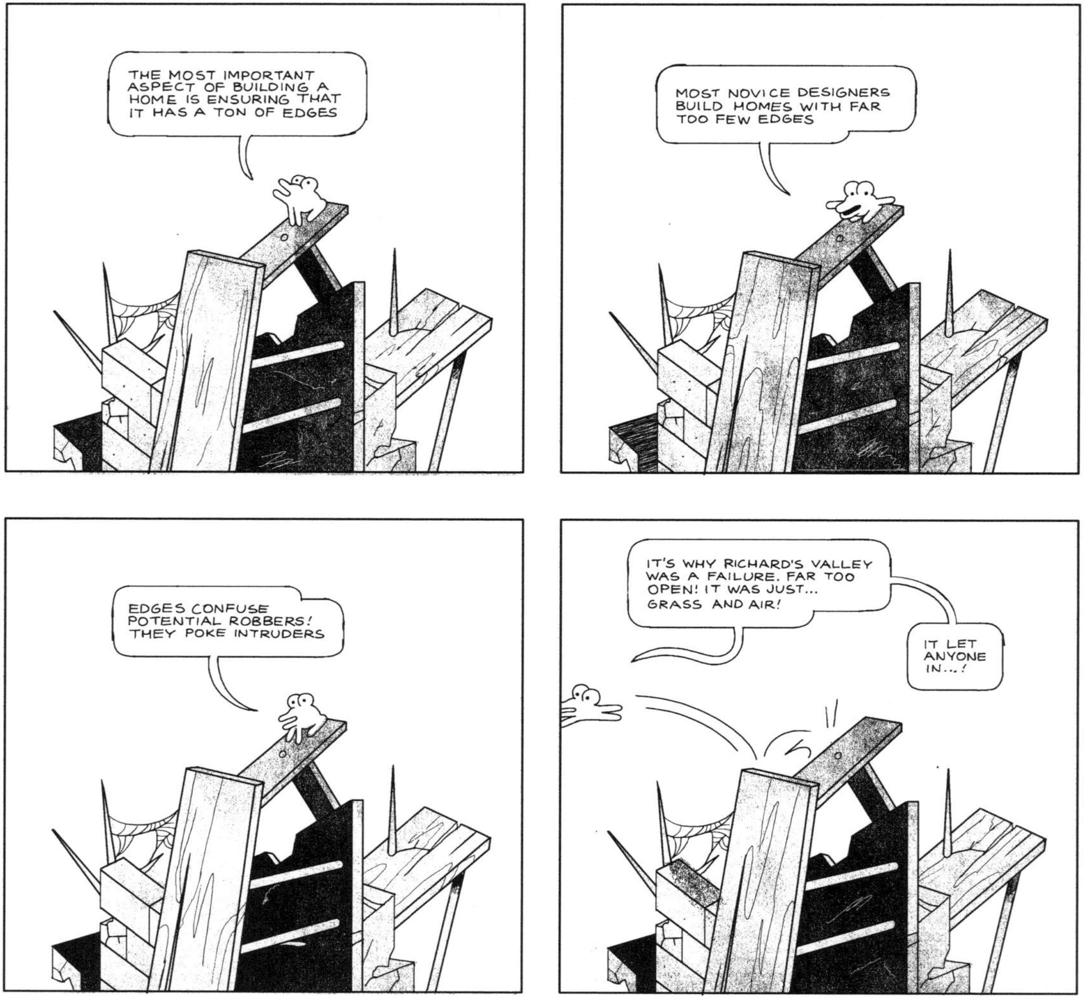
THE MOST IMPORTANT ASPECT OF BUILDING A HOME IS ENSURING THAT IT HAS A TON OF EDGES
MOST NOVICE DESIGNERS BUILD HOMES WITH FAR TOO FEW EDGES
EDGES CONFUSE POTENTIAL ROBBERS! THEY POKE INTRUDERS
IT'S WHY RICHARD'S VALLEY WAS A FAILURE. FAR TOO OPEN! IT WAS JUST... GRASS AND AIR!
IT LET ANYONE IN...!

Leaving Richard's Valley

THERE ARE A FEW MYTHS ABOUT DEPRESSION I'D LIKE TO CLEAR UP!
MYTH NUMBER ONE: I AM NOT DEPRESSED
INCORRECT! I AM, IN FACT, EXTREMELY DEPRESSED!
MYTH NUMBER TWO: A TRUE LOVE'S KISS CAN'T CURE DEPRESSION
AGAIN, FALSE! SCIENCE HAS BEEN UNABLE TO DETERMINE WHETHER OR NOT A KISS FROM MY TRUE LOVE, LYLE, WILL CURE MY DEPRESSION!
MYTH NUMBER THREE: SADNESS IS JUST A FEELING
WRONG AGAIN! HA HA!

Leaving Richard's Valley

I'VE ALWAYS BEEN A MORNING PERSON
WHICH MEANS IT TAKES MOST PEOPLE UNTIL 1 OR 2 PM TO STOP BEING ANNOYED WITH ME
I THINK IT'S WHAT MAKES ME A STRONG LEADER
I'VE SEEN WHAT EVERYONE LOOKS LIKE ASLEEP. IT PUTS ME IN A REAL POSITION OF POWER

Leaving Richard's Valley

I SPY WITH MY LITTLE EYE...
SOMETHING THAT IS FURRY!
NEVILLE!
THAT WOMAN'S COAT!
NO! IT'S THE MEMORY OF OUR FORMER FRIEND LYLE, WHICH I CARRY WITH ME ALWAYS!

Leaving Richard's Valley

HEY! THIS ISN'T YOUR PROPERTY!
THIS PILE OF GARBAGE?
IT'S NOT GARBAGE! IT'S A BEAUTIFUL PIECE OF MODERN ARCHITECTURE DESIGNED BY CAROLINE FROG!
IS SHE ON HER WAY TO KICK ME OUT?
NO! SHE DOESN'T OWN ANYTHING SHE'S MADE!
IT'S AWFUL!

WHAT IF WE HELD AUDITIONS FOR A NEW LYLE?
AFTER ALL, ME AND OMAR ARE BEST FRIENDS. NEVILLE AND LYLE **WERE** BEST FRIENDS. OUR SYMMETRY IS ALL MESSED UP WITHOUT HIM
I... I DON'T KNOW IF I CONSIDERED HIM MY **BEST FRIEND** OR ANYTHING...
NEVILLE, MAYBE IF YOU HAD BEEN A BETTER BEST FRIEND TO BEGIN WITH, THIS WOULDN'T HAVE HAPPENED!

Leaving Richard's Valley

IS THIS ONE OF YOURS, CAROLINE?
NO! IT'S ANOTHER KNOCK OFF. THEY'RE EVERYWHERE NOW! COPYCATS, CHEAP IMITATIONS... TRIBUTES... PARODIES...!
I'M TOLD MY WORK HAS BECOME UBIQUITOUS- ABSORBED INTO THE TEXTURE AND FABRIC OF THE CITY
FINE. GREAT. I'M SO GLAD! I'M SO HAPPY FOR EVERYONE'S "TEXTURE!"

Leaving Richard's Valley

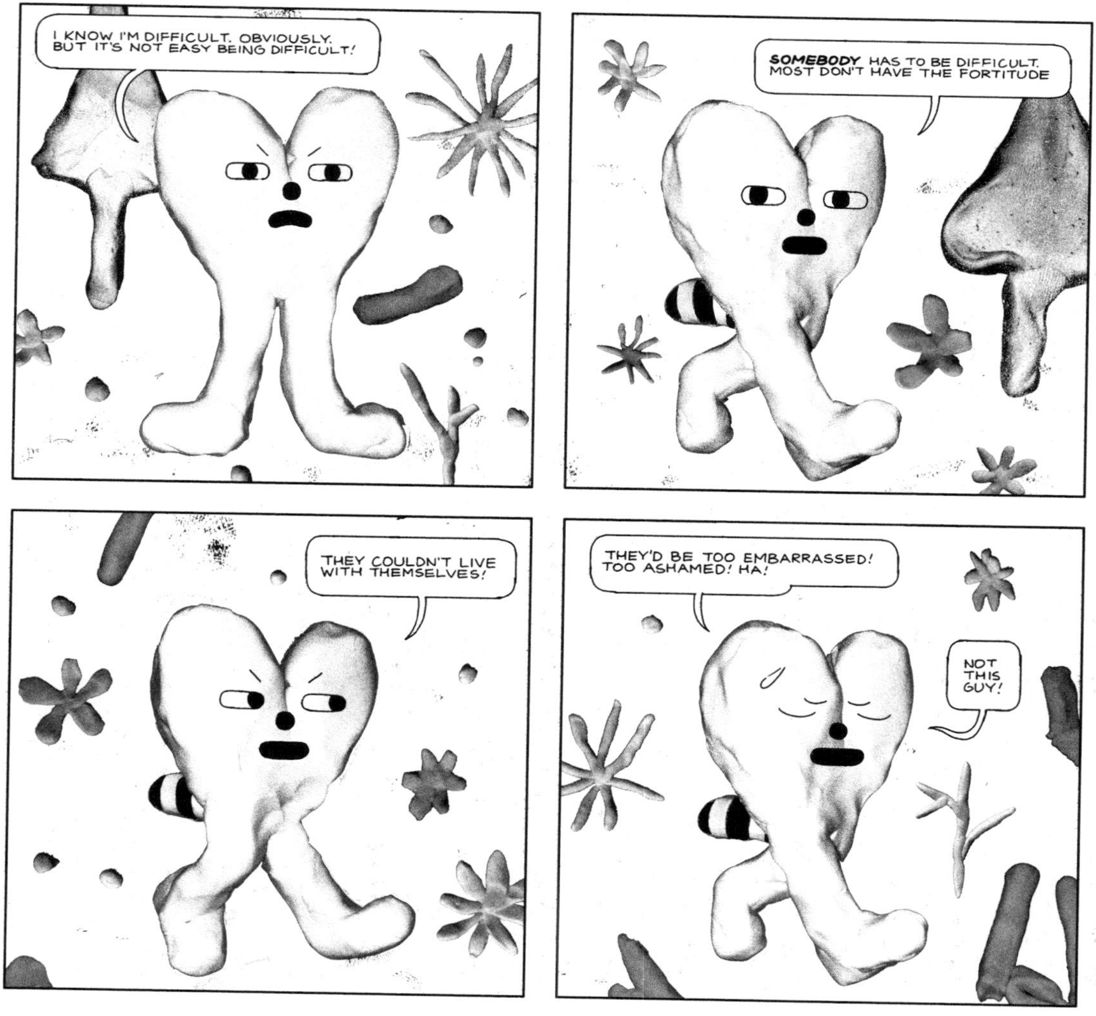

I KNOW I'M DIFFICULT. OBVIOUSLY. BUT IT'S NOT EASY BEING DIFFICULT!
SOMEBODY HAS TO BE DIFFICULT. MOST DON'T HAVE THE FORTITUDE
THEY COULDN'T LIVE WITH THEMSELVES!
THEY'D BE TOO EMBARRASSED! TOO ASHAMED! HA!
NOT THIS GUY!

Leaving Richard's Valley

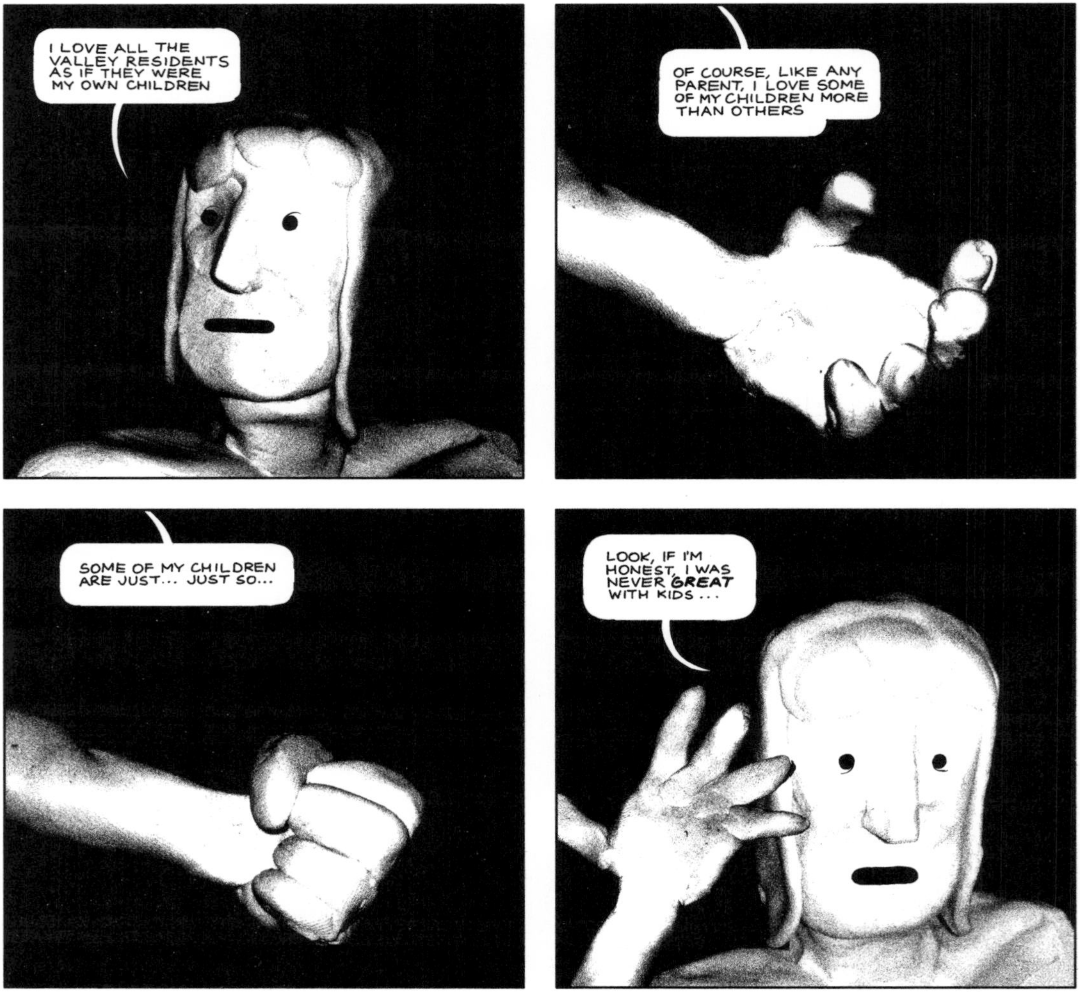
I LOVE ALL THE VALLEY RESIDENTS AS IF THEY WERE MY OWN CHILDREN
OF COURSE, LIKE ANY PARENT, I LOVE SOME OF MY CHILDREN MORE THAN OTHERS
SOME OF MY CHILDREN ARE JUST... JUST SO...
LOOK, IF I'M HONEST, I WAS NEVER **GREAT** WITH KIDS...

Leaving Richard's Valley

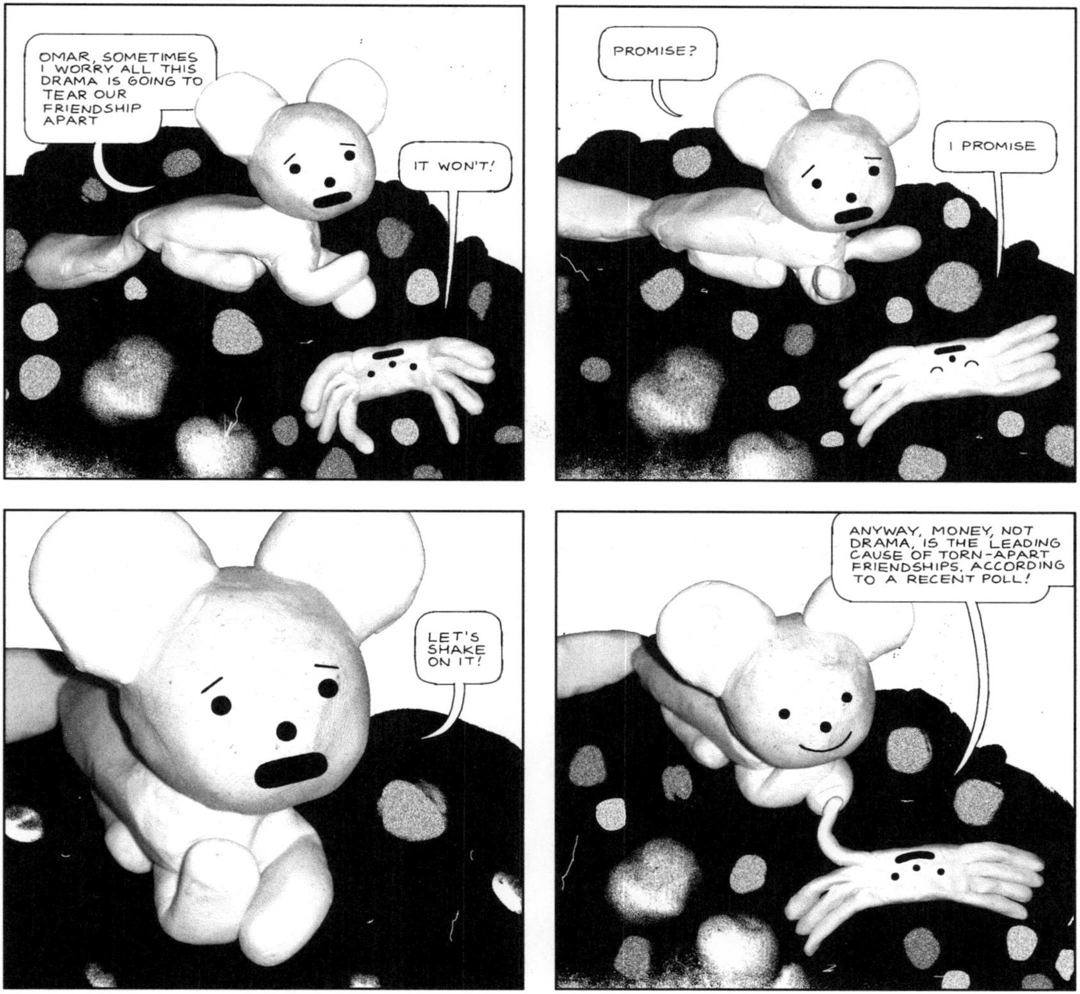

OMAR, SOMETIMES I WORRY ALL THIS DRAMA IS GOING TO TEAR OUR FRIENDSHIP APART
IT WON'T!
PROMISE?
I PROMISE
LET'S SHAKE ON IT!
ANYWAY, MONEY, NOT DRAMA, IS THE LEADING CAUSE OF TORN-APART FRIENDSHIPS, ACCORDING TO A RECENT POLL!

Leaving Richard's Valley

THE PLAN:
TO GO WHERE THE WIND TAKES ME...
I'M AT YOUR MERCY, NATURE!

WE'RE AWARE OF THE MARKSISTS. THE CITY IS MONITORING THE SITUATION
FROM WHAT WE UNDERSTAND, SNAKE MARK AND HIS FRIENDS ARE A BENEVOLENT SPIRITUAL GROUP WHO WORSHIP A MYSTERIOUS DEITY NAMED "LYLE"
COMPLICATING THE MATTER IS THAT A WEALTHY REAL ESTATE MOGUL HAS JOINED THEIR RANKS
SHE'S ALREADY PURCHASED A HALF-DOZEN PROPERTIES IN THE ANNEX ON THEIR BEHALF. NEIGHBOURS ARE CONCERNED THAT A CULT HAS MOVED INTO THEIR BACKYARD

Leaving Richard's Valley

AAAH!
GET OFF THE ROAD, YOU MANIAC!
I'M LETTING NATURE BE MY GUIDE!
I'M SORRY NONE OF YOU HAVE THE RELATIONSHIP WITH NATURE THAT I DO...!

"CULT" MIGHT BE TOO STRONG A WORD. "CLUB?" "THE SNAKE MARK CLUB?"
I THINK THEY MEAN WELL
THEY'RE TRYING TO GET INVOLVED WITH THE COMMUNITY
WHICH IS GREAT! IN THEORY
THERE'S A BIG NEIGHBOURHOOD CLEANUP DAY ONCE A MONTH. WE ASKED THEM TO HELP PILE UP SOME LEAVES
IT GOT WEIRD
THEY STARTED ROLEPLAYING AS, LIKE, RAKES?
I COULDN'T TELL IF IT WAS SUPPOSED TO BE THERAPEUTIC OR FUN...

Leaving Richard's Valley

WHEN DOES IT STOP?!
...?
WHEN DOES IT STOP!??!
I DUNNO!
WATCH OUT!
DOES IT EVER?!
WAH!

Leaving Richard's Valley

THERE'S NO NEED TO VIEW US AS A THREAT
THE PREVIOUS OWNERS OF THESE HOMES WERE FAIRLY COMPENSATED
THERE'S ABOUT A DOZEN OF US PER HOUSE, HUMAN AND ANIMALS ALIKE
WE WANT TO WORK **WITH** THE COMMUNITY. WE'RE HERE TO HELP
I DON'T THINK IT'S TOO MUCH TO HOPE OUR NEIGHBOURS MIGHT ONE DAY EXTEND US A SIMILAR COURTESY
Help me
AND IF THEY DON'T, WELL... LET'S JUST SAY THEY'LL GET A TASTE OF JUST HOW **UNCOURTEOUS** WE CAN BE
WHAT?! **NO,** NO, NOTHING LIKE THAT

Leaving Richard's Valley

AH... ONTARIO'S ROLLING RACCOONS
ONE OF OUR NATION'S MOST ICONIC SIGHTS
ALMOST ANYONE NEW TO THE CITY GOES WITHOUT ANY SLEEP FOR THEIR FIRST FEW WEEKS HERE, KEPT AWAKE BY THE SOUND OF THE BOUNCING
BUT YOU GET USED TO IT
LIKE LIVING NEXT TO A WATERFALL

IT'S NATURAL TO HAVE DOUBTS, CHILD...
IT'S MORE THAN THAT! THIS WHOLE ENTERPRISE HAS GOTTEN AWFULLY FISHY. WHY BUY ALL THESE HOUSES? MARK'S CLUB USED TO BE ABOUT ART AND PHILOSOPHY AND SPIRITUALITY. NOW ALL WE EVER TALK ABOUT IS REAL ESTATE!
AND WHEN DO WE FINALLY GET TO MEET LYLE?! THIS MYTHICAL LYLE FELLOW THAT'S SUPPOSED TO CHANGE ALL OF OUR LIVES?!!
ALL I NEED IS SOME SORT OF SIGN... SOMETHING THAT PROVES YOU'RE NOT JUST CRAZY
CRASH

Leaving Richard's Valley

LYLE! MY LOVE! YOU'VE BEEN DELIVERED TO ME AT LAST!
WELCOME TO YOUR NEW KINGDOM... WE'VE TOILED SO HARD TO BUILD A HAPPY HOME FOR YOU....!
REUNITED AT LAST! TOGETHER, OUR PRECIOUS BOND WILL REINVIGORATE MARK'S CLUB AND INSPIRE HUMANS AND ANIMALS EVERYWHERE TO COME HEAR THE WORD OF LYLE!
COOL
DO I RECOGNIZE YOU FROM SOMEWHERE? YOU LOOK FAMILIAR

Leaving Richard's Valley

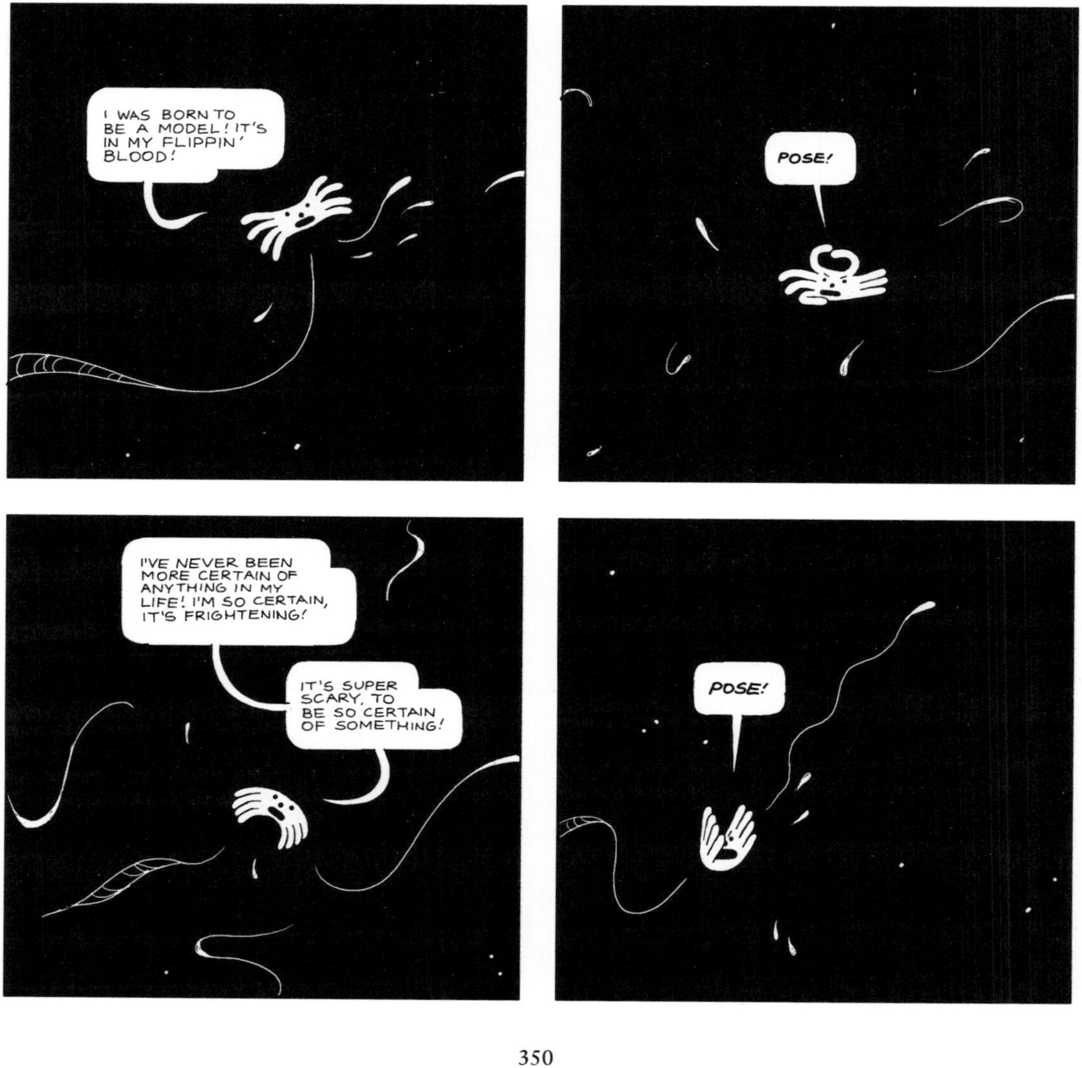
I WAS BORN TO BE A MODEL! IT'S IN MY FLIPPIN' BLOOD!
POSE!
I'VE NEVER BEEN MORE CERTAIN OF ANYTHING IN MY LIFE! I'M SO CERTAIN, IT'S FRIGHTENING!
IT'S SUPER SCARY, TO BE SO CERTAIN OF SOMETHING!
POSE!

Leaving Richard's Valley

OMAR, ARE YOU OKAY?
I HURT MYSELF POSING
IT'S GIVEN ME A CRAZY CASE OF WAVY LEG SYNDROME
IT'S MADE ALL OF THE WEBS I'VE SPUN TODAY TURN OUT SUPER WEIRD
AND I'M SORT OF FREAKING OUT ELLIE

Leaving Richard's Valley

WHAT'S WRONG WITH ALL OF YOU?
WE DECIDED WE SHOULD ALL MATCH

IS HE ASLEEP?
I THINK SO...
HE DOESN'T LOOK LIKE MUCH OF A SAVIOUR
I'M NOT CRAZY ABOUT THE INCESSANT NOISE MUSIC
MARK KNOWS BEST
XXXX ## !!!?

Leaving Richard's Valley

LYLE... I'M HERE TO FEED YOU
NOT HUNGRY
I'D LOVE TO SERVE YOU
S'OK
I WANT TO LOVE YOU!
I'M GOOD
I BUILT THIS ALL FOR YOU!
THANKS ANYWAY

Leaving Richard's Valley

I'M GLAD YOU'RE FEELING BETTER, OMAR!
I FEEL SPIDER-SHAPED AGAIN!
I ALWAYS THOUGHT YOU WERE KINDA SHAPED LIKE A HAND

Leaving Richard's Valley

THE FIRST SNOWFALL OF THE SEASON!

Leaving Richard's Valley

I'M NOT SURE WHAT THE ENDGAME IS FOR OUR LITTLE GROUP. CONTINUED EXPANSION? TO WHAT END?
LYLE WILL COME AROUND. ARE WE BOYFRIENDS? WHY PUT A LABEL ON IT...?
AM I IN OVER MY HEAD? DID I START A CULT? AM I A CULT LEADER?
AGAIN WITH THE LABELS...

Leaving Richard's Valley

Leaving Richard's Valley

Leaving Richard's Valley

IT'S SIMPLE. STEP ONE: CHECK THE WEATHER TO FIND OUT WHEN IT'S SNOWING NEXT
STEP TWO: STEAL EVERYONE'S SNOW SHOVELS OFF THEIR FRONT PORCHES THE NIGHT BEFORE
STEP THREE: ADVERTISE A SNOW SHOVELLING SERVICE
STEP FOUR: I GUESS... OPEN UP A STORE
SHOVEL STORE

Leaving Richard's Valley

THIS SNOW SHOVEL SHORTAGE IS OUT OF CONTROL
I'VE HEARD IT'S A MOB OPERATION
PFFFT, NUH UH. THE GOVERNMENT ORCHESTRATED THIS WHOLE THING. FOR WHAT PURPOSE? ONLY TIME WILL TELL
IT'S NOT SO BAD. IT'S LIKE WE ALL LIVE ON CLOUDS. LIKE WE'VE ALL DIED AND GONE TO HEAVEN!
I HEARD SOME EX-CANADIAN TIRE EMPLOYEES STARTED HOARDING THEM. SELLING THEM FOR 120 BUCKS PER SHOVEL
MADNESS
IT'S A WARZONE OUT THERE
I MADE A SNOW LYLE

Leaving Richard's Valley

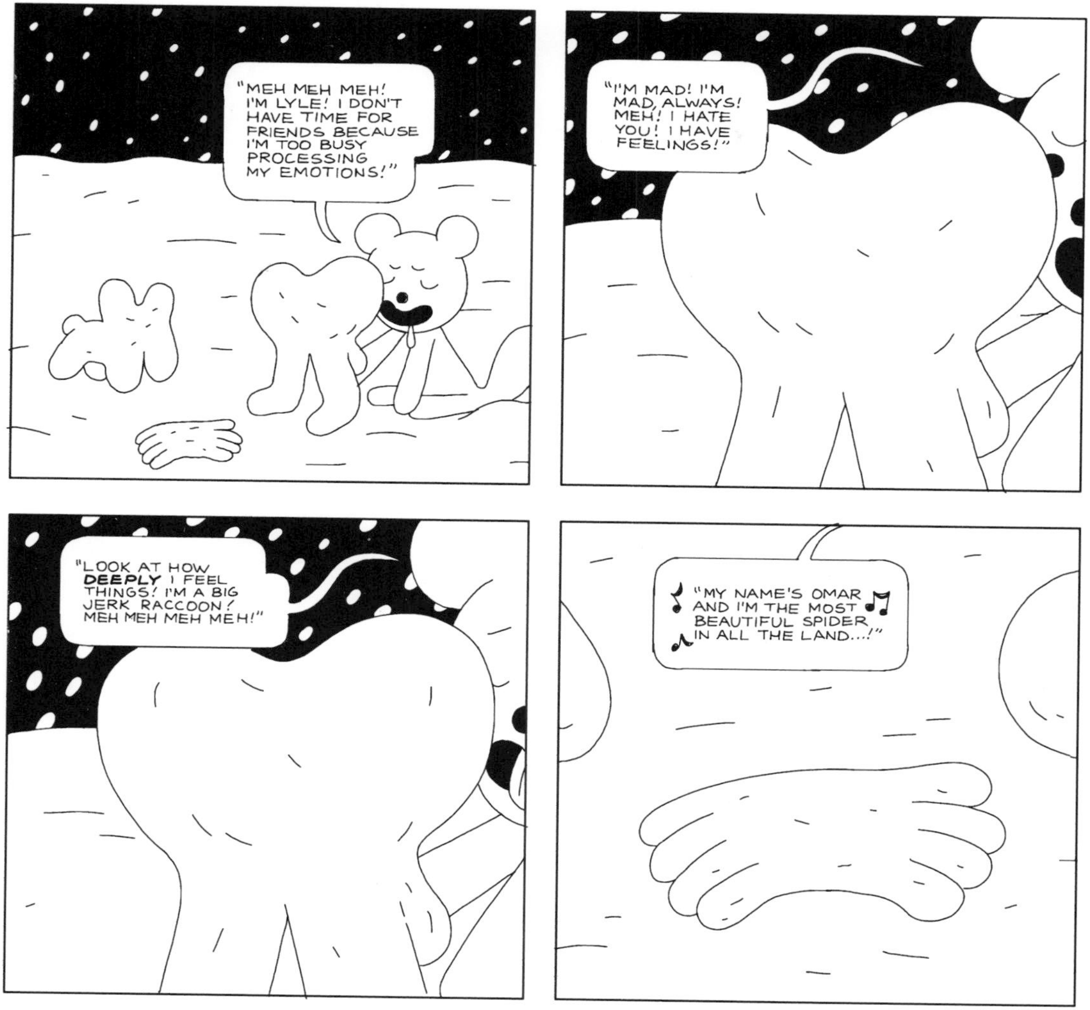
"MEH MEH MEH! I'M LYLE! I DON'T HAVE TIME FOR FRIENDS BECAUSE I'M TOO BUSY PROCESSING MY EMOTIONS!"
"I'M MAD! I'M MAD, ALWAYS! MEH! I HATE YOU! I HAVE FEELINGS!"
"LOOK AT HOW **DEEPLY** I FEEL THINGS! I'M A BIG JERK RACCOON! MEH MEH MEH MEH!"
"MY NAME'S OMAR AND I'M THE MOST BEAUTIFUL SPIDER IN ALL THE LAND...!"

Leaving Richard's Valley

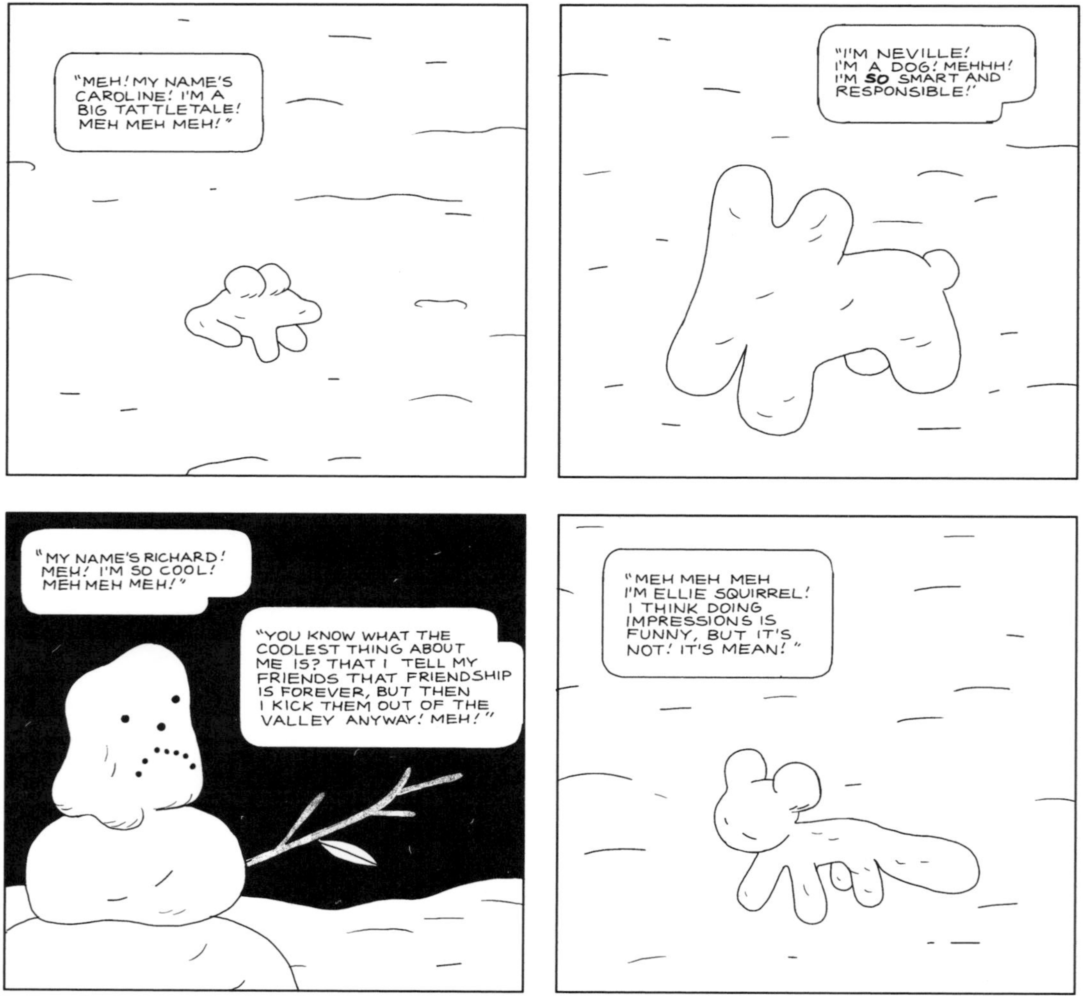
"MEH! MY NAME'S CAROLINE! I'M A BIG TATTLETALE! MEH MEH MEH!"
"I'M NEVILLE! I'M A DOG! MEHHH! I'M SO SMART AND RESPONSIBLE!"
"MY NAME'S RICHARD! MEH! I'M SO COOL! MEH MEH MEH!"
"YOU KNOW WHAT THE COOLEST THING ABOUT ME IS? THAT I TELL MY FRIENDS THAT FRIENDSHIP IS FOREVER, BUT THEN I KICK THEM OUT OF THE VALLEY ANYWAY! MEH!"
"MEH MEH MEH I'M ELLIE SQUIRREL! I THINK DOING IMPRESSIONS IS FUNNY, BUT IT'S NOT! IT'S MEAN!"

Leaving Richard's Valley

SIGH
WHY SO GLUM, LIL' FROGGY CHUM?
I'M JUST FEELING BURNT OUT... I'M A RENOWNED ARCHITECT, CEO OF THE LARGEST SNOW SHOVELLING BUSINESS IN THE CITY, AND A PROFESSIONAL BUSYBODY
BUT I STILL CAN'T MAKE ENDS MEET! NO MATTER HOW HARD I WORK, IT NEVER SEEMS TO ADD UP!
WHAT AN INHUMANE CITY...
YOU'RE TELLING ME. SOMEONE STOLE MY SNOW SHOVEL RIGHT OFF MY PORCH

Leaving Richard's Valley

Leaving Richard's Valley

I WAS A CHRISTMAS GIFT TO ONE OF MY FIRST HOUSEMATES, LLEWELLYN, 15. HE TIRED OF ME DURING OUR EARLY WEEKS TOGETHER AND REGIFTED ME TO HIS YOUNGER SISTER, AMANDA, 8
A MONTH LATER, SHE AND HER FRIENDS FLUSHED ME DOWN A TOILET AT A SLUMBER PARTY. SHE CALLED ME AN "ICKY LITTLE GRINCH THING"
THOSE FORMATIVE EVENTS WOULD COME TO DEFINE THE REMAINDER OF MY TIME IN THIS CITY - AN UNENDING SERIES OF HOSTILE ROOMMATES, VICIOUS LANDLORDS, CON ARTISTS, CRASH PADS, RENT STRIKES, EVICTION PARTIES, COLLECTIVES, COMMUNES, CO-OPS, FLOPHOUSES, FALSE STARTS, FAILED EXPERIMENTS
I'M NOT FOR EVERYBODY. I KNOW IT! BUT I THINK I MAKE A PRETTY GOOD GIFT! I'M NOT THE WORST, AT LEAST!
THERE ARE A LOT OF FROG LOVERS WHO WOULD BE LUCKY TO HAVE ME!

IN 1953, RYERSON UNIVERSITY STUDENT PATRICIA SOON BECAME THE FIRST PERSON TO DOCUMENT AN OCCURRENCE THAT HAD BEEN HAPPENING HUNDREDS OF TIMES DAILY FOR CENTURIES:
A HUMAN-ANIMAL CONVERSATION
SHE USED THE WAVE-TRANCE METHOD TO ASK HER TERRIER GED ABOUT HIS DOG FOOD BRAND PREFERENCE
SPIDERS PRACTICE THE MOST ADVANCED FORM OF WAVE-TRANCE COMMUNICATION, SPEAKING TO EACH OTHER THROUGH BOTH THE DESIGN AND VIBRATION OF THEIR WEBS
THEY SPENT DECADES TRYING TO USE THEIR WEBS TO REACH OUT TO MANKIND. WE USUALLY CLEARED THEM OUT
WITH BROOMS

Leaving Richard's Valley

ELLIE... WHY MAKE A RICHARD SNOWMAN?
SO HE CAN BANISH SNOW ELLIE, SNOW LYLE, SNOW NEVILLE, AND SNOW OMAR

Leaving Richard's Valley

I CAN'T TAKE THIS WEATHER MUCH LONGER
BLECH... DIRTY SNOW
I'M WEARING LITTLE DOG BOOTIES. IT'S DEMEANING
MAYBE WE CAN AT LEAST MOVE TO SOME HIGHER GROUND
BUT WHERE?

Leaving Richard's Valley

WHAT'S GOING ON WITH YOUR SNOW CHARACTERS NOW, ELLIE?
IT LOOKS LIKE THE OTHER SNOW ANIMALS ROSE UP AND OVERTHREW SNOW RICHARD
NOW THEY GET TO RUN THE SNOW VALLEY THEMSELVES! EVERYONE IS MUCH HAPPIER
EXCEPT FOR SNOW LYLE! NOTHING COULD MAKE HIM HAPPY. JUST LOOK AT THE EXPRESSION ON HIS FACE!

Leaving Richard's Valley

Leaving Richard's Valley

MARK SAYS TO USE THE WARMING EFFECTS OF NOISE MUSIC TO KEEP WARM
Why Lyle?
What is Mark's Club?
Markism?

Leaving Richard's Valley

MY NEW YEAR'S RESOLUTION IS TO AFFECT REAL CHANGE IN THE WORLD!
IT DOESN'T HAVE TO BE SOME HUGE, MONUMENTAL GESTURE. IT CAN BE SMALL. LOCAL!
LIKE, FOR INSTANCE, SINGLE-HANDEDLY DISMANTLING CAPITALISM
OR TEACHING AN OLD, CROTCHEDY LONER GUY ABOUT THE POWER OF KINDNESS
OR VOLUNTEERING AT A COMMUNITY CENTRE
AND WINNING A BIG AWARD FOR IT
AND THEY MAKE A MOVIE ABOUT ME AND IT INSPIRES MILLIONS

Leaving Richard's Valley

WHEN RICHARD KICKED LYLE, ELLIE, OMAR, AND NEVILLE OUT, I LEFT TOO
IN SOLIDARITY
I DON'T THINK ANYONE REALLY NOTICED
I HAVE APPREHENSIONS ABOUT MARKSISM, BUT I JOINED MARK'S CLUB AS A SYMBOLIC SHOW OF SUPPORT
I DON'T THINK HE RECOGNIZED ME, THOUGH
IT'S NO EASY THING ... TO HAVE EVERY ONE OF MY ACTIONS BE SO COMPLETELY LOADED WITH MEANING

Leaving Richard's Valley

IT'S GETTING A BIT CROWDED AROUND OUR STATUE
MUST BE THIS AWFUL WEATHER
I LIKE IT. THE MORE THE MERRIER, RIGHT?
I GUESS SO...
I COULD ALWAYS STAND TO BE MERRIER
YES. HONESTLY, I DON'T THINK I'M ANYWHERE NEAR MY MERRIMENT THRESHOLD YET

Leaving Richard's Valley

Leaving Richard's Valley

I'M SEEING A LOT OF NEW FACES HERE AT THE STATUE AND I THINK THAT'S FANTASTIC!
I JUST WANT TO REITERATE A FEW HOUSE RULES TO ANYONE WHO WASN'T HERE ON FRIDAY
PLEASE DON'T TOSS YOUR LITTER AT THE BASE OF THE STATUE
YOU CAN ASK OMAR ABOUT OUR RECYCLING AND COMPOST PROGRAMS, OR USE THE LOBLAWS DUMPSTER UP THE STREET
ELLIE WOULD LIKE TO HUMBLY REQUEST THAT PEOPLE STOP REARRANGING HER SNOW FIGURES INTO LEWD TABLEAUS
AND FINALLY, WE'D PREFER IT IF ALL BLACK MARKET SNOW SHOVEL SALES OR TRADES TOOK PLACE OFFSITE
WE'RE TRYING OUR BEST TO NOT ATTRACT THE ATTENTION OF THE POLICE OR ANIMAL CONTROL

Leaving Richard's Valley

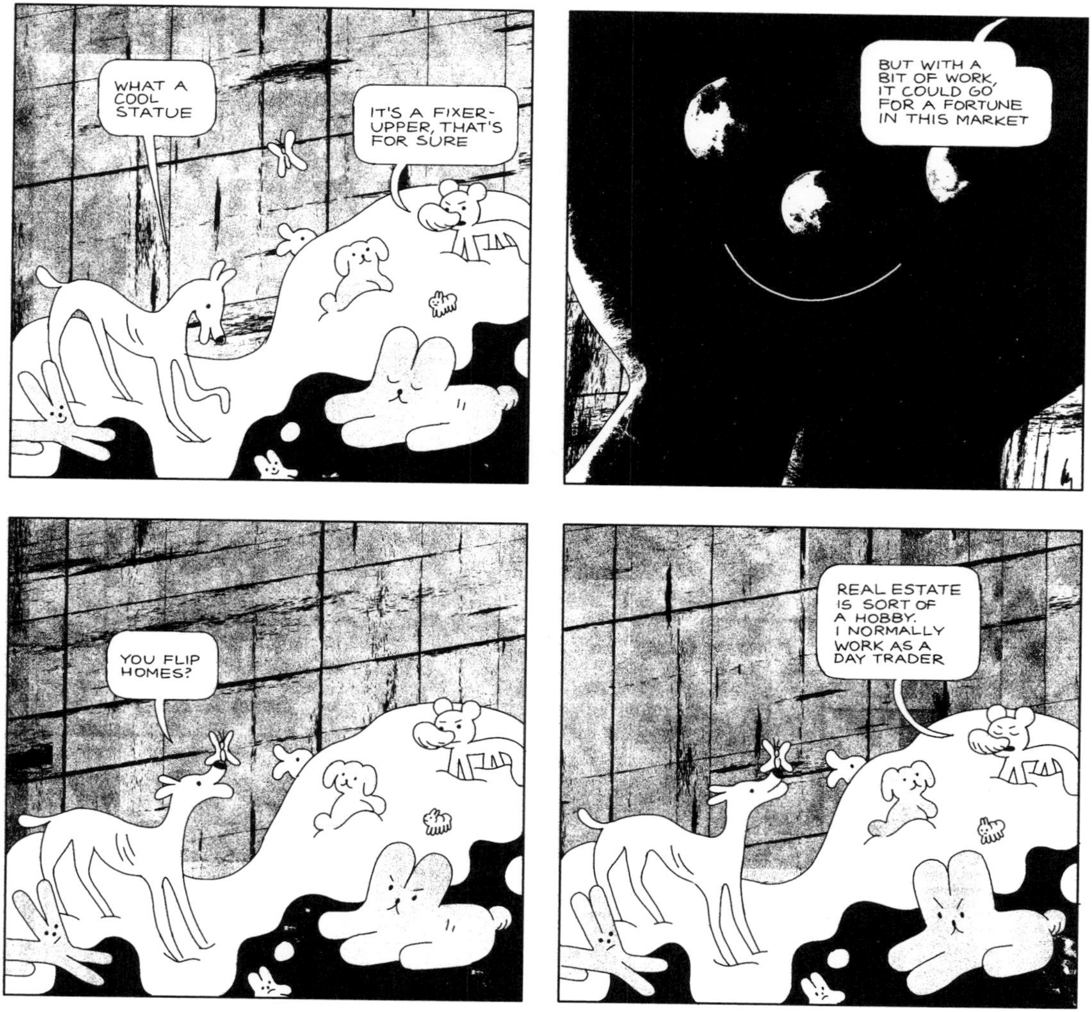
WHAT A COOL STATUE
IT'S A FIXER-UPPER, THAT'S FOR SURE
BUT WITH A BIT OF WORK, IT COULD GO FOR A FORTUNE IN THIS MARKET
YOU FLIP HOMES?
REAL ESTATE IS SORT OF A HOBBY. I NORMALLY WORK AS A DAY TRADER

Leaving Richard's Valley

PEOPLE SAY WE LOOK ALIKE
I GET CONFUSED WITH YOU A LOT, ELLIE
IT MUST BE THAT WE BOTH HAVE GIGANTIC NOSES
OUR ENORMOUS, BULBOUS, FREAK-LIKE HONKERS...

Leaving Richard's Valley

LYLE, SOMETIMES I SUSPECT YOU DON'T TAKE MARKSISM VERY SERIOUSLY
I ABSOLUTELY DO NOT
TELL ME THE TRUTH: IS MARK'S CLUB JUST ONE BIG JOKE TO YOU?
YES
NO, PLEASE, THAT'S NICE OF YOU TO SAY, BUT DON'T JUST TELL ME WHAT I WANT TO HEAR. BE BRUTALLY HONEST WITH ME
YOU'RE PATHETIC
IT MEANS A LOT THAT YOU'D SAY THAT, LYLE. I CHERISH YOUR PRESENCE, TOO

EVERY MORNING I LIE AT YOUR FEET. I FOLLOW YOU NO MATTER HOW FAST YOU RUN. I DIE EVERY NIGHT. WHAT AM I?
A SHADOW!
WHY DO THESE BRAIN TEASERS HAVE TO BE SO SCARY?
A FATHER AND SON GET INTO A CAR ACCIDENT AND ARE HORRIBLY INJURED. THEY ARE TAKEN TO SEPARATE HOSPITALS. WHEN THE BOY IS BROUGHT TO SURGERY, THE DOCTOR EXCLAIMS "I CANNOT OPERATE, FOR THIS CHILD IS MY SON!" HOW IS THIS POSSIBLE?
A CAR ACCIDENT? DON'T YOU HAVE ANY NICE RIDDLES?!
THIRTEEN MEN DROWN IN A LAKE. THE POLICE SEARCH THE WATER AND ONLY FIND ELEVEN CORPSES. WHERE ARE THE OTHER TWO BODIES?
NEVILLE--
A CHILD IS BORN WITHOUT A MOUTH, YET HER SCREAMS ARE HEARD CONSTANTLY--
STOP! ENOUGH!

SNOW LYLE IS MELTING!
ALL OF THEM ARE!
THEY CAN'T--!
IF THEY MELT, I WON'T KNOW HOW ANY OF IT ENDS!

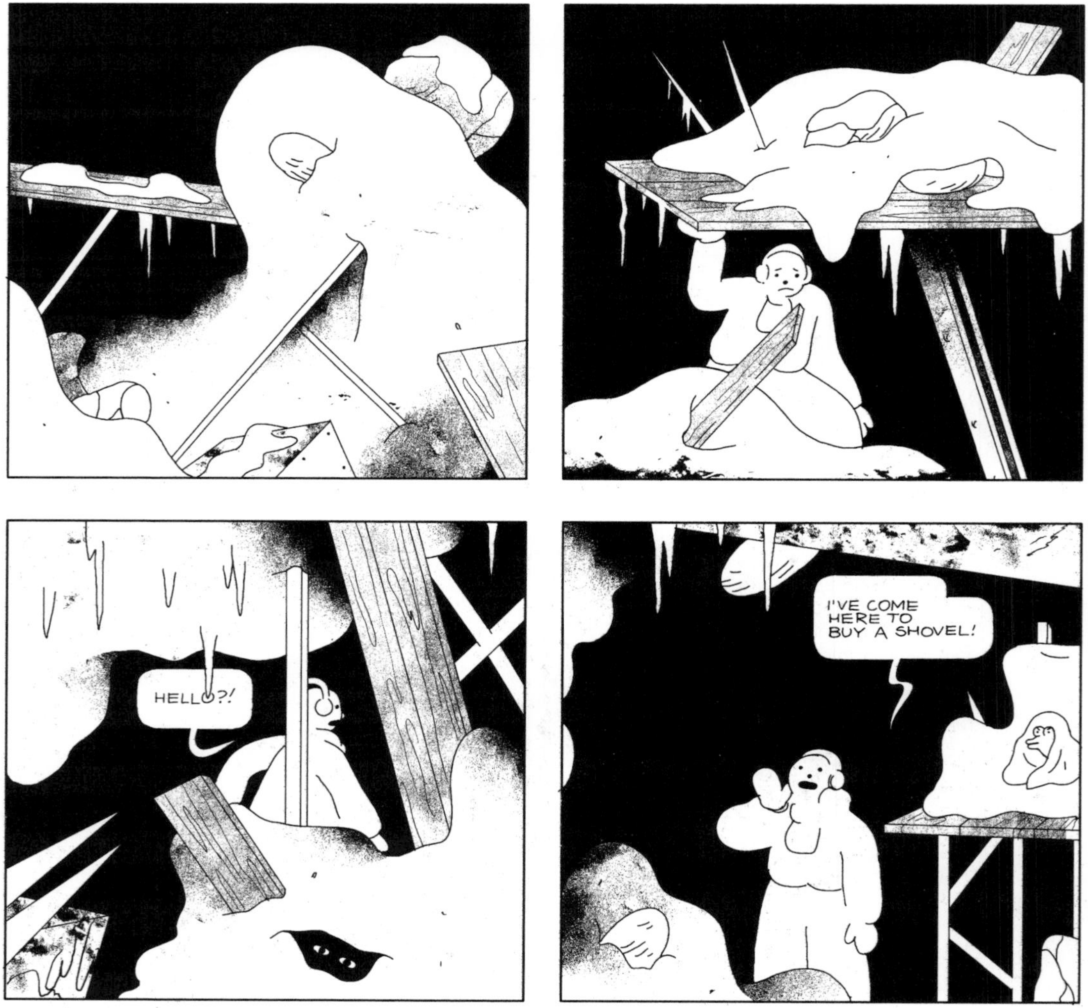
HELLO?!
I'VE COME HERE TO BUY A SHOVEL!

Leaving Richard's Valley

WELCOME TO CAROLINE'S SHOVEL EMPORIUM
FOR ALL YOUR SHOVEL NEEDS
WE'RE HAVING A GOING AWAY SALE
A DEVELOPER IS PUTTING A CONDO HERE
ALSO, THE WEATHER TURNED. WE'RE MELTING

Leaving Richard's Valley

THIS HAS BEEN A DIFFICULT YEAR FOR THE VALLEY
AND FOR ME, FRANKLY
A RECORD NUMBER OF DESERTIONS. BANISHMENTS, TOO
ALTHOUGH TO BE HONEST, THE SHAPE OF THINGS ... THE WAY THE YEAR HAS WORKED OUT, ITS DAY TO DAY...
IT FELT MORE OR LESS THE SAME AS ANY OF THE "GOOD" YEARS

Leaving Richard's Valley

HEY. NEW GUY
THAT STRUCTURE
IN THE DISTANCE BEYOND THE VALLEY
ACROSS THE ROAD
WHAT IS IT?
OH! THAT'S A CAROLINE FROG STATUE. HER WORK IS EVERYWHERE
THE CITY KEEPS COMMISSIONING THEM
THEY'RE BEAUTIFUL, I GUESS. I'M TOLD THEY'RE VERY BEAUTIFUL

Leaving Richard's Valley

YOU SEEM VERY TENSE
YEAH, PAUL
MAYBE IT'S SOME SORT OF SEASONAL DISORDER THING
I'M SUPER DOWN LATELY
I THOUGHT YOU SAID THE VALLEY CURES ALL ILLNESSES
WELL. SURE. I MEAN, IT'S JUST A PARK, REALLY. IT'S NOT LIKE IT'S MAGIC

Leaving Richard's Valley

* SNF *
NOTHING
WHAT ARE YOU DOING SO CLOSE TO THE VALLEY'S EDGE?

Leaving Richard's Valley

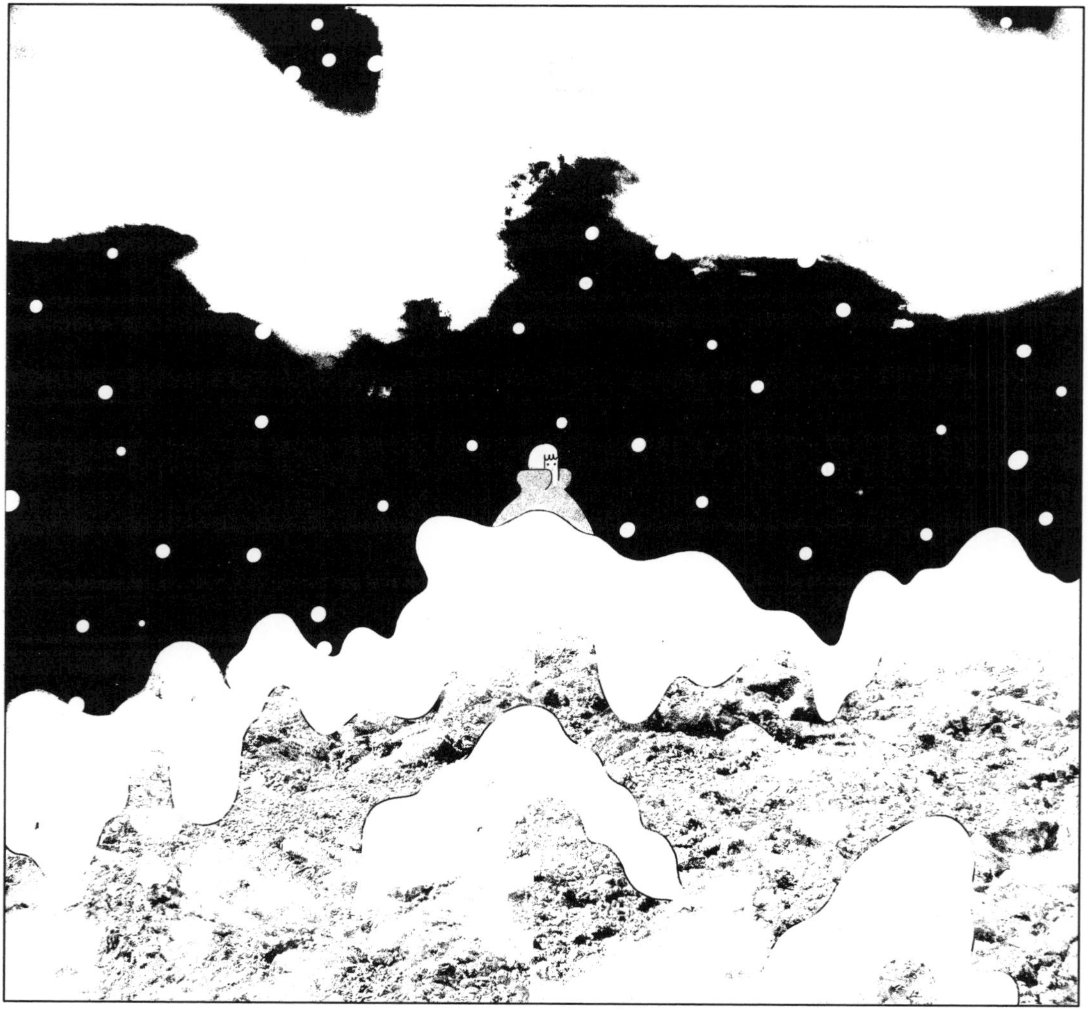

Leaving Richard's Valley

WHEN I LOOK BACK AT THIS TIME IN MY LIFE, I'LL BE ABLE TO SAY:
"I WAS A PART OF SOMETHING"
AS I'M DISTINCTLY AWARE THAT I'M FAST APPROACHING A POINT WHERE I WON'T BE A PART OF ANYTHING AT ALL
OTHER, YOUNGER PEOPLE WILL BE PARTS OF THINGS WHILE I'LL SIMPLY BE... AFLOAT.
YES, I'LL REMEMBER THIS TIME FONDLY
UNFORTUNATELY, I'M COMPLETELY UNABLE TO APPRECIATE ANY OF THIS IN THE MOMENT

WHY DO WE NEED TO THROW OUT EVERYTHING THAT WORKS ABOUT MARK'S CLUB FOR JUST ONE RACCOON?
WHAT YOU'RE TALKING ABOUT IS MUTINY
MARK'S CLUB IS BIGGER THAN LYLE! BIGGER THAN MARK! IT'S AN IDEA
BUT... TO JUST GO ON WITHOUT THEM...?
MARK IS OUR FRIEND! HE'S A LIVING CREATURE WITH REAL FEELINGS, NOT SOME "IDEA!" HE'S NOT SOME... ABSTRACT CONCEPT!
YES, BUT FOR THE PURPOSE OF CONVERSATION, WHAT IF HE WAS?

Leaving Richard's Valley

NEVILLE, YOU NEVER TALK ABOUT LEAVING THE CITY
WELL, I HOPE TO ONE DAY SEE THE SEVEN WONDERS OF THE WORLD
THE PYRAMIDS... NIAGRA FALLS... THE... SPACE NEEDLE
N.Y.C. A.K.A. "THE BIG APPLE"
THE SMALLEST HOUSE IN THE WORLD... SASKATCHEWAN...
A REALLY HUGE HOT TUB...

Leaving Richard's Valley

YOU KNOW WHAT I LOVE MOST ABOUT OUR CURRENT LIVING SITUATION?
WHAT?
HOW PERMANENT IT IS! HOW WE'LL ALL BE ABLE TO KEEP ON LIVING HERE INDEFINITELY
I WAS GETTING EXHAUSTED BY ALL THE BIG SHAKE-UPS AND SWEEPING CHANGES!
I'M SURE GLAD I'VE SEEN THE LAST OF THOSE FOR MY LIFETIME
YUP, IT'LL BE SMOOTH SAILING FROM HERE ON OUT

Leaving Richard's Valley

IF I HAD TO LIST THE ONE THING I MISS MOST FROM RUNNING A SNOW SHOVEL EMPIRE
IT'D BE THE POWER
IF I HAD TO LIST A SECOND THING, IT'D BE THE MONEY
IF I HAD TO LIST A THIRD THING, IT'D BE THE SHOVELS
LOVED THOSE SHOVELS

Leaving Richard's Valley

MAKE ME CONFUUUSED
MOCK ME WITH PRAAAISE
LET ME FEEL USED
VARY MY DAYS
BUT ALONE... IS ALONE...
NOT ALIIIIIVE

Leaving Richard's Valley

CHANGE IS IN THE AIR! I CAN SMELL IT. ALTHOUGH I CAN SMELL A TON OF OTHER STUFF, TOO
INCLUDING... INERTIA
STILLNESS
THE AIR IS THICK WITH . . . A TON OF COMPETING SMELLS
EVERYTHING STINKS, ESSENTIALLY

Leaving Richard's Valley

AND SO THE WISE OWL REPLIED TO THE DOG,
"IF IT'S YOUR OWN FUR YOU'RE SMELLING --RUN!"
HAHAHA
AHA
HAHA HA
A HA HA HA HA
HA HA
OH, RICHARD
WHAT A WONDERFUL FABLE
HA HA HA HA
HA HA HA
HA HA HA
HAHA HA HA HA

Leaving Richard's Valley

PAUL, AM I FUNNY?
SURE
SOMETIMES I SUSPECT THAT PEOPLE LAUGH AT MY JOKES EVEN IF THEY THINK THEY AREN'T FUNNY
OR THAT PEOPLE WILL JUST GO ALONG WITH WHATEVER I DO OR SAY, NO MATTER WHAT IT IS
UM... ISN'T THAT THE POINT
OF YOUR WHOLE... THING?

Leaving Richard's Valley

AND SO THE WISE OWL REPLIED TO THE DOG
"IF IT'S YOUR OWN FUR YOU'RE SMELLING-- RUN!"
I DON'T GET IT
I THOUGHT YOU COULD EXPLAIN IT TO ME. I THINK THE ANIMALS ARE SYMBOLS
WHAT DO YOU THINK WE'RE SYMBOLS FOR?
I SYMBOLIZE HOTNESS. YOU'RE A SYMBOL FOR SQUIRRELS

SOME INSIST MARK'S CLUB SHOULD REMAIN A SPIRITUAL GROUP, THE WAY IT WAS INITIALLY INTENDED TO BE
PEOPLE USED TO SAY THE SAME THING ABOUT MY OLD BOOK CLUB
BUT CHANGE IS NATURAL. GROWTH IS ORGANIC. THINK ABOUT IT:
IF WE NEVER GREW, WE'D ALL STILL BE BABIES
NOT EVEN OUR PARENTS COULD TAKE CARE OF US, SINCE THEY'D HAVE STAYED BABIES TOO!
A WORLD FULL OF BABIES?
NOT ANY WORLD I'D LIKE TO LIVE IN
THAT OLD BOOK CLUB IS NOW THE THIRTEENTH-LARGEST SOFTWARE DEVELOPMENT COMPANY IN ONTARIO

Leaving Richard's Valley

WHAT DOES IT SAY?!
MAYBE IT'S A LOVE LETTER!
FROM A SECRET ADMIRER!
"NOTICE OF EVICTION"
OUR SECRET ADMIRER... IS EVICTING US?

Leaving Richard's Valley

SO WE HAVE TO LEAVE?
OR GET BULLDOZED
LET'S STAGE A BENEFIT CONCERT. TO SAVE THE STATUE!
IT CAN BE P.W.Y.C.
WHAT'S P.W.Y.C.?
UM. "PLEASE WEAR YOUTHFUL CLOTHING?"
CLOTHING THAT PROVES TO THE CITY THAT WE'RE A VIBRANT, VITAL PART OF ITS CULTURE!

Leaving Richard's Valley

TORONTO
A change has been proposed for this site.
A Development Application has been submitted to amend the Official Plan and Zoning By-law to permit a 7 building development for residential, office and retail use.
Proposal summary:
For information & to tell us what you think:

Leaving Richard's Valley

I MET A TRAVELLER FROM, UH... HAMILTON
WHO SAID-SOMETHING ABOUT A STATUE. IN A DESERT?
WITH A FROWNY FACE. REALLY SCREWY FACE. I DUNNO. ETC.
ANYWAY, BESIDE THE STATUE WAS ANOTHER THINGY
THE THINGY READ: "MY NAME IS CAROLINE FROG, KING OF KINGS!"
"LOOK UPON THE COOL STUFF I MADE AND FEEL, LIKE, SUPER LAME"
BUT ALL THE COOL STUFF WAS GONE, ACTUALLY
CAROLINE'S COOL STUFF WAS ALL GONE. THE END
WOW

Leaving Richard's Valley

WHAT DO YOU THINK THEY'LL TURN OUR STATUE INTO?
PROBABLY SOMETHING DUMB
LIKE A BARF CAFÉ
HA HA HA
I LOVE YOU, OMAR
I WONDER IF THE BARF CAFÉ IS HIRING

Leaving Richard's Valley

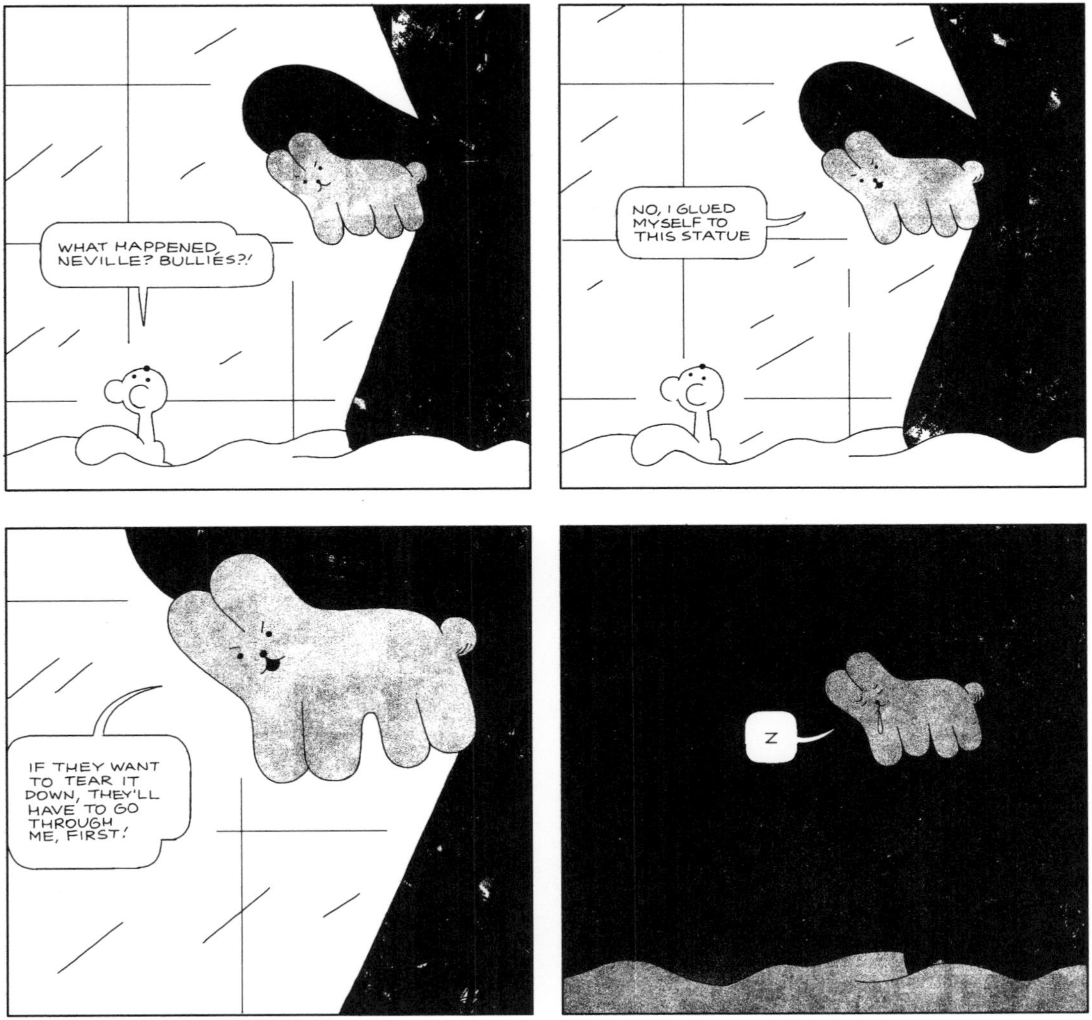
WHAT HAPPENED, NEVILLE? BULLIES?!
NO, I GLUED MYSELF TO THIS STATUE
IF THEY WANT TO TEAR IT DOWN, THEY'LL HAVE TO GO THROUGH ME, FIRST!
Z

I THINK IT'S VERY BRAVE WHAT YOU'RE DOING, NEVILLE
THANK YOU. I AGREE
DO YOU HAPPEN TO KNOW WHEN THE DEVELOPERS ARE DUE TO COME?
THREE WEEKS

DON'T
HURT
STATUE

Leaving Richard's Valley

IF I'M HONEST, IT'S ALWAYS ON MY MIND
MY POOR BABY
I KNOW THE VALLEY WAS A FARCE. I KNOW RICHARD WAS JUST SOME SNAKE OIL SALESMAN
BUT WHAT'S SO WRONG WITH SNAKE OIL?!
YEAH!
I GOTTA GET MY SNAKE OIL FROM SOMEWHERE!
LET ME BE YOUR PROVIDER

Leaving Richard's Valley

MY FIRST AUDITION IS THIS TUESDAY! AN AGENCY WANTS TO TRY ME OUT AS A HAND MODEL
A TALENT SCOUT SPOTTED ME HOLDING A PROTEST SIGN
SOON, I'LL BE A PROFESSIONAL MODEL!
I CAN'T WAIT TO GROW JADED AND BITTER!
WITH ANY LUCK, I'LL BE COMPLETELY SICK OF THE INDUSTRY BY THE END OF NEXT YEAR!

Leaving Richard's Valley

I THINK I'D GIVE A GOOD MOTIVATIONAL SPEECH! I'D BE A GOOD MOTIVATIONAL SPEAKER!
I THINK THAT'S A GREAT IDEA, ELLIE!
A PROMISING CAREER PATH
I COULD TRAVEL THE WORLD AND TALK ABOUT MY PATH TO SUCCESS!
"HOW TO BE OMAR'S BEST FRIEND: THE ELLIE SQUIRREL STORY"

Leaving Richard's Valley

LOOK: A SIMPLE ACORN
BUT! BOOM. ACORN'S ON HEAD
WOW
NOT SO SIMPLE NOW, EH?
SO MANY VARIATIONS! INFINITY --!

Leaving Richard's Valley

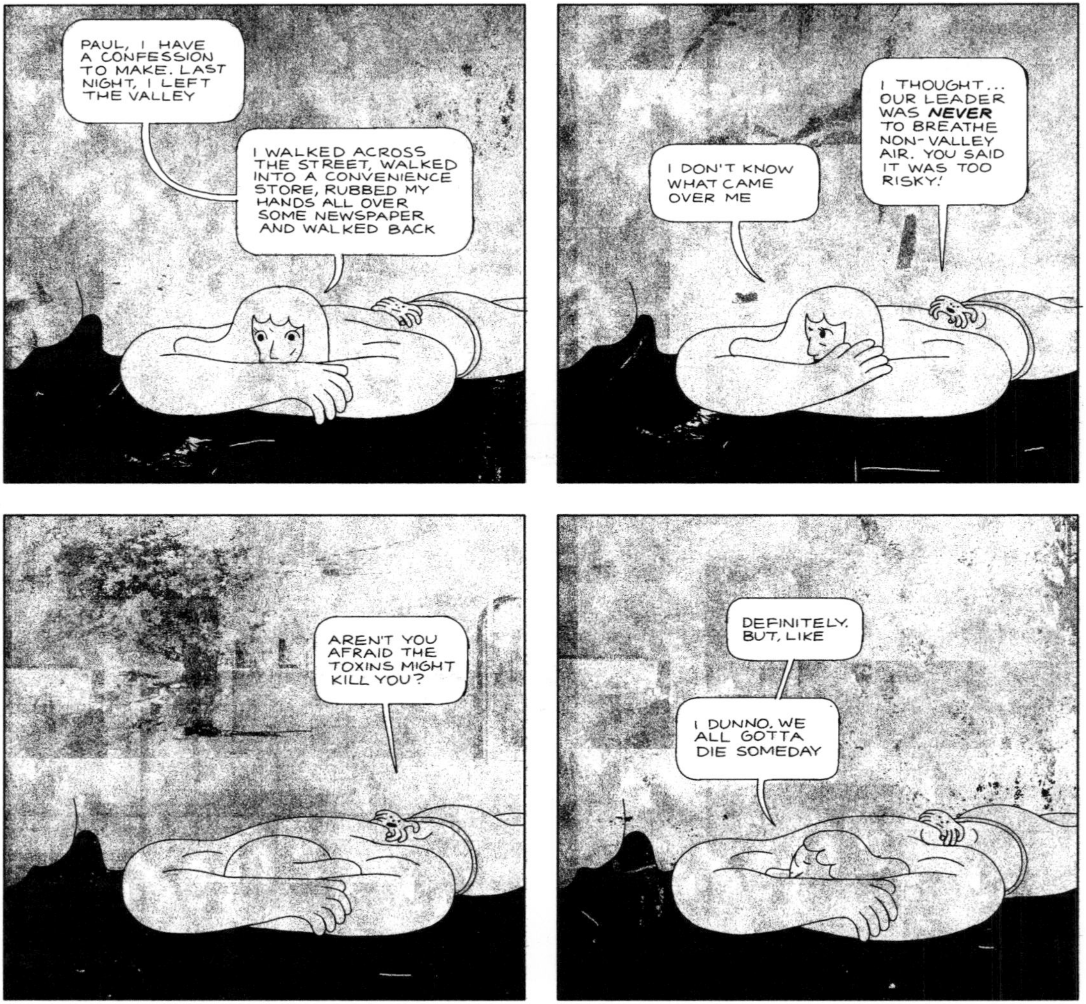
PAUL, I HAVE A CONFESSION TO MAKE. LAST NIGHT, I LEFT THE VALLEY
I WALKED ACROSS THE STREET, WALKED INTO A CONVENIENCE STORE, RUBBED MY HANDS ALL OVER SOME NEWSPAPER AND WALKED BACK
I THOUGHT... OUR LEADER WAS **NEVER** TO BREATHE NON-VALLEY AIR. YOU SAID IT WAS TOO RISKY!
I DON'T KNOW WHAT CAME OVER ME
AREN'T YOU AFRAID THE TOXINS MIGHT KILL YOU?
DEFINITELY. BUT, LIKE
I DUNNO. WE ALL GOTTA DIE SOMEDAY

Leaving Richard's Valley

THANK YOU FOR DOING THIS, ELLIE
I HOPE YOUR TRYOUT GOES WELL!
IT'S CALLED A "GO-SEE"
I THINK YOU'LL MAKE AN AMAZING HAND
OKAY, THIS IS KIND OF SPOOKING ME

Leaving Richard's Valley

Leaving Richard's Valley

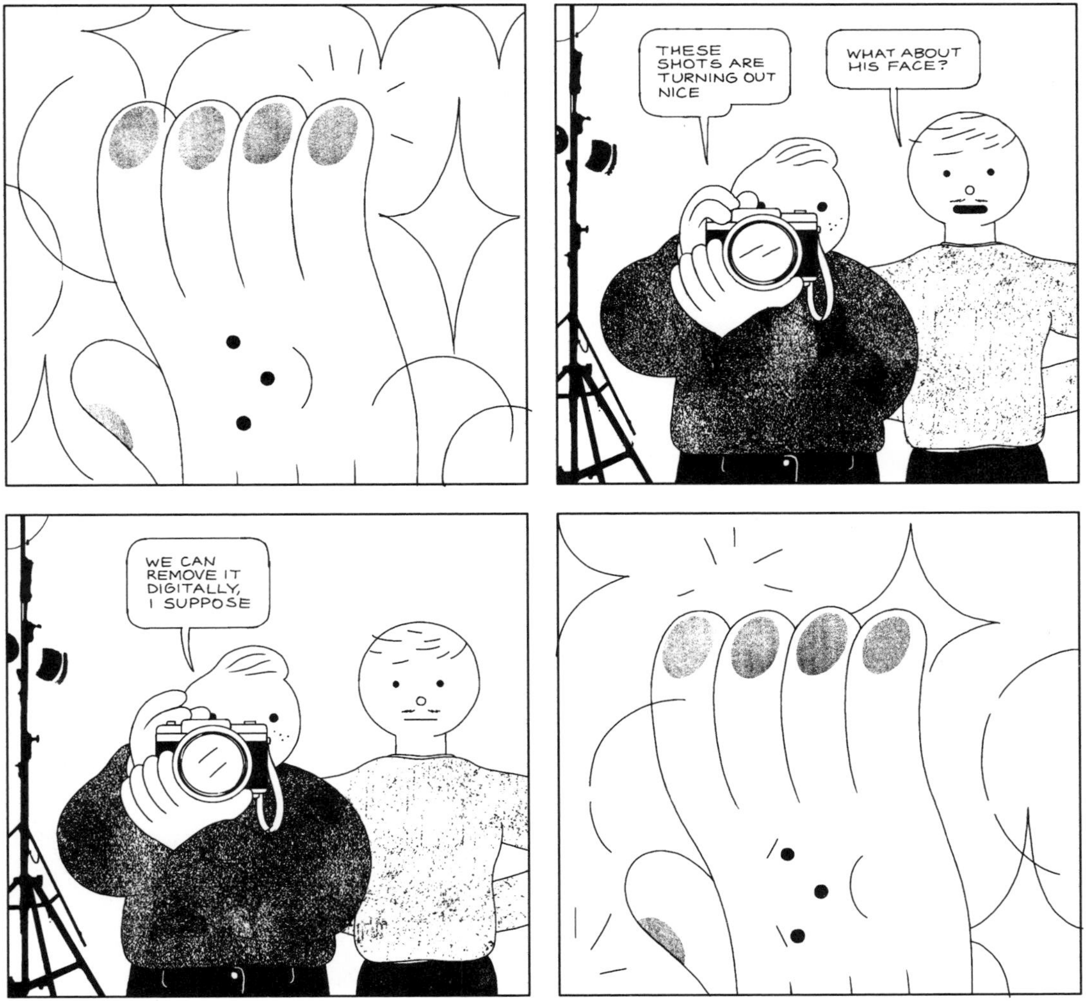

THESE SHOTS ARE TURNING OUT NICE
WHAT ABOUT HIS FACE?
WE CAN REMOVE IT DIGITALLY, I SUPPOSE

Leaving Richard's Valley

SIR... ARE YOU LOST? DO YOU NEED A SHIRT?
I'VE BEEN... WALKING... FOR... HOURS
?
WHAT IS THAT... YOU'RE EATING
A BEEF PATTY. FROM RANDY'S
IT'S UP THE ROAD
BEEF... ROAD...

Leaving Richard's Valley

COOL

Leaving Richard's Valley

HEY
HEY, AREN'T YOU THAT GUY?
YOU ARE! YOU'RE TOTALLY HIM, AREN'T YOU?!
HEY RAJ! PHOEBE! KIM! CHECK IT OUT! IT'S THIS GUY!

Leaving Richard's Valley

RICHARD?
RICHARD...?!
RICHARD?!!
HE'S GONE

Leaving Richard's Valley

PAL, THIS STATUE'S COMING DOWN WITH OR WITHOUT YOU ATTACHED TO IT
YOU'LL NEVER TAKE ME ALIVE--!
RAAA--!
I FAILED
I LED MY FRIENDS ASTRAY. AGAIN
AND MY BACK IS COLD. AND ITCHY

Leaving Richard's Valley

Leaving Richard's Valley

Leaving Richard's Valley

YOU'RE LOOKING CHIPPER TODAY, CAROLINE
I HEARD A RUMOUR ABOUT RICHARD
WORD IS HE LEFT THE VALLEY!
AND TRIPPED ON HIS SHOELACE! AND FELL INTO A TRASH CAN! AND POOPED HIS PANTS! THEN ATE HIS OWN POO AND EVERYONE LAUGHED
I DON'T LIKE GOSSIP

I KEEP HOPING THIS IS ALL JUST SOME HORRIBLE DREAM I'LL WAKE UP FROM
OR THAT IT'S A TEST... THAT RICHARD IS JUST HIDING BEHIND SOME BUSHES, WAITING TO SEE HOW WE'D GET ON WITHOUT HIM
I THINK A RIVAL GROUP KIDNAPPED HIM. THAT SNAKE MARK LUNATIC AND HIS BAND OF CRAZIES
MY THEORY? "RICHARD" HAS BEEN A PAID ACTOR THIS WHOLE TIME. THE REAL RICHARD, THE ONE PULLING ALL THE STRINGS, HAS YET TO REVEAL HIMSELF...
EH, MAYBE THIS IS ALL FOR THE BEST. I WAS THINKING ABOUT GOING BACK AND FINISHING MY DEGREE...

Leaving Richard's Valley

Private property
No parking
JESUS SAVES
Coca-Cola
HAMB
Vehicle Arrival
352
8882

Leaving Richard's Valley

YOU KNOW, THERE'S SOMETHING ROMANTIC ABOUT ALL THIS IMPERMANENCE
ON THE OTHER HAND, THERE'S SOMETHING EXTREMELY SUCKY TO IT AS WELL
I'D SAY IT'S PROBABLY TWENTY PERCENT ROMANTIC AND EIGHTY PERCENT SUCKY
I'VE ALWAYS WANTED A LIFE OF ROMANCE...

Leaving Richard's Valley

OMAR STOLE SOME MAKEUP FROM ONE OF HIS MODELLING JOBS FOR US TO EAT
I'VE EATEN THREE LIPSTICKS TODAY
I STILL ONLY GET PAID IN "SWAG"
I THINK I SWALLOWED TOO MUCH CONCEALER
IT MAKES YOUR GUTS INVISIBLE
I FEEL SICK. BUT ... HOT

Leaving Richard's Valley

MY NATURAL HABITAT... AHH
NO FOLLOWERS, NO CULTS...
NO ROOMMATES
JUST... A VERY SMELLY ECHO CHAMBER
IT'S SPOOKY IN HERE

Leaving Richard's Valley

I WONDER IF SNAKE MARK WILL COME LOOKING FOR ME...
OR ELLIE... OR NEVILLE... OR OMAR...
OR RICHARD...
OH GOSH, IT'S SO STRESSFUL! BEING SO SOUGHT AFTER...

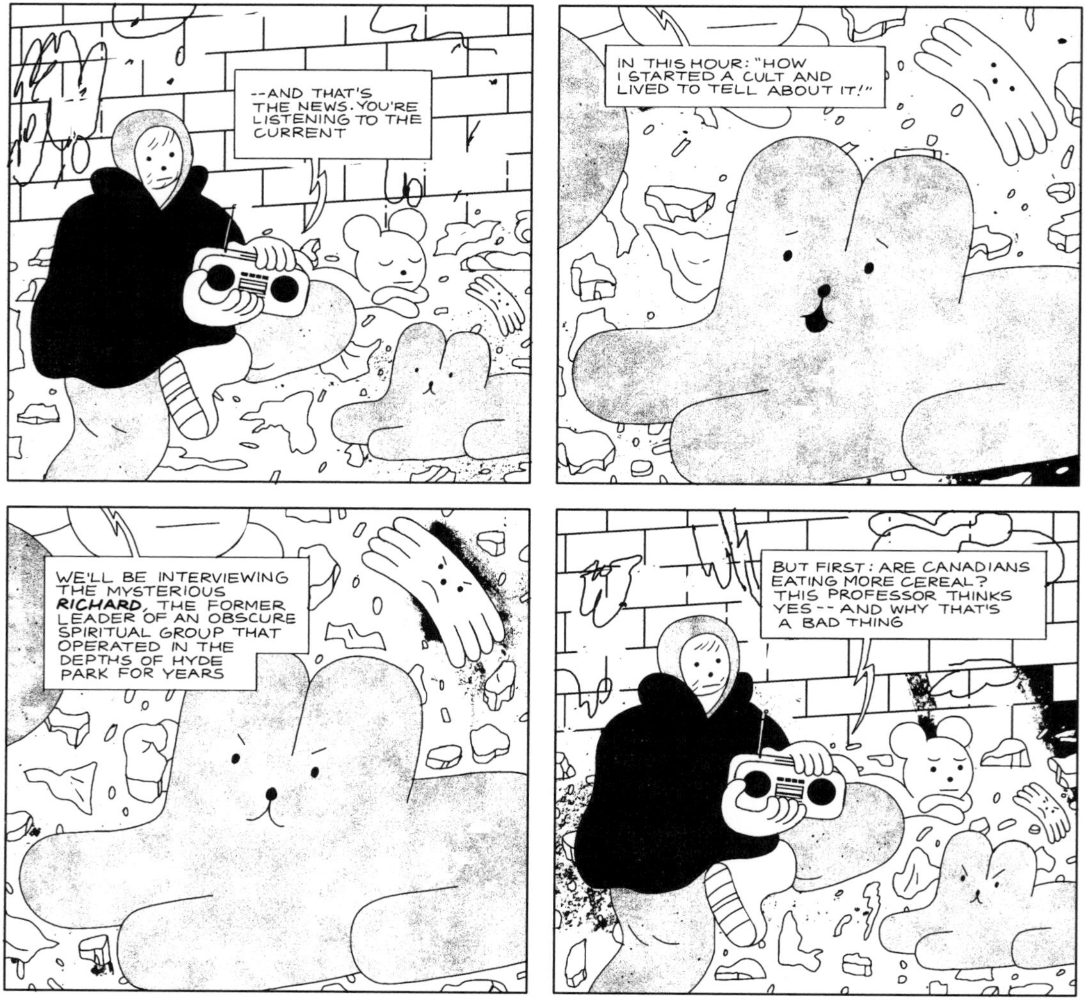
--AND THAT'S THE NEWS. YOU'RE LISTENING TO THE CURRENT
IN THIS HOUR: "HOW I STARTED A CULT AND LIVED TO TELL ABOUT IT!"
WE'LL BE INTERVIEWING THE MYSTERIOUS **RICHARD**, THE FORMER LEADER OF AN OBSCURE SPIRITUAL GROUP THAT OPERATED IN THE DEPTHS OF HYDE PARK FOR YEARS
BUT FIRST: ARE CANADIANS EATING MORE CEREAL? THIS PROFESSOR THINKS YES -- AND WHY THAT'S A BAD THING

ULTIMATELY, I'M A VICTIM OF SELF-BRAINWASHING. I DON'T BLAME ANYONE FOR BEING MAD AT ME. I'M MAD AT MYSELF!
radio one
BUT SELF-IMPROVEMENT, SELF-ACTUALIZATION... PART OF THAT PROCESS IS ABOUT RECOGNIZING YOUR OWN SHORTCOMINGS
RIGHT NOW, I'M EXCITED TO MOVE ON TO A NEW CHAPTER IN MY LIFE
AND WHAT MIGHT THAT ENTAIL
I'M NOT SURE WHAT MY NEXT ADVENTURE WILL BE YET, BUT I KNOW ONE THING-- IT'LL BE INDOORS THIS TIME!
HA HA
ON AIR

Leaving Richard's Valley

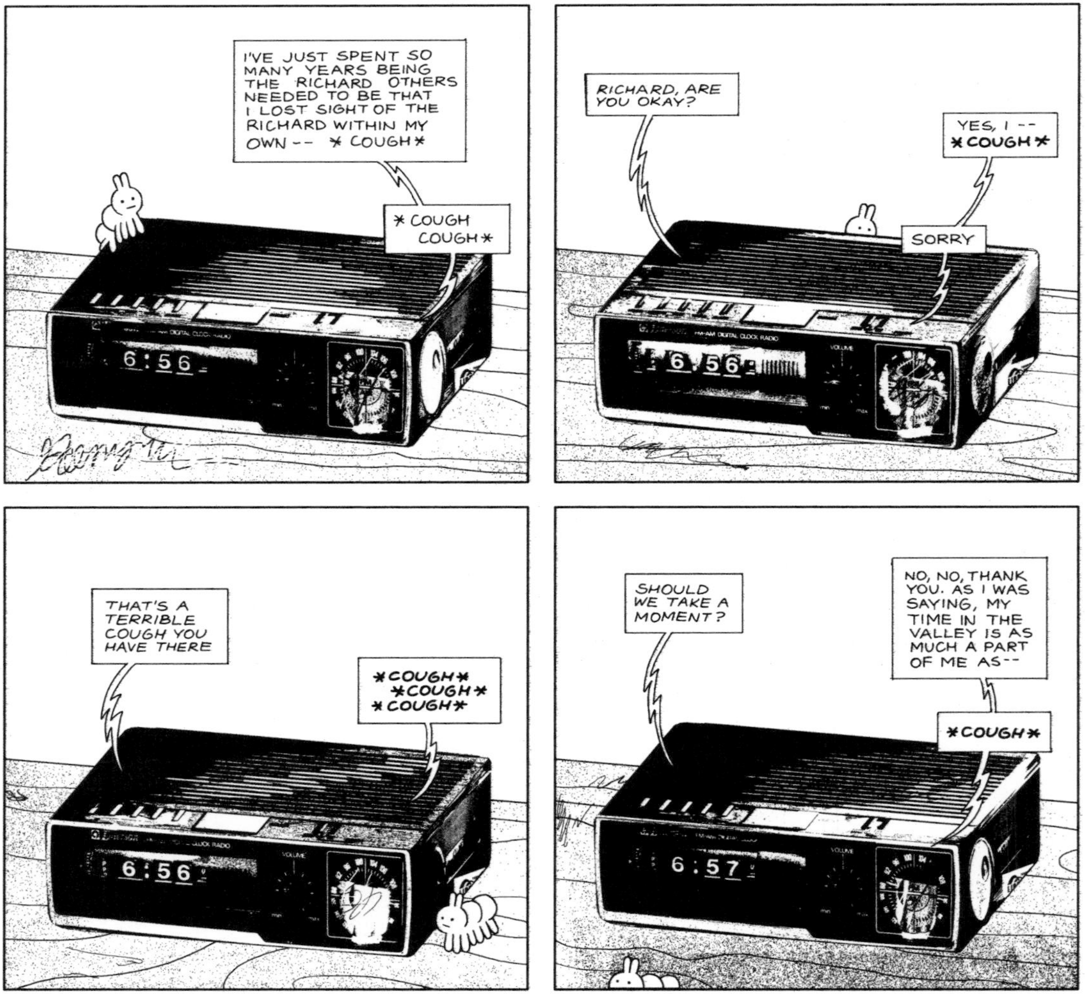
I'VE JUST SPENT SO MANY YEARS BEING THE RICHARD OTHERS NEEDED TO BE THAT I LOST SIGHT OF THE RICHARD WITHIN MY OWN -- *COUGH*
COUGH COUGH
6:56
RICHARD, ARE YOU OKAY?
YES, I -- *COUGH*
SORRY
6:56
THAT'S A TERRIBLE COUGH YOU HAVE THERE
COUGH *COUGH* *COUGH*
6:56
SHOULD WE TAKE A MOMENT?
NO, NO, THANK YOU. AS I WAS SAYING, MY TIME IN THE VALLEY IS AS MUCH A PART OF ME AS--
COUGH
6:57

Leaving Richard's Valley

WE CAN'T GO BACKWARDS! WE'D LITERALLY BE GOING BACKWARDS
NEVILLE, IT'LL BE DIFFERENT IF RICHARD'S GONE! IT WILL BE BETTER
BUT GOING BACK TO THE VALLEY?
I JUST WANTED ... TO BUILD SOMETHING FOR OURSELVES
...
WHY? WHO CARES?
YEAH, I JUST WANT A PLACE TO SLEEP

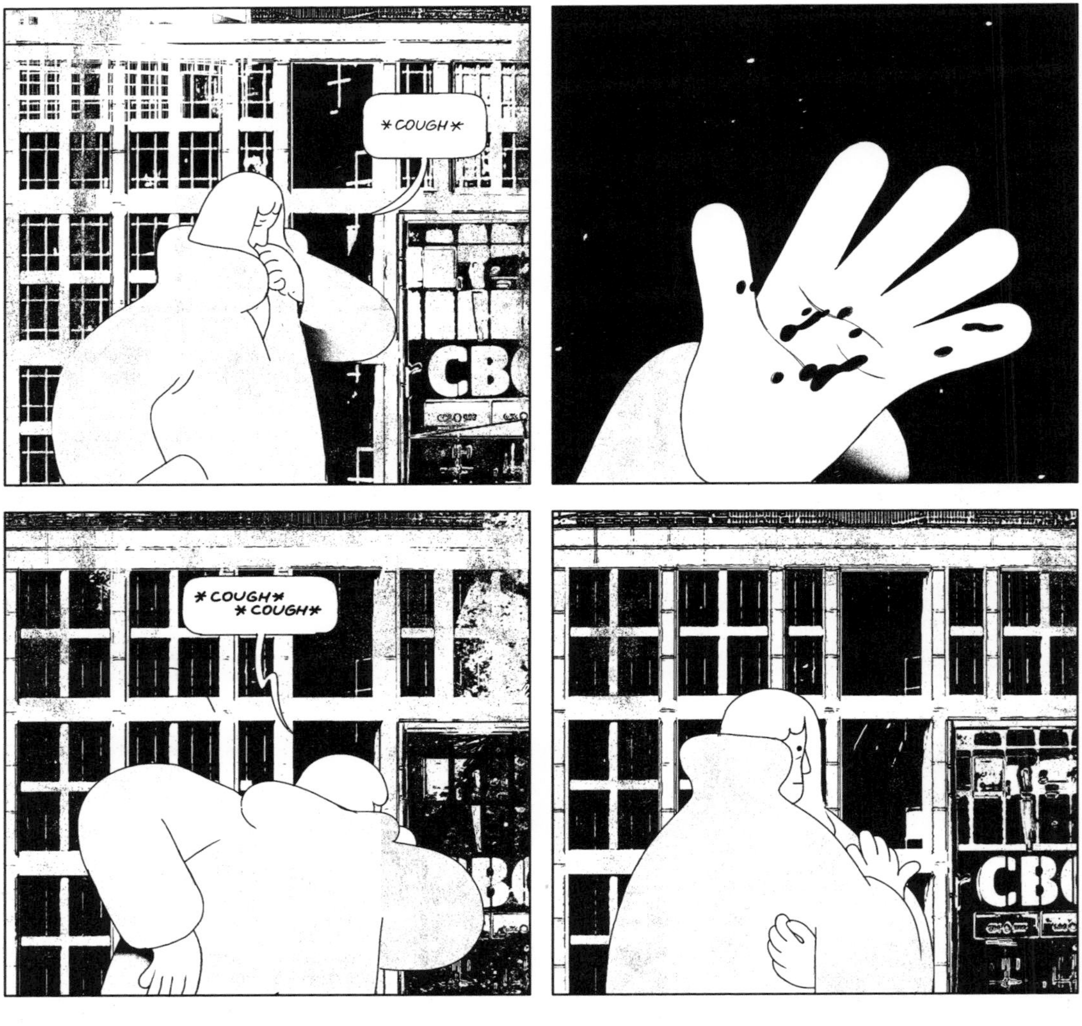
COUGH
COUGH
COUGH

Leaving Richard's Valley

SO WHAT'S THIS FOR AGAIN?
MALE MODEL MONTHLY. OUR "25 UNDER 25" ISSUE
SOME SPIDERS CAN LIVE **UP TO** 25 YEARS!
DO YOU THINK ABOUT DEATH OFTEN?
NOT OFTEN. MAYBE... ONCE AN HOUR? NO, WAIT
ONCE A YEAR?
THRICE A...
FORTNIGHT?
WHAT'S ONE FACTOID ABOUT YOURSELF THAT MIGHT SURPRISE OTHERS?
THAT SOME SPIDER WEBS CAN SPAN A LENGTH OF 80 FEET OR MORE!
I'M ALSO A HUGE MUSICAL THEATRE NERD

Leaving Richard's Valley

NEVILLE, WHAT'S ONE FACTOID ABOUT YOURSELF THAT MIGHT SURPRISE OTHERS?
SOME PEOPLE ARE SURPRISED I'M A DOG
WHEN WE FIRST MET, I ASSUMED YOU WERE, LIKE, A VERY PUFFY RABBIT. THAT YOU WERE JUST SWOLLEN OR SOMETHING
SO WHAT'S YOUR FACTOID, ELLIE?
I'M NOT SURE WHAT A "FACTOID" IS. IT SOUNDS MEDICAL
YES, THAT IS SURPRISING
"I HAD A REALLY BAD FACTOID A FEW MONTHS AGO, BUT A VET HAD IT REMOVED"
"MY FACTOIDS FLARE UP WHEN I EAT DAIRY"

Leaving Richard's Valley

MARK, WHAT'S ONE FACTOID ABOUT YOURSELF THAT MIGHT SURPRISE OTHERS?
I'M A HUGE MUSICAL THEATRE N--
THERE'S NO TIME FOR THIS! MARK, WE'RE KICKING YOU OUT OF MARK'S CLUB. THE BOARD OF DIRECTORS TOOK A VOTE
"BOARD OF DIRECTORS?"
LYLE IS BARELY EVER HERE. YOUR GOD IS DEAD. WE APPRECIATE YOUR CONTRIBUTION TO MARKSISM, BUT WE'VE DECIDED TO GO IN A DIFFERENT DIRECTION
WE'LL BE FIELDING DIFFERENT DEVELOPMENT OFFERS, BUT MOST OF THE MARK'S CLUB PROPERTY WILL BE RENTED OUT AS A CO-WORKING SPACE IN THE INTERIM
INCLUDING YOUR ROOM
WE'D BE HAPPY TO WRITE YOU A GLOWING RECOMMENDATION SHOULD YOU WISH TO PURSUE A DIFFERENT CULT

Leaving Richard's Valley

SORRY YOUR THINGY BROKE UP
IT'S NOT YOUR FAULT, LYLE
WELL. IT'S NOT NOT MY FAULT, Y'KNOW...
THERE'S PROBABLY A LESSON TO BE GLEANED FROM ALL THIS
I HOPE NOT
I'VE BEEN IN FAR TOO DEEP FOR FAR TOO LONG TO START LEARNING FROM MY MISTAKES NOW

Leaving Richard's Valley

I KNOW IT DIDN'T MATTER TO YOU
BUT MARK'S CLUB MEANT ALOT TO ME
NOW THAT'S OVER. IN ANY MEANINGFUL WAY, THAT IS
I'M PITCHING A SORT OF "IN MEMORIUM" FOR THE GROUP TO A LOCAL WEEKLY
I KNOW THERE ISN'T MUCH CHANCE YOU'D SPARE A KIND WORD
BUT KNOW IT'D BE GREATLY APPRECIATED
WOULD IT REALLY KILL YOU TO JUST SAY SOMETHING NICE --?
YES. YES IT MIGHT

Leaving Richard's Valley

YUP, A SOLITARY LIFE...
I FINALLY HAVE THE SPACE AND TIME TO FOCUS ON MY MUSIC
THANK GOODNESS ... A LIFE WITHOUT DISTRACTION... OR INTERRUPTION... OR FRICTION... OR SURPRISE
IT'S JUST ... SO GOOD FOR MY MUSIC ... SO GOOD
I'M JUST... OVERJOYED...

Leaving Richard's Valley

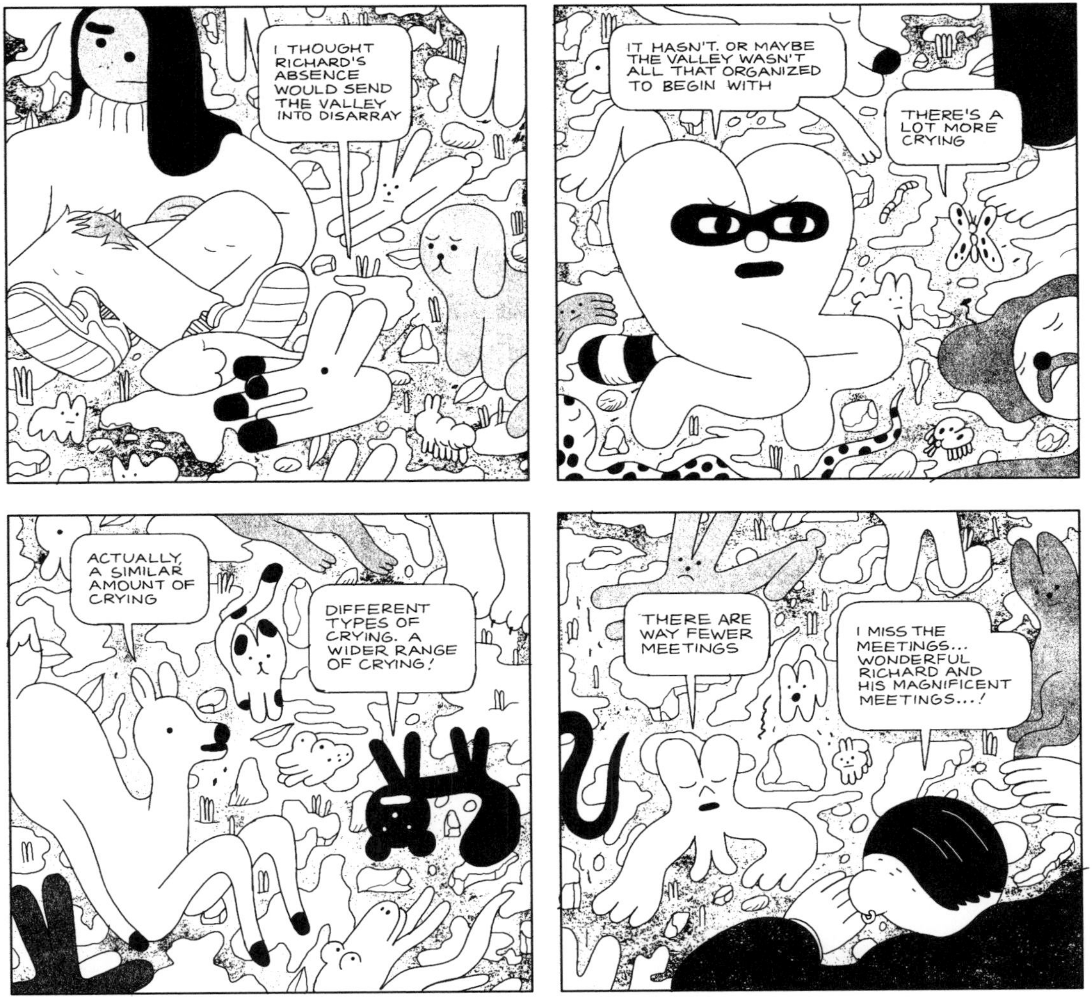
I THOUGHT RICHARD'S ABSENCE WOULD SEND THE VALLEY INTO DISARRAY
IT HASN'T. OR MAYBE THE VALLEY WASN'T ALL THAT ORGANIZED TO BEGIN WITH
THERE'S A LOT MORE CRYING
ACTUALLY, A SIMILAR AMOUNT OF CRYING
DIFFERENT TYPES OF CRYING. A WIDER RANGE OF CRYING!
THERE ARE WAY FEWER MEETINGS
I MISS THE MEETINGS... WONDERFUL RICHARD AND HIS MAGNIFICENT MEETINGS...!

Leaving Richard's Valley

DURING THE FIRST FEW WEEKS, WE TRIED TO HAVE **DAILY** RICHARDS
EVERY MORNING, A RANDOM VALLEY MEMBER WOULD BE SELECTED TO BE RICHARD FOR A TWENTY-FOUR HOUR PERIOD
IT WAS KIND OF A DISASTER
THE DAILY RICHARDS EITHER DIDN'T TAKE IT SERIOUSLY ENOUGH, OR TOOK IT WAY TOO SERIOUSLY
LATER, A BUNCH OF US STOOD ON EACH OTHER'S SHOULDERS TO TRY TO FORM A NEW, SUPER-RICHARD
WE HAD A TRENCHCOAT AND EVERYTHING
IT UPSET TOO MANY OF THE CHILDREN

Leaving Richard's Valley

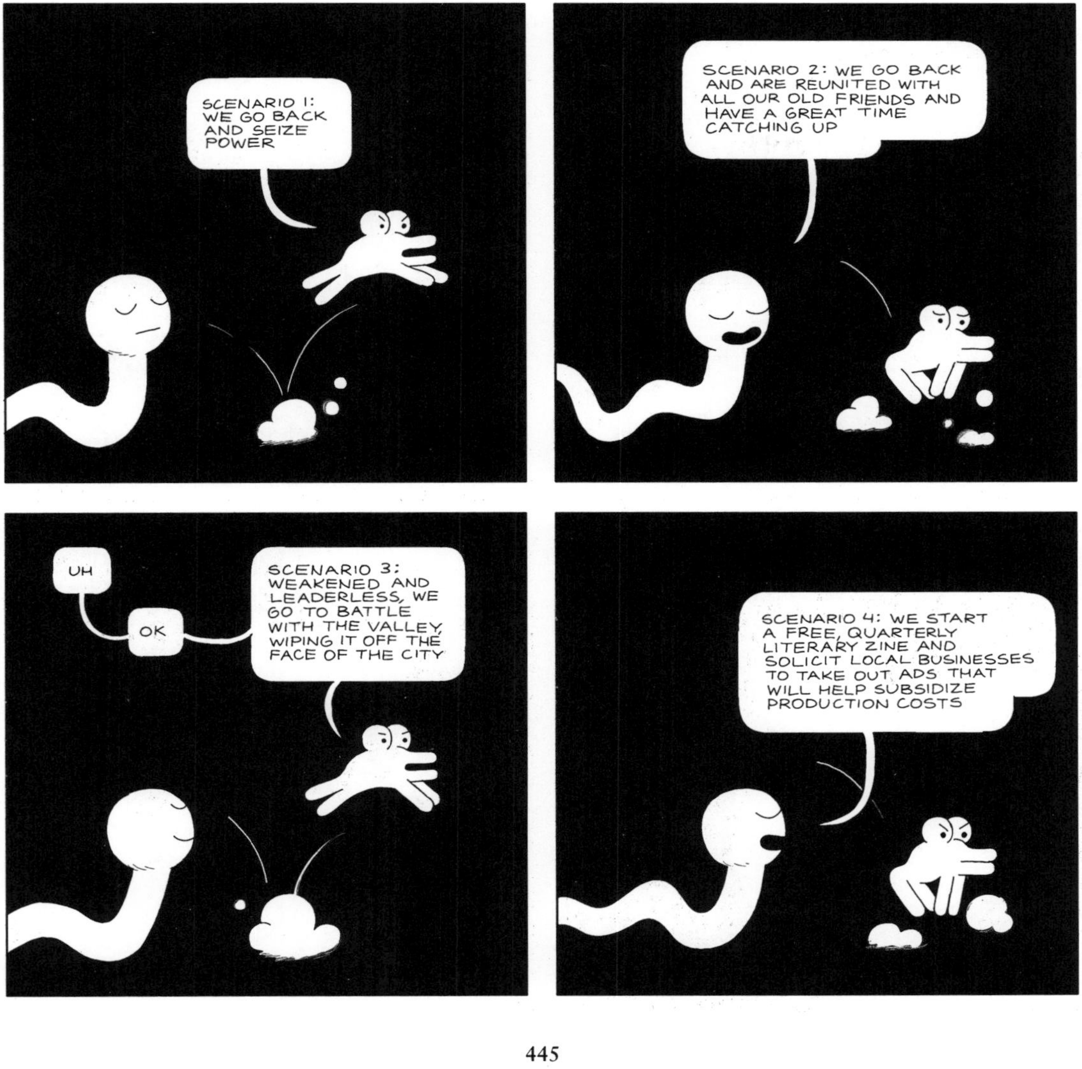

SCENARIO 1: WE GO BACK AND SEIZE POWER
SCENARIO 2: WE GO BACK AND ARE REUNITED WITH ALL OUR OLD FRIENDS AND HAVE A GREAT TIME CATCHING UP
UH
OK
SCENARIO 3: WEAKENED AND LEADERLESS, WE GO TO BATTLE WITH THE VALLEY, WIPING IT OFF THE FACE OF THE CITY
SCENARIO 4: WE START A FREE, QUARTERLY LITERARY ZINE AND SOLICIT LOCAL BUSINESSES TO TAKE OUT ADS THAT WILL HELP SUBSIDIZE PRODUCTION COSTS

Leaving Richard's Valley

DO YOU THINK THEY'LL BE HAPPY TO SEE US BACK IN THE VALLEY?
OF COURSE! WE'RE HEROES
MAYBE MY ISSUE OF "MALE MODEL MONTHLY" WILL BE OUT BY THEN
EXACTLY. WE'RE INSPIRATIONAL
WOW! I'M TOUCHED
ME... AN INSPIRATION! I'M AT A LOSS FOR WORDS
A PARADE?! IN MY HONOUR--?
OH GOSH! NO, NO, THAT'S SIMPLY TOO MUCH!

Leaving Richard's Valley

I WAS SICK ONCE
I'LL BE SICK AGAIN
AND SO IT GOES . . .

Leaving Richard's Valley

GOING BACK? I MEAN, SURE, SOME OF MY HAPPIEST MOMENTS OF MY LIFE WERE IN THE VALLEY
ALTHOUGH SOME OF MY OTHER HAPPIEST MOMENTS WERE OUTSIDE THE VALLEY, IN OTHER PLACES
SOME OF THE MOST MEDIUM EXPERIENCES OF MY LIFE WERE IN THAT VALLEY!
YES, THAT TOO
THE HIGHS AND LOWS REALLY STARTED TO EVEN OUT AT SOME POINT

Leaving Richard's Valley

R

Leaving Richard's Valley

I HAVE THIS VISION OF COMING BACK HOME AND BEING WELCOMED WITH OPEN ARMS
AND THEN LEAVING. NO ONE'S UPSET WHEN WE PART WAYS
AFTER SOME TIME, I RETURN HOME AGAIN. ONCE MORE, I'M GREETED WITH WARMTH AND GENEROSITY
ONCE MORE, I LEAVE
THIS HAPPENS OVER AND OVER AGAIN FOR THE REST OF MY LIFE
COMING AND GOING, NOW AND FOREVER, NEVER IN ANGER

Leaving Richard's Valley

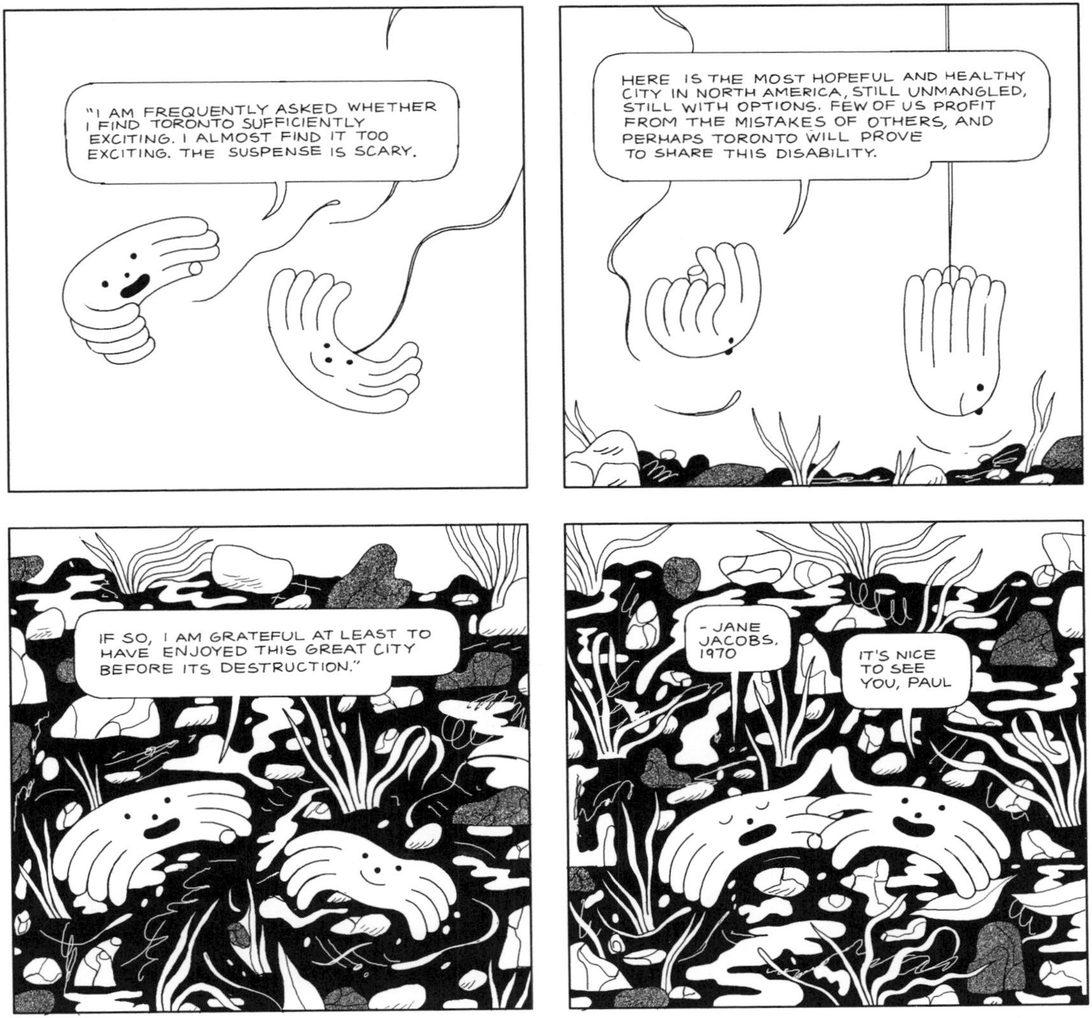
"I AM FREQUENTLY ASKED WHETHER I FIND TORONTO SUFFICIENTLY EXCITING. I ALMOST FIND IT TOO EXCITING. THE SUSPENSE IS SCARY.
HERE IS THE MOST HOPEFUL AND HEALTHY CITY IN NORTH AMERICA, STILL UNMANGLED, STILL WITH OPTIONS. FEW OF US PROFIT FROM THE MISTAKES OF OTHERS, AND PERHAPS TORONTO WILL PROVE TO SHARE THIS DISABILITY.
IF SO, I AM GRATEFUL AT LEAST TO HAVE ENJOYED THIS GREAT CITY BEFORE ITS DESTRUCTION."
- JANE JACOBS, 1970
IT'S NICE TO SEE YOU, PAUL

Leaving Richard's Valley

LONG TIME NO SEE, NEVILLE!
WHAT'S THE NOT-VALLEY LIKE? THE OUTSIDE WORLD...?
IS EVERYONE SICK? SICKER? ARE THERE MUTANTS?
HAS THE U.S. INVADED CANADA?
WELL--
FLYING CARS?
WHAT'S THE ROBOT SITUATION OUT THERE?
IT MUST BE A WASTELAND
WHO DIED IN THE SPACE ACADEMY FINALE?
IT MUST BE LOVELY
HAVE YOU SEEN RICHARD?
WHAT YEAR IS IT
WHO PLAYS REMY IN THE SPACE ACADEMY MOVIE?
DID YOU TALK TO HIM?

Leaving Richard's Valley

I MISSED STEW
WHO?
I MISSED YOU TOO, ELLIE
THE RECIPE'S DIFFERENT FROM HOW I REMEMBER IT
YOU MUST HAVE TRIED SOME INCREDIBLE CUISINE ON YOUR TRAVELS
WE WENT TO A DUMPSTER BEHIND A VERY AUTHENTIC SZECHUAN RESTAURANT
YOU SHOULD OPEN ONE OF THOSE HERE IN THE VALLEY
I DUNNO... THE START-UP COSTS OF DUMPSTERS...
WHY NOT JUST OPEN A STEW PLACE?
WHO'S STU?

Leaving Richard's Valley

CAROLINE. LONG TIME NO SEE
WE WERE WORRIED ABOUT YOU WHEN YOU LEFT
YOU... YOU WERE?
WELL, AT FIRST. THEN WE STARTED HEARING ABOUT ALL THE SUCCESS YOU WERE HAVING AS AN ARCHITECT
WE WERE SO PROUD OF YOU! ONE OF OUR OWN, MAKING A MARK ON THE CITY
SO COOL!
YOU'RE, LIKE, A HERO

Leaving Richard's Valley

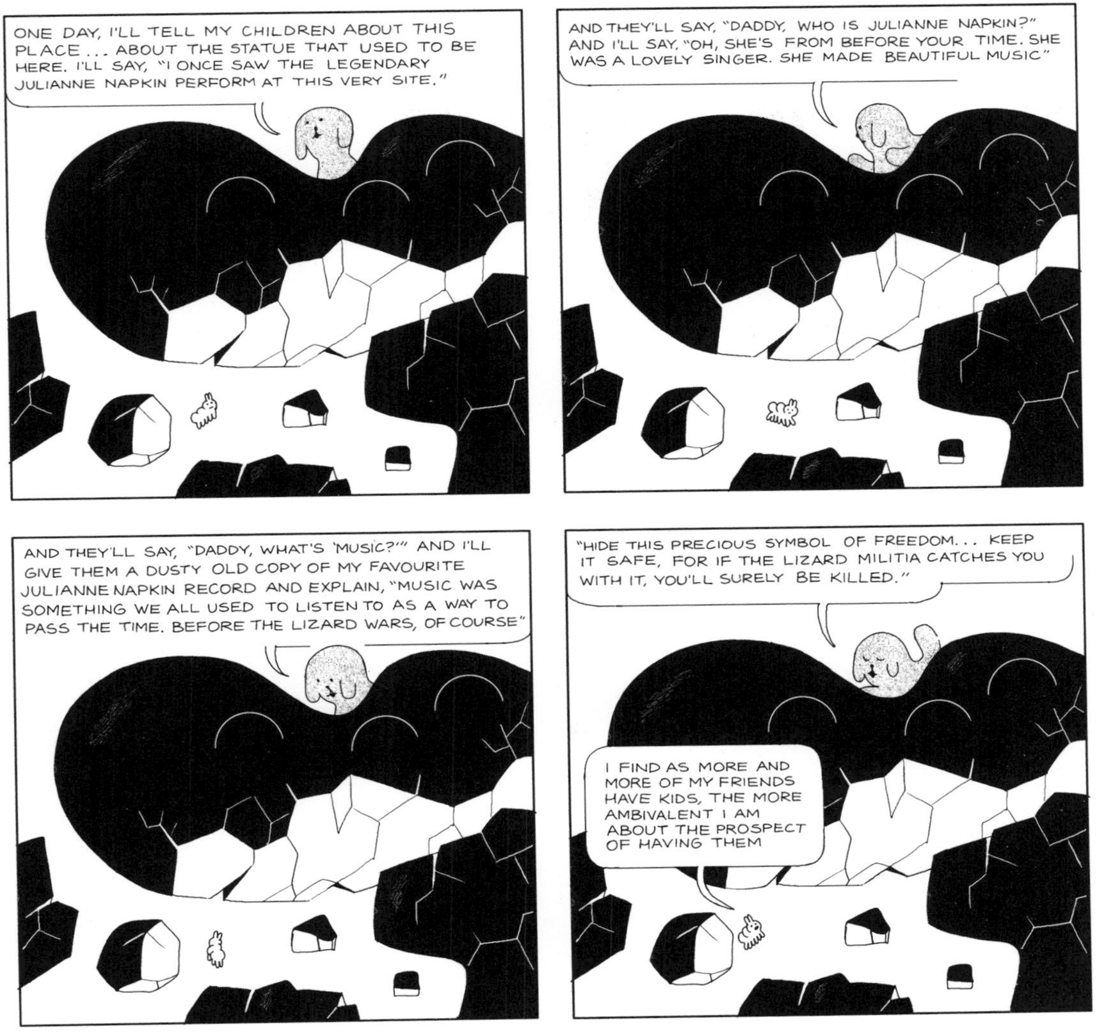
ONE DAY, I'LL TELL MY CHILDREN ABOUT THIS PLACE... ABOUT THE STATUE THAT USED TO BE HERE. I'LL SAY, "I ONCE SAW THE LEGENDARY JULIANNE NAPKIN PERFORM AT THIS VERY SITE."
AND THEY'LL SAY, "DADDY, WHO IS JULIANNE NAPKIN?" AND I'LL SAY, "OH, SHE'S FROM BEFORE YOUR TIME. SHE WAS A LOVELY SINGER. SHE MADE BEAUTIFUL MUSIC"
AND THEY'LL SAY, "DADDY, WHAT'S 'MUSIC?'" AND I'LL GIVE THEM A DUSTY OLD COPY OF MY FAVOURITE JULIANNE NAPKIN RECORD AND EXPLAIN, "MUSIC WAS SOMETHING WE ALL USED TO LISTEN TO AS A WAY TO PASS THE TIME. BEFORE THE LIZARD WARS, OF COURSE"
"HIDE THIS PRECIOUS SYMBOL OF FREEDOM... KEEP IT SAFE, FOR IF THE LIZARD MILITIA CATCHES YOU WITH IT, YOU'LL SURELY BE KILLED."
I FIND AS MORE AND MORE OF MY FRIENDS HAVE KIDS, THE MORE AMBIVALENT I AM ABOUT THE PROSPECT OF HAVING THEM

NEVILLE, WHY AREN'T YOU WITH MY BROTHER? IS LYLE COMING BACK TO THE VALLEY AS WELL?
NO. NO, I DOUBT IT
DID SOMETHING HAPPEN TO HIM? IS HE OKAY?
HE'S PROBABLY... FINE? WE HAD A FALLING OUT
WE TOOK A VOTE AS A GROUP, AND DECIDED TO PART WAYS
YOU... WAIT, YOU KICKED HIM OUT?
IT WASN'T THAT DRAMATIC. THE PROCESS WAS VERY DEMOCRATIC, VERY--
PTOO

Leaving Richard's Valley

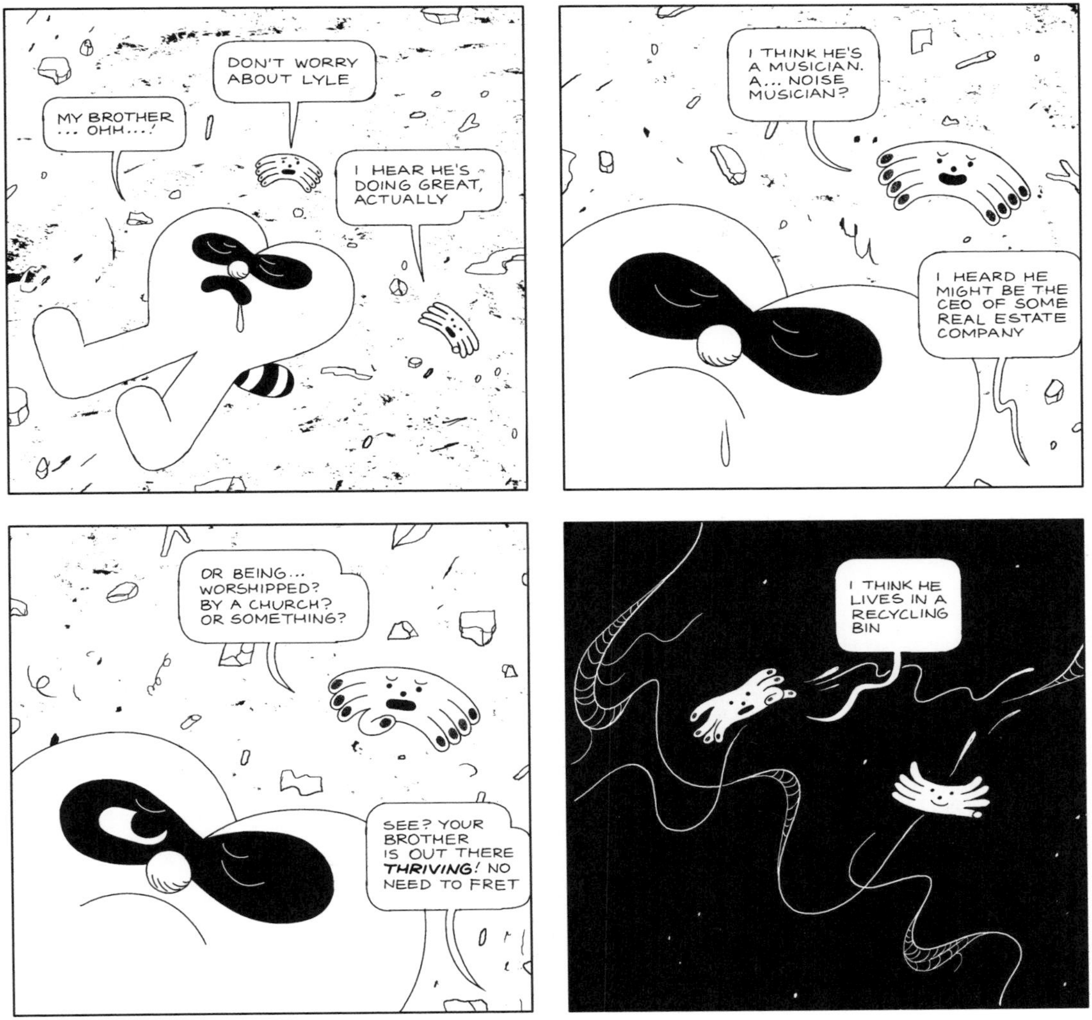

MY BROTHER ... OHH...!
DON'T WORRY ABOUT LYLE
I HEAR HE'S DOING GREAT, ACTUALLY
I THINK HE'S A MUSICIAN. A... NOISE MUSICIAN?
I HEARD HE MIGHT BE THE CEO OF SOME REAL ESTATE COMPANY
OR BEING... WORSHIPPED? BY A CHURCH? OR SOMETHING?
SEE? YOUR BROTHER IS OUT THERE THRIVING! NO NEED TO FRET
I THINK HE LIVES IN A RECYCLING BIN

Leaving Richard's Valley

I DIM THE LIGHTS... I THINK ABOUT YOU
SPEND SLEEPLESS NIGHTS ... TO THINK ABOUT YOU
YOU SAID YOU LOVED ME
OR WERE YOU JUST BEING KIND
TORONTO LIFE
OR AM I LOSING MY MIND...
The rise of the restaurant pati
Top 200 T.O. patios
Jason Patio: A life in patios
Patios - trend or menac
What's in a patio?
Patios: An Oral History
Patios: A Primer
What'
in a name?
New season, new baby names
City's most interesting dog
You won't believe how interesting
I feel sad but I don't know why
Does Mark's Club have the answers?
We Love The Valley - Oh!
Celebrity cults and municipal parks - inside a day in the life of the enigmatic

TORONTO LIFE
ANOTHER YEAR OF THIS
The rise of the restaurant patio
Top 200 T.O. patios
Jason Patio: A life in patios
Patios - trend or menace?
What's in a patio?
Patios: An Oral History
Patios: A Primer
What's in a name?
New season, new baby names
City's most interesting dog
You won't believe how interesting
I feel sad but I don't know why
Does Mark's Club have the answers?
We Love The Valley - Oh!
Celebrity cults and municipal parks - inside a day in the life of the enigmatic Richard

Leaving Richard's Valley

IF THERE'S A MESSAGE I WANT PEOPLE TO TAKE AWAY FROM MY FORTHCOMING BOOK, IT'S THAT WE **ALL** HAVE A VALLEY WE CAN GO TO. IT'S THE VALLEY IN **HERE**
BUT SOMETIMES WE FORGET THE DIRECTIONS, THAT'S ALL
COULD YOU REPEAT THAT LAST PART, BUT SPECIFY THAT THE VALLEY IS IN OUR MINDS? YOU SAY, "THE VALLEY IN **HERE**" AND THEN POINT TO YOUR HEAD, WHICH REALLY WON'T COME ACROSS VIA AUDIO--
SURE. WHEN DOES THIS AIR AGAIN?
DON'S MEATS
FOOD Market
COUGH
--AS ALWAYS, THIS WEEK'S EPISODE OF "SLOW PLAY" IS BROUGHT TO YOU BY YELLOW HAT MATTRESSES. TUNE IN NEXT WEEK FOR--

Leaving Richard's Valley

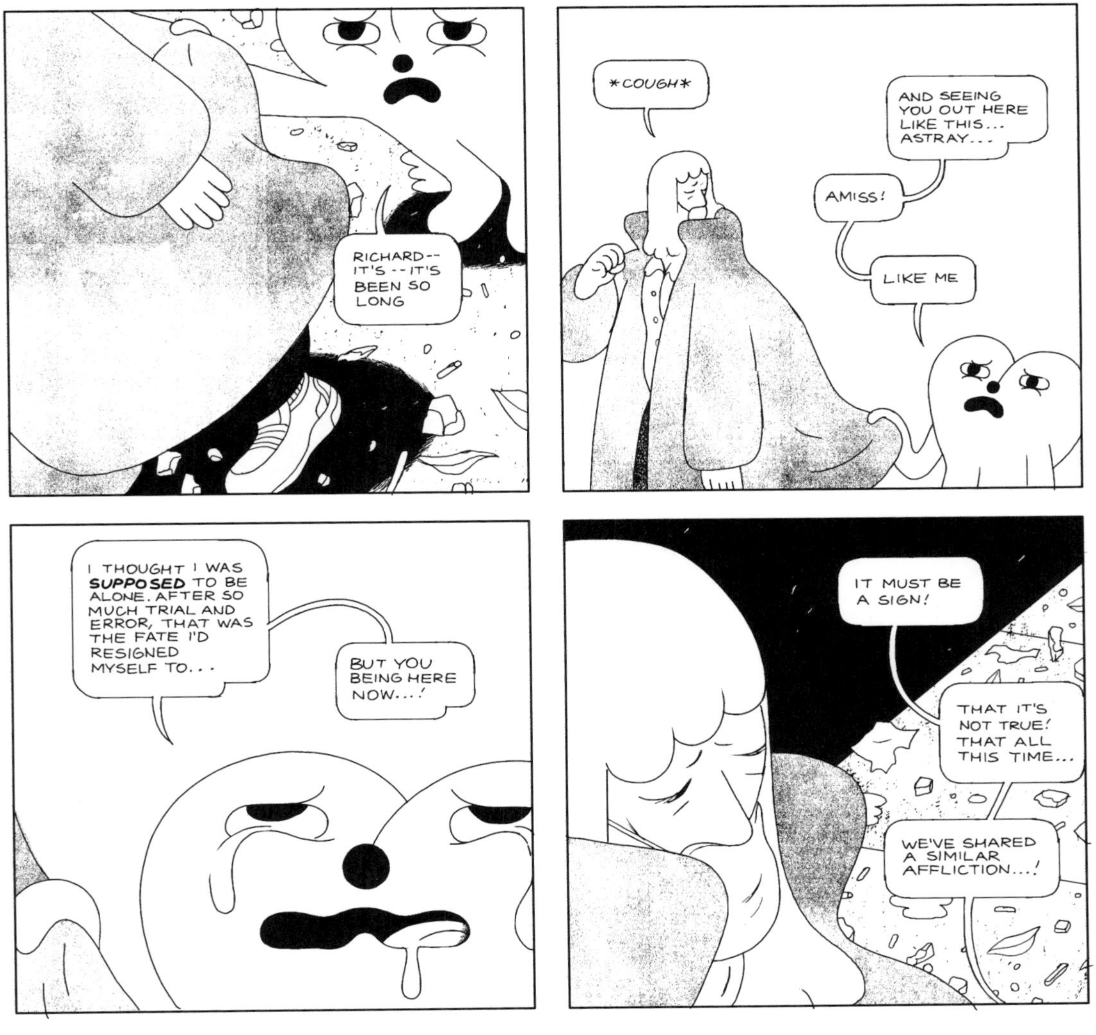
RICHARD-- IT'S --IT'S BEEN SO LONG
COUGH
AND SEEING YOU OUT HERE LIKE THIS... ASTRAY...
AMISS!
LIKE ME
I THOUGHT I WAS **SUPPOSED** TO BE ALONE. AFTER SO MUCH TRIAL AND ERROR, THAT WAS THE FATE I'D RESIGNED MYSELF TO...
BUT YOU BEING HERE NOW...!
IT MUST BE A SIGN!
THAT IT'S NOT TRUE! THAT ALL THIS TIME...
WE'VE SHARED A SIMILAR AFFLICTION...!

YOU'RE LIKE ME ...!
DON'T YOU SEE, RICHARD? WE'RE ALIKE...
THERE'S SOMEONE LIKE ME....!
LYLE. IF I'M HONEST, I CAN'T TELL THE DIFFERENCE BETWEEN ANY OF YOU. PEOPLE, ANIMALS, WHOEVER
YOU'RE **ALL** ALIKE. THERE'S MILLIONS LIKE YOU. BILLIONS
YOU'VE ALL JUST... BLENDED TOGETHER

Leaving Richard's Valley

IT'S NICE TO BE BACK! I MISSED YOU ALL
YOUR FOOD! YOUR FRIENDSHIP! YOUR FARTS!
SPENDING SO MUCH TIME IN THE SPOTLIGHT... IT'S NICE TO HAVE THIS GRASSY, GASSY PARADISE TO RETREAT TO
PEOPLE IN THE CITY CAN BE SO FAKE
AND IF THERE'S ONE THING THAT JULIANNE NAPKIN DEMANDS, IT'S THE GENUINE ARTICLE!

Leaving Richard's Valley

WHAT AN EYESORE!
WELL, THEY TECHNICALLY DIDN'T PUT IT UP **IN** THE VALLEY. JUST ACROSS THE STREET FROM IT
THE TERM "PUBLIC SPACE" USED TO ACTUALLY MEAN SOMETHING
MAYBE WE COULD PETITION THE CITY
I DON'T MIND IT
Radiance.
Refined.
Second Sunrise
Antiques Jewelry

Leaving Richard's Valley

MARK, NO! EVERYONE IN THE VALLEY IS HAPPY TO HAVE YOU HERE AGAIN. IT'S JUST THE CRYING... IT'S KEEPING OTHER RESIDENTS UP AT NIGHT
I JUST LOVE SO MUCH, NEVILLE! I LOVE SO MUCH AND SO HARD
WHAT IF YOU TRIED LOVING LESS? OR LOVING A LITTLE?
SPEAKING FROM EXPERIENCE, I'VE FOUND IT VERY PLEASANT TO BE ONLY A LITTLE BIT LOVED
I FEEL LOVE, BUT NEVER THAT MUCH OF IT. PEOPLE ENJOY MY COMPANY, BUT I'M NOBODY'S FIRST CHOICE. THEY'RE HAPPY TO SEE ME! JUST NOT TOO HAPPY
NEVER THE HAPPIEST, SEE? I KNOW PEOPLE COULD BE HAPPIER WITH ME. IT USED TO BOTHER ME, BUT NOW I APPRECIATE IT
AS IT GIVES ME SOMETHING TO WORK TOWARDS

WILL YOU BE SINGING FOR US TONIGHT, JULIANNE?
WHY DON'T YOU SING ME A SONG INSTEAD, PAUL? I'D LOVE TO BE SERENADED TO
HA HA, GOSH! OKAY, HERE GOES:
NOT A DAY GOES BY... ♫
NOT A SINGLE DAY ♪
WAIT, WAIT. SORRY TO INTERRUPT, BUT COULD YOU START OVER? AND START SOFTER THIS TIME? THAT SONG SHOULD START SOFT, THEN BUILD
HERE, LIKE THIS:
♫ NOT A DAY GOES BY ...

Leaving Richard's Valley

WHEN WE MOVED BACK TO THE CITY, RICHARD HAD DIFFICULTY MAKING NEW FRIENDS. WE SPENT A LOT OF TIME IN THE PARK TOGETHER
WHILE WE WERE THERE, WE'D OFTEN RUN INTO A GIRL RICHARD'S AGE, WHO LIVED IN THE NEIGHBOURHOOD. RICHARD WANTED TO BE HER FRIEND, BUT WAS A LITTLE SHY
RICHARD
LIED
I TOLD HIM, "SON, THE BEST WAY TO MAKE A FRIEND IS TO TELL THEM A SECRET"
WELCOME
TO THE VALLEY
RICHARD LOVED THE PARK. HE ONCE TOLD ME THE PARK KNEW ALL OF HIS SECRETS
NO

Leaving Richard's Valley

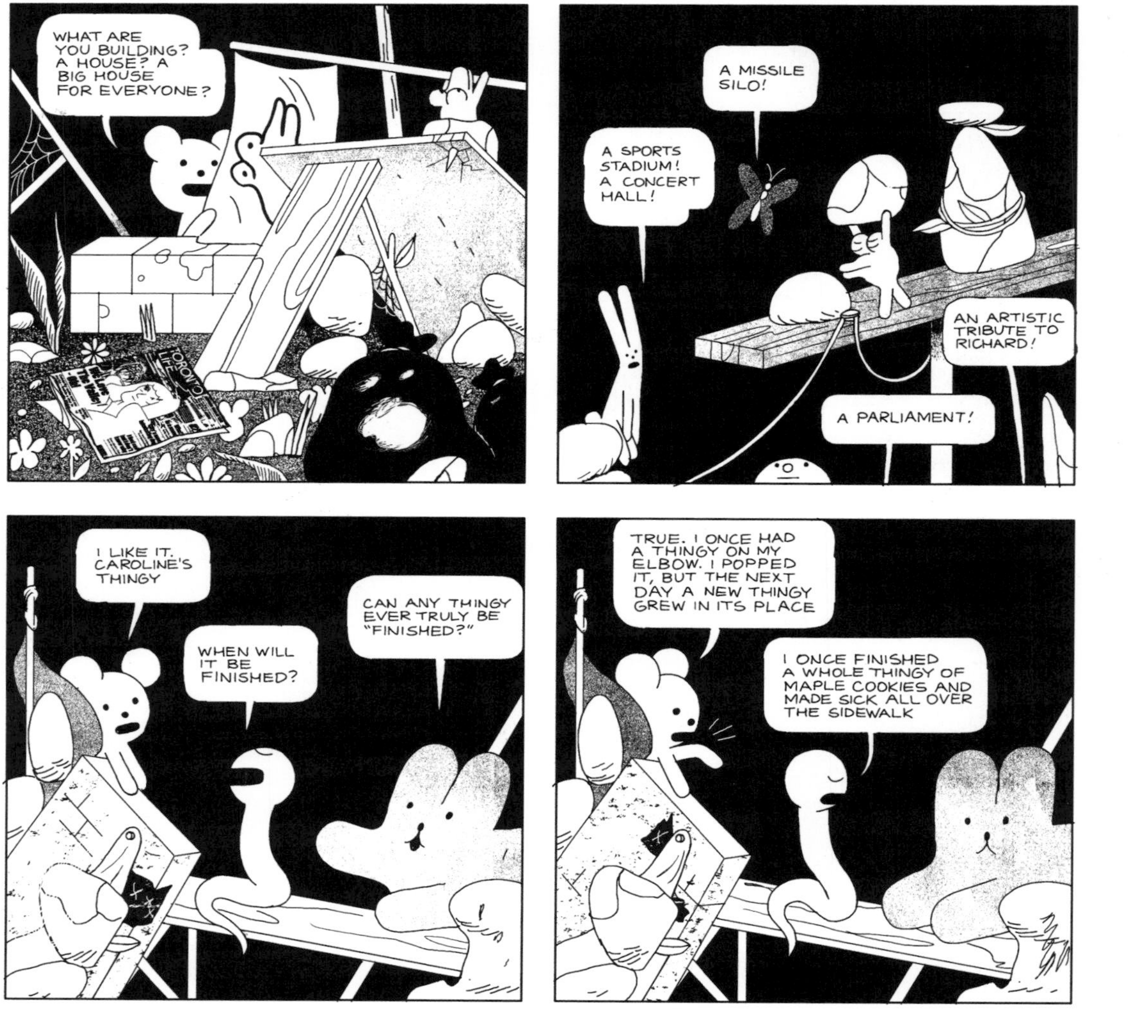
WHAT ARE YOU BUILDING? A HOUSE? A BIG HOUSE FOR EVERYONE?
A MISSILE SILO!
A SPORTS STADIUM! A CONCERT HALL!
AN ARTISTIC TRIBUTE TO RICHARD!
A PARLIAMENT!
I LIKE IT. CAROLINE'S THINGY
WHEN WILL IT BE FINISHED?
CAN ANY THINGY EVER TRULY BE "FINISHED?"
TRUE. I ONCE HAD A THINGY ON MY ELBOW. I POPPED IT, BUT THE NEXT DAY A NEW THINGY GREW IN ITS PLACE
I ONCE FINISHED A WHOLE THINGY OF MAPLE COOKIES AND MADE SICK ALL OVER THE SIDEWALK

Leaving Richard's Valley

THE FIRST TIME I SHED MY SKIN, I FREAKED OUT!
MY PARENTS DID A GOOD JOB RAISING ME, BUT THEY WERE PEOPLE, NOT SNAKES. THEY DIDN'T THINK TO PREPARE ME FOR IT
I SAW MY SKIN AND THOUGHT I'D DIED! I THOUGHT I WAS STARING AT MY CORPSE, HAVING AN OUT-OF-BODY EXPERIENCE
I'VE CARRIED THAT SENSATION WITH ME EVER SINCE. THAT WE'VE ALL BEEN DEAD FOR YEARS...
IT FRIGHTENS ME. THE MISTAKES WE MADE IN LIFE WERE ONLY TEMPORARY
OUR SCREW-UPS IN THE AFTERLIFE ARE ETERNAL

EXCUSE ME, ARE YOU LYLE? LYLE RACCOON?!!
YES...?
OH MY GOD! ME AND MY BROTHER ARE HUGE FANS!
WE SAW YOUR SET AT THE STATUE LAST FALL! YOU WERE INSANE
WE'RE IN A NOISE BAND, TOO! WE DO A COVER OF ONE OF YOURS--WELL, NOT A "COVER" PER SE, BUT WE DO AN IMPROVISATIONAL PIECE STRUCTURED AROUND SIDEWALK DISCOURSE #23
WE DON'T HAVE ANY RECORDINGS YET, BUT I THINK WE CAN BORROW MY SCHOOL'S EQUIPMENT TO MAKE A DEMO
Z
HE WAS KIND OF A JERK IN REAL LIFE
I KNOW, RIGHT?! THAT WAS SO COOL
HATS
BOOTS

Leaving Richard's Valley

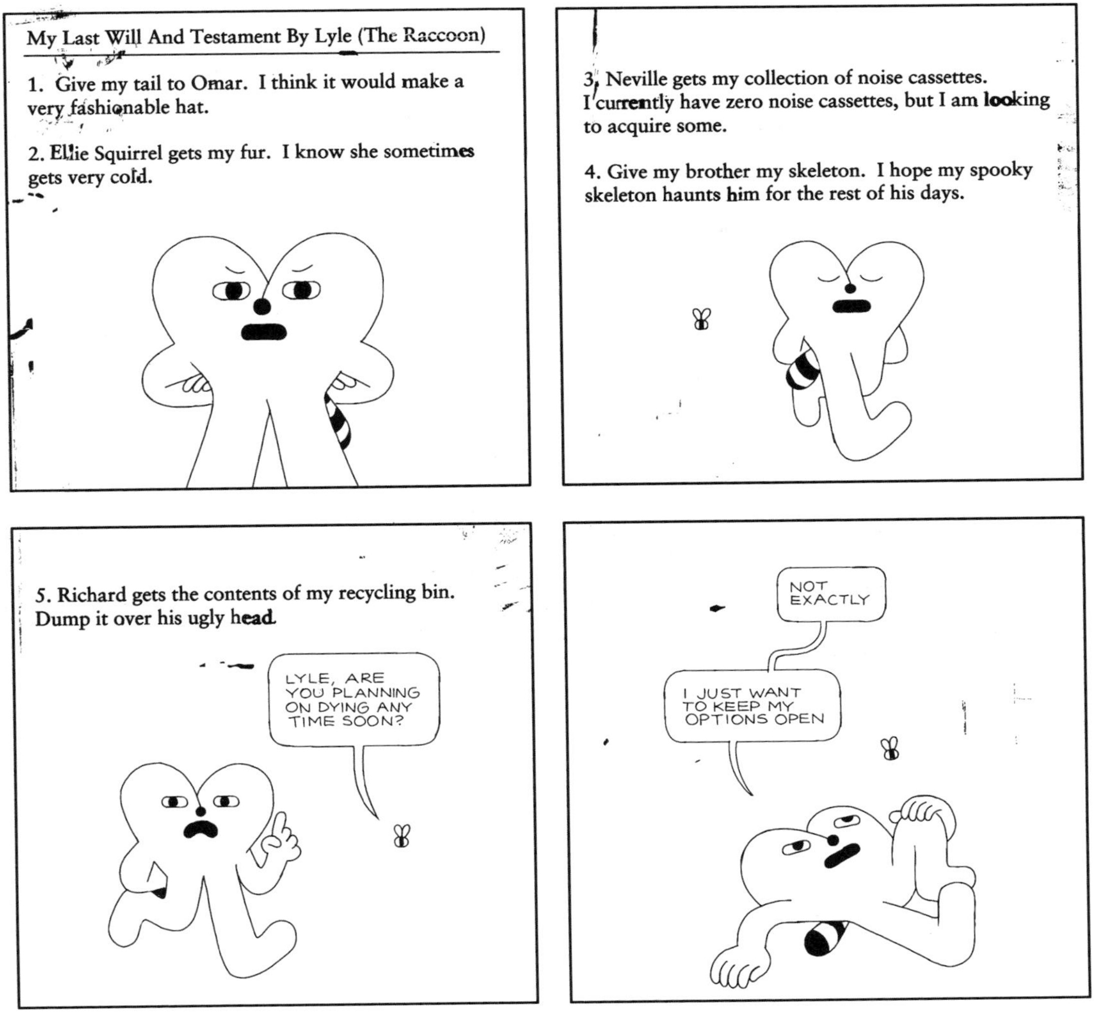
My Last Will And Testament By Lyle (The Raccoon)
1. Give my tail to Omar. I think it would make a very fashionable hat.
2. Ellie Squirrel gets my fur. I know she sometimes gets very cold.
3. Neville gets my collection of noise cassettes. I currently have zero noise cassettes, but I am looking to acquire some.
4. Give my brother my skeleton. I hope my spooky skeleton haunts him for the rest of his days.
5. Richard gets the contents of my recycling bin. Dump it over his ugly head.
LYLE, ARE YOU PLANNING ON DYING ANY TIME SOON?
NOT EXACTLY
I JUST WANT TO KEEP MY OPTIONS OPEN

Leaving Richard's Valley

ULTIMATELY, THE VALLEY IS GOING TO BE REMEMBERED AS EITHER A VERY GOOD OR VERY BAD IDEA
I GUESS?
I USED TO BE ABLE TO TELL THE DIFFERENCE, BUT I DEFINITELY CAN'T ANYMORE
BETWEEN GOOD AND BAD IDEAS
WE'RE BOTH SCHEMERS, NEVILLE. WE BOTH HAVE GRAND PLANS ... GRAND DESIGNS...
IT'S TRUE. I'D ALWAYS RATHER HAVE A BIG IDEA THAN A GOOD ONE
TOTALLY

Leaving Richard's Valley

NO, NO, I'M JUST SURPRISED! I HAD NO IDEA
IT'S TRUE, MARK. ALL THIS TIME, I'VE LOVED YOU FROM AFAR
I'VE... I'VE ALWAYS BELIEVED AFAR WAS THE BEST DISTANCE TO LOVE SOMEONE FROM!
I AGREE! YOU MUST THINK ME CRAZY. A CAT AND A SNAKE? OUR ROMANCE WOULD BE DOOMED FROM THE START
BUT... THAT'S MY FAVOURITE **TYPE** OF ROMANCE!
I AGREE!

Leaving Richard's Valley

IT'S TRUE, I COULD HAVE EXITED MORE... GRACEFULLY. I HAVEN'T ALWAYS ACTED RESPONSIBLY, BUT I'M MAKING UP FOR IT
I'M LEARNING FROM MY MISTAKES. AND YOU'LL LEARN, TOO!
FIRST, ON MY BOOK TOUR AND LECTURE SERIES. AFTER THAT? CITY HALL. THEN TELEVISION
COUGH
COUGH COUGH
THEN, WHO KNOWS? PARLIAMENT HILL? MAYBE EVEN A "WEBSITE?"

Leaving Richard's Valley

I'VE LIVED IN THE VALLEY MY ENTIRE LIFE
IT'S THE MOST BEAUTIFUL PLACE ON EARTH
BORN HERE. RAISED HERE
BUT NO, I WAS NEVER ONE OF THOSE RICHARD PEOPLE
I LOVE IT HERE. I JUST NEVER MADE IT MY WHOLE "THING," LIKE THEY DID
GET A LIFE! GET A HOBBY, JEEZ...
MY THING? AEROBIC GYMNASTICS. I'M **EXTREMELY** COMPETITIVE

Leaving Richard's Valley

SO WHAT'S THIS ALL GONNA BE WHEN IT'S FINISHED? NONE OF US CAN GUESS
JUNGLE GYM
I SEE! A SMALL BUSINESS!
SORTA. I'M NOT CHARGING. IT'LL BE FREE
EVEN BETTER!
THAT'S HOW I'LL GET 'EM HOOKED!

Leaving Richard's Valley

WELL, WE DID IT! IT TOOK SOME TIME, BUT WE FINALLY DID IT
DID WHAT?
HMM
I DON'T REALLY KNOW, BUT I'M PRETTY SURE IT WAS SOMETHING

Leaving Richard's Valley

Leaving Richard's Valley

IT'S STILL COLD
I THOUGHT IT'D BE WARM BY NOW
GET UNDER THE BLANKET
IT FEELS LIKE SPRING IS TAKING FOREVER TO GET HERE

Michael DeForge lives in Toronto, Ontario. His comics and illustrations have been featured in *Jacobin*, *The New York Times*, *Bloomberg*, *The Believer*, *The Walrus*, and *Maisonneuve* Magazine. He worked as a designer on *Adventure Time* for six seasons.

Thanks: Drawn & Quarterly, Ryan, Patrick, Jillian, Anne, Ginette, Robin, Mickey, Sadie, Scott, The Beguiling, S.T. and family

Also by Michael DeForge

Very Casual
A Body Beneath
Ant Colony
First Year Healthy
Dressing
Big Kids
Sticks Angelica, Folk Hero
A Western World
Brat